FREEDOM
FROM THE
STREETS

'To free yourself
from the streets,
you have to
know about the
mind-set which
is keeping you
entrapped to the
streets...'

ROBYN TRAVIS

Solution-Rooted Publications

Published 2019

Text copyright © Robyn Travis 2019. All rights reserved.

The moral right of the author has been asserted.

Cover re-imagined & page layout by David Springer
Editor by James Beckles
Printed by Biddles Books Ltd

British Library Cataloguing in Publications Data
A CIP catalogue record of this book is available from the British Library.

ISBN : 978-0-9569810-6-6

Solution-Rooted Publications
About the author

Robyn Travis

In 2012, Robyn Travis burst on to the writing scene as published author with Prisoner to Streets, memoirs that explored the realities of London's 'postcode wars' and exploded the myths around it. It was his 'foundation solution book' for dealing with the youth violence on our streets. In 2016, he released Mama Can't Raise No Man, an eye-opening exploration of different definitions of masculinity in today's society told from a black male perspective. It raises the issues of being on the margins of society, broken family units and the need for role models It also cleverly and intelligently looks at how personal circumstances and changing social norms can colude to impose a situation of a boy not having the influence of his father in his life. Without underminding the ability of women ability raise boys, it subtlely suggests the importance of boys having fathers in their lives to navigate the journey to manhood. Both books had a huge impact on publication and garnered much interest across TV, radio and press reaching a wide readership Robyn has been a guest speaker at a number of high profile literature festivals including Cheltenham, Harrogate, WOMAD, Bare Lit and Stoke Newington. He has also been on author panels in prisons such as Aylesbury and Wandsworth. He is a passionate speaker and advocate for young people and regularly uses his own life experiences to try and teach, educate, and inspire younger generations. Robyn also featured in the SAFE Anthology which was published in March 2019. Both of Robyn's books have been recorded on audio by Amazon Audible and a featured essay piece was also recorded for audio.

Other books from Robyn Travis

MAMA CAN'T RAISE NO MAN
ROBYN TRAVIS

PRISONER TO THE STREETS
ROBYN TRAVIS

Table of Contents

FREEDOM FROM THE STREETS

"Emancipate yourself from mental slavery only ourselves can free our minds."

Bob Marley

"To free yourself from the streets, you have to know about the mind-set which is keeping you entrapped to the streets..."

Robyn Travis

INTRODUCTION

To wear your heart on your sleeve is a hard thing to do. Especially for those of us who wear short-sleeves in the winter.

Where I grew up many people didn't wear their hearts in the open and many still don't till this day. Truth be told I don't blame them. It makes perfect sense to me. The heart is one of the main organs which keep us alive – so naturally you gotta protect yours. As humans we seem to have this in-built tendency of keeping things close to our heart. We seem to be incapable of talking to, or showing our true emotions to the ones we love, let alone anybody else.

So the fact that I wrote *Prisoner to the Streets* from such an open honest perspective amazes me to this day. I've always been an introvert at heart. So to share any part of my story was never something I planned, or wanted to do. However, the responsibility of writing the story presented itself to me, with a multiplicity of purpose filled reasons. And because of those reasons I knew I had to be obedient and deliver the message – That message was *Prisoner to the Streets.*

Prisoner to the Streets was never a convenient label. It wasn't another way to describe a gang or criminals. It's a description of the mental prison we're trapped in. My intention was to get rid of the labelling not re-label what has been taught to us about the streets up to now. I've always maintained that Prisoner to the Streets is a mentality. And I've always stressed if we address this matter looking at it from a mental perspective rather than a criminal perspective, then we would be much better equipped in understanding the problems to find the solutions. What I'm saying is *Prisoner to the Streets* (PTTS) is a mentality we get trapped into rather than something we consciously choose. Ask yourself - are the choices the youth make coming from a criminal mind-set or the mind-set of an infant learning to survive the environment around them?

Somewhere between the lines of those pages, the messages which were written in Prisoner to the Streets got lost in translation. People looked at me sideways when I said my book had nothing to do with gangs or fighting knife crime. Some people looked at me like I was in denial of my own story. As if to say I was naïve to what my own street experience was. So many people couldn't comprehend what

I meant by the term PTTS so they dismissed it completely. And how do I know they dismissed my example? Because people who claimed to be doing the same work as me were still going on the news proclaiming to be in this fight against knife crime. And that's not something I can co-sign to. If I wanted to fight crime I would've joined the police, not written a book. The reality is you can't fight someone with an imprisoned mind-set; you can only enlighten them about the trap they're in and show them the key to freedom.

Seven years after the publication of *Prisoner to the Streets* I came to the hard realisation that a lot of people didn't get what I set out to achieve in it. The book was somewhat misunderstood. I suppose in some ways I'm responsible for that. Maybe writing a book in story format wasn't enough to explain something that's so complicated and intricate. Or maybe the book was just ahead of its time? I don't know. What I do know is that I'm no longer angry at people for not understanding or for not wanting to understand. At the end of the day I was the person who wrote the book. And I'm the one who's trying to explain what I've learnt. And as a teacher I must be patient. I can't say nobody got the initial message because a lot of people did. But nowhere near enough people in the right places to make the changes we need to see.

I now feel a sense of responsibility to write something with more depth than the first book had, if that's even possible. Some people may not understand this process, but writing about your past isn't as easy as it looks. The process includes the writer having to go back to places in their mind, where they don't really want to be. But I get it now; it's no longer up for discussion. I have to dig deeper in to those past thoughts to bring forth more clarity. This book will not only breakdown *Prisoner to the Streets*, this book will also breakdown how one gets their freedom from the streets. Freedom for the prisoner to the streets is why I've committed to go back to the drawing board. I have to write this one with my heart on my sleeve, to finish off what I started.

This is my final say on the subject matter before I get to free myself completely from the topic of the streets. They say, **'You can lead a horse to water, but you can't make him drink.'** So here I am passing on the baton in the hope that you can maintain our position to the end. You don't have to run the race but here's the baton just in case!

> *'Don't be in such a hurry to condemn a person because he doesn't do what you do - or think as you think - or as fast. There was a time when you didn't know what you know today.'*

Malcolm X

CHAPTER 1

THE JOURNEY WITHIN THE REASON

*'The journey of a thousand
miles begins with one step...'*
©Lao Tzu

Journey...

The first steps on this journey happened long before the idea of picking up a pen. In fact, my first steps to freedom started when I was in the pen. Before I got convicted I was convinced I was a changed man. I'm not saying I made the complete change because I didn't. I was still in transition, but a lot had changed within me. And now that I was a father there was no going back to a PTTS mind-set. Or so I thought.

At the end of 2003 I did the same thing that the hash taggers of today are telling the youth to do. Before social media existed, I put the hash tag Gun Down and the hash tag Knife Down. At the time I was 18 and if you asked me then or now, putting the weapons down wasn't and still isn't the solution to the problem. It might be a solution to fighting knife crime. But it's not enough to unlock the chains and free the minds of the prisoners. Remember in the Bible how Cain killed Abel with a piece of rock from off the streets. Well, he wasn't rolling with it. In case my point isn't clear enough - putting down the weapons didn't give me the freedom I was looking for back then.

Fast forward the journey to 2006, I ended up in a prison cell over ignorance and karma. No words could ever explain the way that setback dented my motivation and desire to change for the better. Prior to my conviction I was like a young Michael Jackson looking for the man in the mirror. But before I could find that man, karma came and took me to a place where they had no mirrors – Spanish Town Prison. It was there the real journey of reflection began.

Imagine being addicted to a harmful drug for over 10 years. And then one day you decide to go cold turkey. You manage to give this drug up for 3 years with only a handful of minor relapses. And then boom, you find yourself locked in a room alone with drugs all around you. Well that's what it felt like when I got locked up. The only difference was that my addictive drug was violence and temper. Adding to that the island in which I was incarcerated had just recorded the highest number of murder rates worldwide the year before. So this was the ultimate test to see if I could stay clean and say no to violence, however strong the urge was to relapse.

Sometimes I had to revert to my old behaviours and mind-set but only in the form of self-defence. I tried my best to avoid violence but prison isn't the best place to be if you're trying to learn how to avoid conflict, or is it? Well in my case it was. I learned from my cell mates that I lacked the skills to deal with verbal conflict. Every other day, my Nigerian cell mate Elijah would get frustrated with me and shout,

'You will die Travis, they will kill you.' He would say that every time I gave in to the death threats of other inmates and in turn made my own. Over time I learned that he wasn't insinuating that they were a threat to me. But he was shouting out of love, trying to teach me how not to react to every escalating situation.

As pitched black as that cell was Elijah found a way to read books in the darkness. One day Elijah caught me watching him read. He looked at me, flicked through a few pages quickly, laughed, and handed the book to me.

The book cover was entitled, *'Purpose Driven Life'* by Rick Warren.

'Travis, tell me, what is your purpose?'

I looked at the book fully knowing I had no interest in reading it, but something in the title grabbed me. Even so there was nothing else to do. I read the first chapter and it made me curious thinking about knowing why God had created me. The chapter explained that we were created for a reason and not necessarily one of our own choosing. It explained how God created every single one of us for a purpose. I wasn't totally sold by that idea but it made me think. Before I went to sleep that night my brain went into overdrive. I started to think about why the decisions I made in life left me hurting. I began to think did God have a purpose for me. I scanned the cell and saw other inmates sleeping on the floor with the cockroaches. Questions quickly began to fill my mind.

'Where the hell am I?

'Really, what type of shit is this? This can't be life.'

I asked the most high to give me a purpose for living, because other than my girlfriend and son back in England, I really can't say I had a purpose to live. That night I prayed hard about my purpose. I asked God to give me the desire to care about my own life.

Elijah wasn't the only cell mate who taught me some key philosophies about life.

There were days when I would be locked up in the pitched black cell with other prisoners. But while they were resting to stay strong, I was up shadow boxing getting ready for a possible beef in the shower as it was a place where old and new tensions could blow up. An older cell mate from England turned to me one day and told me that I looked like a pretty sharp fighter. Then he added that I may need something as sharp as what the next man has if I was planning to be fully prepared come shower time. To which I replied,

'I'm prepared for whatever comes, big man.'

At that point the older cell mate sat up and taught me something I'll never forget.

'You young boys like to say the word switch don't you?'

'Huh?' I replied.

'Well, when you lot get vex, you call it switch, right?' he continued.

'Yeah, I suppose.'

Then he said, *'Ok, whenever you find yourself getting heated I want you to do this. I want you to imagine a light switch on the wall. That switch represents your temper. Try to keep that switch off while you're in here. You control that switch. If somebody attacks you then cool turn the switch on, but remember you control the switch. When you finally get out of here and return to the boxing, I want you to do the same thing in the ring. I want you to box smart by keeping the switch off. Once your opponent is hurt, you can turn that switch back on and throw controlled combinations. If you can learn how to control that switch in here, you can control it anywhere.'*

Who would have thought a story about a light switch could help me be free of a violent mind-set whilst surrounded by other violent prisoners? I practised that concept every day, believe me. It didn't get rid of all my problems though, but it helped me to avoid everyday conflict. I didn't realise it at the time, but I wasn't just free from prison physically. Unknowingly, I was becoming free from the prison mentality on a whole.

'You don't need walls around you to be imprisoned, remember?' - Quote on cover of PTTS.

When I returned to England I was a free man, ready to live by that switch concept. Did prison rehabilitate me? Hell no, prison is a business. So what I had to do was rehabilitate myself. I was out of jail for a few months when one of my childhood mates from London Field's Primary School asked me to come to Haggerston to kick some ball. My initial reaction was, *'Cool let's do this.'* Then I remembered that a lot of the guys I had beef with was going to be on that pitch. I began to have mixed feelings about it. The first feeling was, I didn't want to go there and let my enemies think I was begging friends with them. Then on the flipside I didn't want to go there and put myself in a position where I'd have to react violently. Then I thought about what rumours could circulate if people heard that me and the Fields' boys were playing football together, especially after all the ill feeling between us. Then I thought, *'Fuck all that. I don't care what people think or say.'* I wanted to play a football match and nothing was going to stop me from going to my local to do so. So with that last thought I said, *'Cool, let's go.'*

When we arrived I saw a whole heap of man who didn't know how to react to my presence. I can't say I was surprised because the beef between our areas weren't squashed. I then remembered the last time the two areas, Holly Street and London Fields were on that pitch together. I remembered it well cos I was getting chased across the halfway line between the two areas by police for bringing tools with me for protection that day. Some of the same people who witnessed the chase were on that football field. So naturally one's enemy might think I was tooled up again but I wasn't. This time, I didn't bring anything but my Arsenal top and my football boots. Why? Because I didn't want to be a prisoner to the streets anymore, and bringing a gun or knife wouldn't have been constructive to my rehabilitation.

I walked on the pitch feeling completely fearless but aware of the position I was in. After a minute of receiving the odd stare I shouted, *'What team am I on?'* Some people weren't happy to see me and what I said could have been interpreted as disrespectful. But looking back to 2007, when I walked on the football pitch that day, it was probably the realist thing I'd ever done. I didn't realise the power in what I did that day. But I get it now. I was unconsciously setting pace and making peace through my actions. That moment was the moment I freed myself from being a prisoner to the streets. *How?* By going against the mind-set which was keeping myself and others shackled to the streets.

It wasn't as straight forward as I've written it though. You have to understand the entirety of the situation to get the full picture. You see, it had been rumoured that some of the people on that pitch had something to do with a death of my close friend. There were a lot of people on that pitch who I had done negative things to in the past. And these guys were still good friends with a guy who stabbed me when I was younger. My friends also killed their friend in a drive by shooting, who was actually a friend of mine. Not to mention my name was caught up in a rumour as one of the shooters involved in the shooting of their friend, also my friend. So to say it was technical on both sides is a bit of an understatement. But there I was, playing football, something I'd always loved with the people I once hated. The same people who could have still had hatred for me.

The team I played for didn't have any of my enemies on it, which was good. There were quite a few teams and the settings were: first 2 goals wins and the losing team comes off or 10 minutes on and if scores remain level then penalties would settle it. There was a strange vibe in the air from the get go and I could sense things might kick off. But my thoughts were, *'I never come 'ere to find trouble so trouble shouldn't come find me.' And of course my mind-set was still 'prisonerish'* so if trouble did come then boy, every man has the right to survive.

I can't remember exactly how the day went down but it was hot and in terms of football, I was on fire. The inner child had come back to the surface. I was banging in goals for fun. I must have twined up one player and scored a spanker and sent the losing team off the pitch. Then I heard an old enemy shout out my name, *'Oi Robin.'* When I turned around he had a serious look on his face, but he was clapping, *'That was sick cuz.'* Initially I didn't know what the big deal was. Call it ego if you like but I was just thinking, *'What's the big deal? I've been doing this'* Even though Hackney man had its inside beef, we always knew who the ballers were. Ego aside though, I was still surprised by his feedback cos that's the first time we had ever communicated positively. When the next team came on the feedback wasn't so positive.

One older guy in particular kept getting frustrated by my aggression used in tackling him. And I kicked his leg once or twice by accident. He started hyping so I stood firm. He was running his mouth swearing but nothing directed at me. I started thinking of that switch again, the prisoner in me wanted to turn it on. I thought to myself, *'Alrite, cool. Imma keep playing my game and if it kicks off it kicks off -whatever.* Then I thought, *'Oh, I know why he's going on so stink. It's not about the aggression in my game.'* It was because when I was about 15 I saw him jamming on Kingsland high road near *'my block'.* The guy I was with at the time (Rip-Dunni) said hello to him. I interrupted their little chit chat and told him to move from the block. Long story short, he did.

At that time I was still a PTTS. The way I saw it was this guy was an older Fields boy of the guy who stabbed me back then, so I felt it was my hood right to send him home. My once misguided-pride of a mind-set couldn't let this older brudder, feel safe and comfy sitting on *'my block.'* So I knew his actions weren't about the tackling, he was still carrying feelings. What nearly made my switch blow was deep down I knew he was only going on like a G because of the numbers behind him. Not saying I'm Wolverine or nothing but I knew and I'm sure he knew too, he would've never raised his voice if it was just me and him in an alley way, because it would've been curtains. I call this type of be-haviour *prisoner tactics.* Anyway, I managed to control the switch that day. I played a few games and went home feeling strangely proud about myself.

I couldn't explain it at the time, but that day I knew I had achieved something to do with freedom. On the way home my bredin told me the same guy who I twined up and got a clap for, was actually a professional baller. I was semi-gassed by that news, I won't lie. I had no idea. I saw him on BBC's Match of the Day playing against Liverpool the night before. The craziest thing was the sense of pride I got to know that a younger from the hood had made it as a pre-miership football player. *'That's BIG!'* I thought. I didn't care that he was from Fields; he was a brother who made it. He wasn't my younger but the next time I saw him I spoke as a big brother would. *'Yo, you need to stop coming to the block to play football bro. You got too much talent to get caught up out here. Worse still what if you get injured?'* Soon after that conversation I stopped going to play football in Haggerston. In the few weeks I played there I kept having this strange day dream like a vision. All of us were playing on that pitch, Holly Street, Fields, Hackney and Tottenham. That vision included the brothers in jail and the brothers in the clouds. The day dream seemed so real I could see their faces clearly. Somehow we all put down our egos and hatred to play a game of football in peace.

The thought of peace was only a day dream though. At this part of my journey peace between us on a whole was never anything I thought could happen. For sure, it wasn't something I thought I could influence or change. The way I saw it, *'I'm still mentally a D Cat Prisoner myself I can't help anyone.'* I believed if peace or freedom was to be achieved the people involved would have to a) want peace, and b) want true freedom. Nonetheless, on a personal level this was another massive step toward the journey of my freedom. Progress was made.

About two months after the football experience, I took another massive step out of my comfort zone when I decided to get into education. I went to college to study social work. Then I got a job working as a door supervisor and a second job as a learning mentor/boxing coach. Things were starting to look up for once. I got invited to come to church by my friend Adrian who was trying to walk a righteous path. He knew I weren't into the church business, but I felt so blessed just to be breathing, that I decided to roll up and give thanks.

This is what the pastor of that church had to say:

'I'm going to start off talking about me. And as I continue to do so you'll understand why I start off with me. In my early days way before I became a pastor. I was involved in certain things. Like Robin says I wouldn't say a gang but a group of friends. We were forced at times to call ourselves a gang, but we weren't really that. We just grew up together in an area where we ended getting up to no good. And so I knew what it was like to be on the street. I knew what it was to be involved in criminal activity.

So by the time I had met Robin, to me it was quite obvious that he was the real deal. I would listen to how other people talked about the streets. And because of my family I knew what the street life was about, so for me hearing Robin's journey, I knew he had really lived that life.

I met Robin in 2007 when he came out of jail from Jamaica. At the time I hadn't realised he spent time there. He came to my church service a few times with his friend Adrian who had recently gotten saved. Many times I had to initiate the conversation with Robin because it seemed like he really didn't want to talk about his past. I could see that he wasn't trying to touch on the subject. At the time I sensed it was the memories of it all why he didn't want to go there.

There were times when we began to talk and we talked quite deep. But on hearing some of the stories straight away in my mind I knew. I could hear that this was someone who knows from start to finish what it means to be in the street, or the so called street life. He played a part in the things that the government might call gang wars or whatever. But as he got a little more comfortable talking to me about his past and growing up in Hackney it just came to me. The more I heard him speak I thought a lot of the stuff he was saying, if it was written down it would really be helpful to those who would read it.

And so, I began to encourage Robin to write a book *but he was very reluctant. And I guess at the time I wasn't really sure why he was so against it. It was only in recent conversations that I kind of got to understand why. By me encouraging him to write a book I was kind of forcing him to relive, some of the events that I guess he wanted to forget. Plus there was also an element that he did mention to me at the time. He said even if he wanted to do it he couldn't do it because he wouldn't want to mention people's names dates or times. He told me he couldn't do it because there could be repercussions for people and that it would be a dangerous thing to write unless he could protect their identity. And with that he disregarded the idea. I then realised it was going to be a dangerous thing asking him to write the book. So I stopped pushing the idea on him.*

Over time I hadn't seen or heard from him. I just assumed he was staying out of trouble and getting on with his life. Little did I know he was doing a lot more than staying out of trouble.

He rang me one day in 2012 and said, 'Kev I did it, I wrote that book still.'

This book has been in my opinion a success. And the fact that he's writing his third one goes to show that this was always his calling.'
Pastor Kevin.

Pastor Kevin was a proper cool guy. Kinda *'like'* mandem. I don't know if it was the God in him or the old G in him but he spoke to me like he knew me. I came back to church for a little while and every time I came back I noticed he would ask me about my past life. He never assumed anything negative of my past, he just kept on asking about it. One day I broke some things down to him and the conversation went kind of deep. Pastor Kevin turned to me and said he thinks I should write a book. I told him I wasn't interested in that. That didn't stop him from pursuing the matter though. Every Sunday I came back he would say the same thing. You need to write this book. It wasn't annoying to hear him say it though. I just couldn't see what good it would do. I was more focused on doing my youth work course than writing about it.

Then soon after I met Kevin I met another older man called Neville Watson.
This is what Neville had to say to me after we met:
'Nearly 12 years ago I met what could be best described as an angry, frustrated and slightly troubled young man - he's name was Robin Travis. And he even doubted that his very name had validity. After a few enlightening conversations, I realised that

*this young man's life was a testimony that needed to be shared. So I told him, '**Robin, you need to write a book!**'*

When I first broached the idea of a book Robin didn't appear to be surprised. I believe the idea of doing a book had been mentioned to him before. I remember before even doing so he doubted his ability to write one and questioned the value of doing so. I believe there was so much going on in this young man's head. Unanswered questions, self-doubt and moreover anger. He probably felt the very notion of a book was too over-whelming to think about. Thank God, as it is by God's grace and mercy that the light that Robin has found can continue to be a beacon of hope for many and not the few!'
Neville Watson

For some reason Nev had the same idea as Kev. And without being preachy, Nev also insisted I write a book. To be fair this type of conversation wasn't foreign to me. My mother had told me the same thing. She was always telling me to write my story I just couldn't see the purpose in it.

Adrian, my old school friend who invited me to church also had this to say:
'Basically, me and Robin go back from like, I don't know like 2001 times. Just after secondary school. I think since I've known him I've always known him to be like... I don't know like he's names always been out there.
He's always been involved in something street. Not in like a fol-lowers sense or a drug sense. Just in the sense where he was always involved in some violence on road. Like, way before I knew him I knew him, if you know what I mean? So to be his

friend before the change and watch his transition was mad to witness.

I remember before he went to Jamaica he was still trying to battle with dead-ing off the road life. Like he was really trying to leave the road ting behind...

At the time as a friend I thought it was inspirational to see somebody that's been that deeply involved and who could still technically be a target for some man to try and change his life and stand up against it. So from when I saw he was serious about making the change. I said to him, **you know what you need to do Trav, you need to write a book!** *Cos the stuff that he'd been through I thought not only could it be inspirational for certain man, but it could help change people's minds about the roads. But he wasn't having it, he was always against it. Like, anytime I told him to write the book he said, 'Nah, nah, nah.'*

And I fully understand why, it's a big thing to ask. But I thank God. The way I see it, God had a different plan for him. Over the years I spoke to him about it. Then eventually the time came when he said, 'Cool, I'm gonna write the book.' but yeah he was dead against it at first.'
Adrian.

Talk about potentially being a target for some people? A few weeks after my mate Adrian was trying to convince me to write a book for the streets, it just so happened I was about to be tested by the very same streets. I was working a security shift at a fun fair in Finsbury Park. Me and my colleague (an older black woman) were supervising our section whilst talking about life and its purpose. As we were speaking she praised me for turning a negative into a positive. Then she said, *'Be mindful when making big changes; we get tested'.* Before I even got the chance to process what she said we were surrounded by twenty or more brothers playing some intimidation game. But we weren't phased or intimidated. We continued to walk while the 'pack of sheep' walked in a circle around us. The guy in front of me started to back step and said something with a smirk on his face, *'Robin from Holly Street, you remember me yeah?'* I honestly didn't. But when I went to spud him he left me hanging. So I took a deep breath and said, *'I guess it's not love then'.* Then another guy walked past laughing, *'He's a youth worker now'.* I know the fella meant it as a diss but I took it as a complement. As far as I was concerned I was woke to the bullshit. I was no longer what rapper Nas would call a *'Black Zombie'.*

A couple of the 'sheep' started putting their hands down their waste, to show me there tools, but me and the lady carried on walking strong. One 'sheep' from the flock walked past and shouted, *'He's a mouse.'* That's when I started to feel that switch go. Then I smiled because I remembered I was with a woman old enough to be my mother. And I couldn't let her witness me switch and get jumped, stabbed or possibly shot dead by some youths who got wicked overnight. And when I say overnight I don't mean that in a disrespectful way. It's the truth. After they took shots at me verbally, they bounced. I told my manager that I was going home but the black lady I was working with sensed I was lying.

She felt I was up to something so she held me back and said, *'Don't pay them boys any mind. And don't do anything stupid, you hear? Nothing happened to you, you're blessed. It's just a test.'*

Out of respect I said,
'I know Aunty it's just a test.'

Minutes later, that switch my cell mate taught me about exploded within me. I went to my car and sat down trying my best to remember where I knew that yute from. Then it came to me. I drove to their block immediately. I sped past and saw him and another two guys standing there looking shocked to see me. I slowed down put my face out of the window. Then I drove past smiling to see I had made them nervous. Then I drove off. The thoughts of the things I planned to do to him that night were so evil I can't even bring myself to write it. The idea was so evil I don't want to remember it, or share it. I'd like to think I'm not capable of such wicked things. But when I remembered who he was, I wanted to make an example. The 'prisoner' in me felt like I had to do something extreme. It was that same old battle again - *Voice of the streets vs Voice of reason.*

The voice of the street was saying, 'Hold up, isn't that the same guy that you stuck it on in the Chinese shop when you were 14, and he was 15? He wasn't acting wicked back then. Now 7 years overnight the man turns wicked because of numbers and weapons? That isn't gangster.' This behaviour is what I call, 'prisoner tactics'.

–The voice of reason kind of said the same thing as the voice of the street, which was strange. The only difference is the voice of the streets wanted me to do something about it. I got a call from an older guy who watched me and this other guy grow up and he wanted to squash it.

I told him, *'Truth be told bruv these man are newbies to me. What they're doing at 21, 22 me and my boys were doing at 13, 14. These youths can't have beef with me. There's only one way to squash this bro. You're their older, so let's set it up. I'll scrap with every single one of your youngers one on one. I wanna punch up these fake arse Suge Knight's quickly. Then I'll be more than cool to squash it.'*

I was raging. It's like people really started to think they were bad because of the numbers. Deep down I knew punching up anyone was a distraction from my purpose. All it would do is put my name back in the hype. I would have had to take it to other levels because people are scared to take a L. The lady was absolutely right. Nobody touched me, so really I didn't lose anything. I stayed angry for a long while and then I worked hard on letting it go.

A couple weeks later, my mate Wale asked me to follow him to his college in Kentish Town, north London. He said something about one boxer coming down to do a talk. And he thought I might get something positive out of it. Before, I wouldn't have said yes to going to events. I was so anti-social in public spaces outside the ends. But since JA I was becoming more open minded to experiencing new things and different sceneries. I was learning that if I wanted to be free

I couldn't restrict myself to only being sociable in the neighbourhood.

When we reached the Whack Performing Arts College I was in admiration of the way Wale spoke to his teachers. He switched up from talking slang with me and went into professional voice. I remember laughing to myself thinking, *'Rah, Wale's woke - my mum used to do that'.* I was impressed because Wale was from where I was from. So to see him be able to conduct himself confidently in professional environments was impressive.

We walked in and sat at the back of the lecture hall quietly, because we were a few minutes late. A man by the name of Mark Prince was on stage talking about losing his son to knife crime. Everyone in the room was glued to Mark's every word – except me. At first I couldn't understand why. I started to think something was wrong with me emotionally. I sat up and made a conscious effort to pay attention. Mark went on to talk about the background of his 15 year old son. He described his son as a loving caring young man who always looked out for people. When he said that I began to reflect on a few of my dead friends, who I felt had those same characteristics. Mark went on to describe the incident itself. He said how his 15 year old son was breaking up a fight at school. Then the guy took out a knife and stabbed him.

At this point Mark started to break down and a lot of the people, mostly girls were crying too. Even the teachers, but for some reason I wasn't moved. Don't get me wrong, I knew it was a fucked up thing to happen to him, but my heart was too hardened to be moved by other people's pain. The reason was that nobody seemed to care about the pain of the prisoners to the streets.

As Mark found the strength to continue talking, I began to shut off again and went all into my feelings. I started thinking,

'I remember this guy's face from the news. It's crazy though. When I was getting stabbed in the chest at 14 nobody cried about that, no media gave a fuck. And why should they give a damn? A life like mine isn't important. We're the children who got kicked out of school with criminal records, so obviously our story doesn't matter. My close friend all got his head blown off at close range. That barely got a mention in the media. Not to mention JD, Poops, Dunni, and all the Murder mile victims, gone before their time.

Maybe if they were promising footballers their deaths could've been considered worthy of media coverage and empathy? It's sad what happened to this guy's son no 'buts', it's fucked up. However, why is it nobody cared or cares about the pain of me and my brothers?' We've been dying since the 90's. Nobody cared about stopping the violence until a celebrity or a parent lost a loved one. Joke ting! Fuck all that though. Rest in Peace, young brother Kiyan. To all of my brothers who lost their lives whose death wasn't positively reflected in the media. May you also rest in peace'

As Mark continued to talk I started to come out of my feelings and listened with an open mind. I could feel this brother's pain. But I was thinking, *'This guy don't look simple, why don't he just duppy the yute?'* But at the same time I respected him for following his belief trying to practice forgiveness. I felt it was a great talk about forgiveness and the courage of a man wanting to spread peace but that was it. It seemed sincere but it didn't explain any of the problems or solutions to the streets on which I grew in and was still partially imprisoned. Then I started thinking this isn't really a street thing. It was a talk about the pain of a man who lost his son. And for some reason I drifted back to thinking about my own pain. All my dead friends who were murdered would have never had their legacy remembered because they were perceived as 'street children' at their time of death.

After the talk everyone from the audience swarmed Mark and praised him for the work he was doing. But like I said I wasn't moved. My bredrin Wale went to big up Mark. Mark saw me standing behind Wale in my own world, he gave me a high five and tried to give me a man hug. But I wasn't feeling that, I was open to coming out the ends, but I wasn't open to embracing people I didn't know. He then said,
'Yes soldier, you good?'
I didn't say much. I just nodded.
Then he said, *'What did you think about that talk?*
I said, *'Yeah, it was alright still.'* Then I added, *'I honestly don't get why you haven't murdered this yute yet but I can respect it.'*
He looked at me and said,
'There's something about you bruv, your energy I can't explain it.'

Then he put his hand on my shoulder and said,
'God's' gonna use you for something special. Something just told me I had to tell you that.'
I looked at him thinking about the book and then I pushed the thought to the back of my mind again.

Not long after I came back from Jamaica I bumped into my old friend Chemaine. She took me on a trip down memory lane and reminded me of how we first met. This is how she remembered it.

"I've known Robin for 17 years. Before I actually met him I heard about him and certain things he was involved in. I use to get my info from a friend of mine who he nicknamed the Hackney Gazette. He used to call her that because she used to talk about him and he never knew who she was. And I've never revealed to him who that friend is. Now before I ever met Robin this girl told me so much about him. She told me that he used to walk around with a strap. Fights that he's had girls that he was seeing. So before I even knew him as a person I already had an opinion of him and what he was about. Just because all the things I had heard about him. Then I finally met him myself.

Me and Robin used to speak on the phone and he seemed like a really cool person. Though secretly I was scared of going to meet him because of all the violent things I heard about him. I didn't want to be around the type of lifestyle he was living. But I soon got past that and after a while I realised he wasn't a threat to me.

I remember he was living in Clapton and there was a rave at one pub near his hostel on Clarence road. I came with a few of my girl's one of them unknowingly to him being the Hackney Gazette. I remember he found me in the rave and he told me 'Get your friends and go home the clubs gonna get heated.' So I did I went home, because obviously I didn't want to be in the middle of all that madness. When I got home I was like whoa I'm really friends with this guy who's living a madness. When I spoke to Rob about the shoot-out years later he said he doesn't even remember the rave.

I remember another night when he got stabbed in the head and shot at outside Palace Pavilion. And I remember telling him to go to the hospital, but he wouldn't listen. I even said I would come down and drop him myself, all he was saying was: 'Nah, nah forget all that. I'm not going hospital until I find these yutes.'

*After that day I spoke to him and he told me he was cool. But just to know he was bleeding from a stab wound to the head and still didn't go hospital made me think. I thought this guy's crazy he was more focused on getting revenge than living. And from that day I knew the Gazette was right. I realised - no he's actually a mad-man. He was really living this lifestyle. Like, this is something that you see in the movies. **And it was from then that day that I said Robs, you need to write a book!** You need to write a book on your lifestyle cos this is a madness!*

It's funny looking back because when the gazette first spoke about him I was fearful of him to tell the truth. It's funny cos it really was a big misconception of who he is. The Robin I got to know was quite a calm and humble guy. I have to say the only time he would let go or get rowdy was if someone troubled him first but apart from that he had a good heart. But as a young girl hearing about him people gave the impression that he was this menace of a gangster. But becoming friends and getting to know him one on one. I learned it's not that black and white.

Robin was like two completely different people. There was this side to him that was easy... or how could I put it. He would buss joke, reason about things in life, and just be that good friend. Then he had the roadside that I've seen but like I said that's not the Robin I know. Deep down I always knew there was a different side to him, not just the roadside. And this is why I'm so proud to see that he finally did it. He actually wrote the book. It might've taken you a good 16 years to listen bro, but you actually did it, well done.

There's an old saying that goes, 'The devil finds work for idle hands'. So I knew I had to stay away from the block and focus on game. From the second I came out of jail I did my best to stay actively busy I was still boxing and playing football in Tottenham. And it was this part of the journey where I met the mental farmer - Lyndon Walters, referred to as Lyn in some parts of the book.

The first time I met Lyndon I was playing 5 a side football at Tottenham Power League. One of the players called Nathan told Lyndon that I was a baller and he wanted me to join Lyndon's team. I didn't know Lyn personally but everyone from Tottenham who played football seemed to know this guy. Anyway, I joined his 11 aside team and brought my bredin Winston from Hackney. We were losing 2-1 with like 15 minutes left to go. I was thinking to myself, *'How's this Rasta man got me standing in the cold watching football? I didn't come out my yard for this shit.'*

Then he put me on and I scored straight away. I was still a little vex but then I scored again. After the match, me and Lyndon spoke. He joked with me saying that he knew I was getting frustrated on the bench but he wanted to teach me about discipline. He said he thought I lacked discipline. I didn't know how to take that.

The 'Mental Farmer' was never afraid to tell me about my flaws, but only because he saw something in me that he couldn't keep to himself.

*'I remember the day when I turned to you and said **Robin you need to write a book...** You looked at me kind of curiously and you said, 'You know what Lyn? When I was younger my Mum said I should write everything down, she was the first one to tell me to write stuff down.' And I thought wow, fantastic Mum. You also told me that a couple other people were saying the same thing - **WRITE A BOOK.***

Well I suppose, I don't know what made you determined that you were NOT going to write a book. Even though people told you that it might be helpful. But I know I had to tell you to write a book. Because you have so much to offer that it had to be done, we talked and talked and I said to you,
'Well, I'm an I' coach' and if you want me to I'll coach you.'
But you weren't interested you said you didn't need coaching.

Then I told you if you write a book you could relay some of that inner stuff and triggers that was causing you to get so angry. And I saw the surprise on your face when I said to you I understand about anger. You turned to me and said you think you need anger management. To which I replied – no son you don't need anger management, nobody does, how can you manage anger? Think about that. You looked at me kind of curiously as if to say what the hell is this man on? He must be crazy, I've heard of anger management. But when I explained to you that anger is a given. It is meant for our survival. I think you got it. And I said to you all you need to do is to be better aware of the triggers that made you feel angry, and in that way you don't have to manage it. Once you're aware of it you make the decision whether to stay angry or to calm down.

I saw the look on your face 'lol' and we progressed on the day to talk about how you go about writing this book if you ever did it. Eventually I said to you well as a coach I believe you writing this book could possibly be the therapy that you need. You looked more confused as I said that. I think you were asking yourself questions about therapy. So I said to you therapy's not a bad thing. In fact it will give you clarity. After that day we progressed and you came back to check me and you said, 'Lyn if I decided to do this would you be my ghost writer?' And I laughed and said, 'to be honest with you Robin I'm not a ghost. I might be a writer but I'm not a ghost.' And we joked for a bit. Eventually I suggested that I got a tape recorder and I could just let you speak if you wanted.

Then you called me one day and said, 'Lyn I don't know about doing this book thing. My memories pretty bad I can't re-

member anything.' And I responded, 'Robin memory is never missing, it's just not accessible. And that was that.

One day you called me and said do you really think I can be an author, and I said yeah. How great would that be for you to be in control? Then you said to me, 'Well how do I write a book?' And I said write the first word and it will go on from then. And I'm proud to say it from then you just blossomed. You found a way not only to remember but to write. Everything you did you sent to me to read over and feedback to you. And you always got the same feedback from me 'Keep writing son, keep writing...'

Following on from that you carried on writing. Then we met up and you told me that you were going to write the book with an old friend who stabbed you. And I thought wow that sounds terrific. Kane invited us up to his flat and we were reasoning everything seemed to be getting on fine. I remember admiring the both of you thinking how you two were once enemies and now you're here reasoning like brothers, it was fascinating. And you were really serious about doing this book with Kane. But sometime to come after that I remember you called me and said Kane was backing out saying he doesn't want to do it anymore. You lost your patience with getting him on board and in the end decided to do it on your own. And I'm glad that you did. You took it up on yourself as you told me to change from being a Prisoner to the Street. And I'm honoured to know you shared with me.

Lyndon Walters – I coach (The Mental Farmer)

So Lyndon got to know me and suggested that I should write a book. I told him if I had a penny for every time I was told that I wouldn't need to write a book. He said something about it giving me clarity, but I wasn't interested. He then told me he was more than a football coach; he also said he was an I-coach. He went on about the importance of me writing the book and how it would be good for therapy.

When he said therapy I thought to myself,

'I am a bit of a mad man maybe I do need help.'

So I said to him, *'Yeah can you help me, I think I need anger management.'*

His response was priceless.

By 2008 Lyndon was the fifth person that told me to write this book in the space of a year. However, Lyndon was the most consistent in sowing seeds of wisdom in my mind. And when those seeds eventually grew I would go on to start believing that there was a greater purpose in writing the book. Now the journey had evolved. It was way bigger than just freeing myself. I thought that if I decided to write it and I could get the story right then many more could avoid this prisoner's mind-set. Many more prisoners could be freed.

The Reasons...

'The heart has its reasons of which reasons mean nothing...'
Pascal

Five different people in one year told me to write a book, but I still wasn't on it. I just couldn't see enough strength in their reasons to justify bringing up the past. In addition to that I hadn't read a book since primary school. I didn't care about books and I seriously doubted I was capable of writing one. I think it was late 2008 when me and my Mum were holding a reasoning. I told her how all these random people keep telling me to write a book.

She said, *'I've been telling you this for years. You're a natural born writer. But you don't listen to me when I talk.'*

I went silent after that, my Mum probably thought I was taking it in, but I wasn't. I didn't respond cos I got that feeling you get when you regret bringing up a subject to your Mum.

'So are you going to write this book or not?'

Me, *'Not, what am I writing a book for Mum? I'm not some celebrity. And I haven't made it at nothing in life. Look I'm still in the hood.'*

She exhaled some smoke from a cigarette, while laughing at my response.

'You haven't made it? Don't you have life? Some of your childhood friends are gone. Most of them are either in jail, the cemetery, or the mental hospitals, and you don't think you made it? Look how much time's you've been stabbed. Issues with your Dad, things you've seen me go through. You've had it hard boy, write the damn book!'

She wasn't lying we had seen a lot, but that still wasn't reason enough for me to write a book about it.

'Mum... half the guys I grew up with had it hard in life. And in case you didn't notice, not having a dad isn't exactly breaking news around here. Seriously mum, nobody cares

about all that.'

I was hoping that statement was going to finish the conversation – but nope.

'That's the problem; none of you talk about the pain or what you go through. You need to make people care about all that.

'No mum I actually don't, it's not my place. Someone else can write it.'

My mum just laughed at me, and then she got deep with it.

'So, five people told you to write a book in one year! Five! Do you really think that's a coincidence? You're too stubborn to listen to anyone. You can't even hear when Gods talking?'

She made a good point, but I still wasn't feeling it. Truth be told, anytime my mum told me something was a sign from God I wrote it off. Growing up I used to express to my Mum that God doesn't chat to me. I believed if God wanted to talk to me, he would talk to me directly not through others. I believed if God is all knowing then he would know I'm not a fan of the he say she say God said. My mum's words had fallen on deaf ears. At this point of the journey my focus was still about doing the work not writing about it.

Between 2008/2009 I managed to get a job in youth work. My first real role in the field was as a detached outreach worker in Stoke Newington. I loved working with these youth. Some of them were prisoner minded, they reminded me of the younger me. They were also the youngers of some guys I used to hang around with. So I always had a reference to reinforce my point. Alongside doing this, I was working as a youth mentor in my old estate Holly Street. I felt like I was finally doing something constructive with my past experiences. I mean, seriously? Who would've imagined someone like me trying to free myself? As well as trying to help free other prisoners from the same estate? Not me, I never saw myself doing this work, the experience was surreal.

On the other hand I was beginning to learn what working in the youth field was about. I didn't like it. I remember I was mentoring one younger Holly street boy in the room, but I kept hearing loud noises coming from outside the room. It became distracting to our session so I came out to see why the other youth workers hadn't settled it. When I got to the pool table room I saw a few olders who I used to ride for, acting like pickney in the youth club. One of the olders, older than me, was ramping throwing snooker balls with the kids. I couldn't understand it myself. I mean, I was 23/24 years old so I couldn't understand why people over 25 were in a youth club with youngers, acting younger than the young-ers. It's like the mandem my age were still living in the past holding on to some street rep. I was baffled.
I shouted at everyone in the room, *'Fix up and keep the effing noise down.'*

It could have gone either way because the older guy ramping was my old friend who I had stabbed in the past, and vice versa. But I didn't care. I felt ashamed for my old friends. They couldn't see any ignorance in their own behaviours. They couldn't see the foolish examples they were setting to the youngers who looked up to us. What pissed me off more was that the youth workers just let the olders come in and chill, like it was a social club for the badly behaved. At that moment I started to dislike youth work. There was no discipline, no structure and my work felt ineffective in that setting. But I didn't give up.

It was February 2009 and I had one of them long hard days at uni and work. To unwind, I went to see my children who were staying in Tottenham at their grandmother's house. By now I was on child number three. My son was 4 years old, my daughter was 1 year and my unborn child was two months away from joining us. But a week before that I remember coming in that same house to a different vibe. Then I remembered my Misses older brother had come out of jail. And some of his youngers who followed him around needed a few lesson in manners. I wanted to teach them too because my children lived in that house. But it wasn't my house, so it wasn't my place.

When I walked in the house I saw my son playing a DS game and I knew I never brought him a DS. So I grabbed it off him and said,
'Whose game are you playing?'
Then one hard face yute with his arm crossed looked at me and said, *'Mine cuz.'*
I wanted to slap 'cuz' with his DS. But I kept my cool, gave him back his DS and said,
'Don't give my son anything without asking me cuz.'

Some people might read that and think why the hostility?
Well to me it's simple. I don't know this yute from Adams. I was trying to keep my son away from a certain lifestyle. I never said cuz or spoke slang around my son, I never smoked weed around my son, and he wasn't allowed to play

violent video games. I came off the street to be an example for him and I didn't like what he was seeing in my absence. I didn't like the fact that this yute was jamming in the kitchen were my children lived like he was jamming on the block. I soon eased off the hostility and started running joke with my childhood friend from Tottenham.

My girlfriend's brother came in the kitchen and was running joke with us too, which in itself is a tale you couldn't make up, unless your name was William Shakespeare. You see, I repped Hackney when I was a prisoner to the streets and my children's Uncle was viewed by older Hackney guys as a main Tottenham guy. And my older brother was viewed as a Hackney man. So the fact that me and my Misses got together was a story within itself. Not in a bad way but we probably would've never got together in the first place had I known her brother repped Tottenham. Not because I had any problems with Tottenham but because I left the roads to get away from the drama. And now I could sense a pending drama in that household. Imagine being caught up in my scenario. It was like some ghetto version of Romeo and Juliet. Hackney's Capulet's and Tottenham's Montague's all under one roof. But up until this day it wasn't a thing - it was all love.

Then a fight broke out upstairs. I won't go into the details of why or what happened but I wasn't happy. I ran upstairs and got into an argument with my girlfriend's older brother and his mother. I was fuming but I hadn't switched yet. Then my children's uncle pulled a knife on me and called me a Hackney boy. If I'm honest, I was angrier about him calling

me a Hackney boy than him pulling a knife on me. My seven
months pregnant girlfriend came storming in the room
pushing her brother and started shouting,
'What the hell are you doing?'
I told her, *'Get my kids out of here before I murder someone.'*

Then I walked out the room and went to get my kids. I
took my son downstairs and put him in the backseat of my
car then I went back inside to get my daughter. As I was
coming downstairs I remember all this shouting going on. I
think my brother in-law called me a pussy or something as
I reached the door. I just remember saying, *'I'm the pussy?*
That's funny but you got the knife right?'
I turned my back on him then I put my daughter in the car.
Then I heard my girlfriend shouting at her brother,
'You're going to attack my man while he's holding my daugh-
ter; you're a sell-out.'
I put my daughter in the car and saw my girlfriend arguing
with her mum and brother. So I walked up to her told her'
'Don't worry just pack your stuff and come stay at mines.'
So she went upstairs to pack. Her brother was by the front
door still making up noise. At that point I felt an old feeling
come back. I walked in the kitchen to get a knife from the
wooden knife holder on the side. As I reached out my hand
in rage at the last second I decided to box the knives down
instead. What happened was I had a flashback of when I
picked up a knife from the kitchen at my Nan's house and
I didn't want any more regrets. I stormed out the house to
wait for my girlfriend to get ready. Then I heard her brother
shouting'
'Nah but he disrespected my Mum.'

And that's when I lost it. I started walking towards him clapping my hands shouting, *'What? How am I disrespecting your Mum? You got a knife in your @@@@ing hand. You're the one disrespecting your Mum.'*

I got close enough to touch foreheads with him. Then he swung the knife with his right hand and it came in the direction of my heart. I lifted up my left arm to defend it and literally blocked it before penetration. Then his little brother, his cousin and a few other people present jumped in the middle to break it up. After all the commotion, he ran off and I was shouting some negatives in his direction. Then the police turned up.

They jumped out of the van and asked me what was going on. They had received a call from neighbours who witnessed an attempted stabbing. I just looked at them and told them nothing happened. I told them it was a family dispute but its resolved now. Most people might think, well why didn't I just tell the police what happened? Well I didn't believe the police cared about my personal safety. I believe they came to do one thing, enforce the law. Although I was vex with my brother in law I didn't want him to go back to jail off the back of me, so I did what comes naturally. I went home that night trying not to fall victim to my pride. Once again I was tested but once again I wasn't hurt. That battle of the voice of reason and the voice of the streets came back to taunt me. I knew that my reaction to this could cause a bigger reaction to spark off the same wars I was trying to free myself from. Like I said, William Shakespeare himself couldn't write a ghetto romance like this. Jokes aside though, this affected the relationship and my mind in a massive way.

I slowly began to lose all interest in youth work and my frustration in studying youth justice and criminology was at an all-time high. I was fed up of hearing the constant use of the word gang or knife crime. Every other lecture I found myself rolling my eyes when I heard those labels to describe the problem. I couldn't see the connection between a criminal mind-set and the life that myself and the mandem lived as children. I stopped engaging in lessons and lost all focus. I think this was partially to do with the fact that I was having constant thoughts of returning to the streets to deal with my girlfriend's brother. *'Hackney bwoy, kmt!'* I thought of the damage my actions could do to the family. In my mind one of us had to go. Not because I wanted to take it there, but the man could've killed me. And I knew most guys on road are scared to fight one on one in case they lose. So they'll stab or try to kill you, rather than take the L. My trap was, I'd rather kill you than let you kill me, either way it's still a catch 22 right?

I started behaving like a prisoner again but not a high risk one. Two months after that incident I was riding my super-bike past McDonalds in Bruce Grove Tottenham. I had just finished boxing and I sighted my girlfriend's brother driving past the snooker club. I'm one-hundred per cent certain it was ego that got the better of me. I childishly wanted to make his heart skip a beat. So I sped up to the side of the car with my blacked out superbike and tinted visor and tapped the driver's window,

'You see how easy it would've been?' I shouted, whilst smiling with my hand in the shape of a gun at the same time. He looked baffled. I was in stitches thinking about it. Then I bussed a lil' wheelie in front and breezed off. Then when I got to Broadwater Farm I noticed he was chasing me with the other guys in the car. I turned down a side road, exchanged verbals and hand signals. I wanted him and his mates to chase me to Hackney but that was never going to happen. I went home laughing about it. In a childish way I felt like I got him back by my actions, but I hadn't. It was a reminder that I wasn't free from that mind-set yet - my ego still controlled me once violated.

A few weeks later I heard he went back to jail for some other madness. I had mix thoughts about it. I didn't really want him dead not at all, but I really wanted to throw hands with him. I could see my girlfriend was getting stressed about the whole thing. Regardless of my rage it was still her brother at the end of the day. She felt trapped in the middle so I tried to push it to the back of my mind whenever I was around her. People on the road who heard about the incident would see me and ask me about what happened. I would try not to say too much, because I've never forgotten how mix up people on the street can be.

The July of 2009 was the month which many would simply call 'divine intervention'. I somehow passed my first year of uni, even with all the distractions and the draw outs. Neville Watson, the same man who told me to write a book in 2007 had set up a boxing trip for me to go to in Wolverhampton. My bags were packed and I was good to go. One of my old friends dropped me to the train station in Euston. But after I reached the platform I was told my train was cancelled so I asked him to come back and grab me. Apparently a man had killed himself by jumping in front of the train at Birmingham. I remember thinking to myself, *'Rah, that's crazy.'* Then me and my old friend concluded that it might be a sign of some sort. He said, *'Maybe you weren't meant to go today!'* I agreed. *'They say everything happens for a reason.'*

I called my girlfriend because I needed the keys for my motorbike parked outside her flat. When I finally got through she said she was at a barbecue across the road from her Mum's house in Tottenham. I was vex because she knew I didn't want my children anywhere near her mums house after the incident with her brother. When I got there I walked in the house like I had no manners. No hello to anyone. I just took the keys out of my girlfriends hand and walked right back out. As I was leaving, I heard the soft voice of a lady,
'Robin?'

 I turned to see who it was. The lady walked up, hugged me then she whispered,
'I'm Kaiya's Mum. You nearly killed my son.'
It was ironic that she hugged me. As she held me, my face rested on her shoulder facing the exact same place where I was nearly stabbed by my girlfriend's brother.
I stepped back from her hug, confused by who she said she was and what she was talking about. Not bragging over my sins but I had so much beef growing up her son could have been anybody. The more she spoke the more it came back

to me. The old me wouldn't even have cared about her pain. Not because I was a heartless person but because the old me was too caught up in his own pain to care about others. Plus I knew I didn't start the beef that day. But when I saw his mother crying, I thought how could I not be respectful enough to hear her out? Especially after knowing I was a massive part of what her tears represented. We spoke for a while that day and she wanted to pray with me. I wasn't really up for praying but I humbled myself before this lady or what my mum would have claimed was God speaking.

We stayed in contact for a few weeks and I can't really re-member who suggested it. But a few conversations later it was suggested that I write a letter to her son who was in jail. Initially I wasn't on it. Then I thought, 'let me humble myself and do the righteous thing. I was raised on the old saying,

'You can't be wrong and strong.'
So considering I might have been wrong and I was working towards being strong, I knew I had to reach out. I wanted freedom from the streets, so I had to face all my old demons if I really wanted to be the difference.

I also wanted to find out if the rumour was true. I kept hearing it was my friend Darker who started the beef that night but I didn't want to believe that. I needed answers. I needed clarity and I didn't trust my friend to believe he would tell me the truth. So I took another massive step towards the journey of freedom and wrote my enemy the letter. If you read *Prisoner to the Streets* then you already know how that letter impacted. You will know that the power of that letter brought forth a lot of revelations.

The power of that letter helped set a fellow prisoner free. It helped to free a man from the thoughts of revenge. It freed him from the thoughts of feeling like a victim. It freed him from the confusion of why he got stabbed. His response letter not only revealed to me that the friend I was defending started the beef but it also helped to free me from the burden of my wrong doing. The letter he wrote said he forgave me and wanted to meet in person.

After his release, we met, and since that day we have become like brothers. And as for the friend who I defended against him, well we don't see eye to eye no more. What gets me is that people who read those letters still have the cheek to say we don't have a solution. How can you ignore what took place here? Youth justice was restored and peace was made in the community without the hands of the law. The power of writing a letter to my enemy and getting that response gave me more reason to tell my story. I still hadn't decided yet but I started the see a clearer picture of what the book could do for people if I wrote it. I was becoming more convinced that I had a powerful story to tell if I chose to write it. At the time I still had a lot going on in my own life. So I just needed a bit more convincing to be 100 per cent certain.

September 2009
Although my girlfriend's brother went back to jail I still felt I had to stay vigilant while in North. Without getting into

detail, being from Hackney and having a child with someone from Tottenham didn't guarantee one's safety. Because when shit hit the fan, people didn't recognise you as anything other than a Hackney boy.

So I wasn't taking any chances.

One day I was in Wood Green shopping centre minding my business when I saw an older Wood Green boy who I recognised. It was my brother- in -law's co-d. They spent quite some time in jail together. There were about six of them. We made eye contact. Because of the rumours on road, I just assumed they knew who I was and what had happened. I didn't know how else to deal with the conflict so I reverted to my old ignorance and offered the group of boys outside to have it. When we got outside I grabbed my helmet tight and said, *'My man's boy, yeah? What is it?'*

The guy was surprisingly cool though. He didn't even know about the situation. When I told him he got vex and said he was going to have a word with him. He said, *'That's not right. You lot are family he shouldn't have done that'.* We spoke for a bit and he realised I was from Hackney but mistook me for my older brother. He then told me that him and my brother was cool from the 90s. We touched fist and then I rode home. At the time I felt so evil on and off I couldn't even talk to my girlfriend most days. I wanted to look past the incident with her brother. I really did. But I was still brainwashed to think like a prisoner. And in that mind-set I thought, *'Why are people on road taking my kindness for weakness? Maybe I should do madness and weaken my kindness?'* (Ali Vegas)

Being tested constantly didn't just affect me, it also affected the relationship with my loved ones. I couldn't be as loving as I wanted to be, my spirit was in constant limbo. How was I supposed to love or live righteously while surrounded by wickedness? Negative thoughts of revenge for everyone who had tested me infiltrated my mind to the point where I began to lose focus at uni. The module assignments and essays kept coming in and my head couldn't take it. I got frustrated and decided to drop out the uni thing and work full time.

It was October 2010 and I was still close friends with the mental farmer otherwise known as Lyndon Walters. I got invited to do a talk at College of North East London to a group of youths. The group of youths were just the right group to talk to. They were hyped about living this road life. My job was to do a talk to deter them from thinking like this. Some people might think, *'How the hell can this guy be doing talks when he himself gets caught up in conflict?'* To which I would have to agree is a good point, but I found a way to listen to my own advice when talking to people. And who says we can't help people heal while being completely broken ourselves? Anyway I decided to invite Lyndon to the talk, but that wasn't it. I decided to pick up my old 'frenemy' Kane who stabbed me as a child. I wanted to show the young people not only through chat but through proof that peace could be achieved. All I can say is that we smashed it. And I'm sure everyone who talks would say the same thing, but this was something special. Rather than take my word for it you can always visit Solutionrooted. com to see a testimony from a veteran youth worker named

Hesketh Benoit. He saw my talk with his own eyes and was happy to write a few words on what he saw.

At the time, this talking in front of people stuff was still new to me. I didn't like doing it but I saw the power in the response from it. Though it was newish, it wasn't the first time I had spoken publicly or openly. A few months prior to this I got a new job as a project worker in Hackney. At first I believed the position would give me the room I needed to be more effective in working with the youth. Solely because it wasn't working under the control of the council's rules; it was an independent organisation. But I soon came to discover that the new job had restrictions of its own in working effectively or even caring about the youth. The only good thing they did was let me go to City and Islington College where I got to do my first set of talks. And that's where I first realised the power of what I bring to table in this field. But it was the talk I did in Tottenham College with the guy who stabbed me and the letter I wrote to the guy I stabbed which kick started everything. It motivated me to pick up the pen and write my truth - Prisoner to the Streets.

By the end of 2010 I called the mental farmer Lyndon Walters and asked him,
'Do you really think I can be an author?'

And he said yes. Then I asked him, *'Well, how do I go about writing a book?'* His response was, *'Write the first word and it will go on from there.'*

From that conversation I began to write the book, but not in book format. It was July 2011 when I decided to go into my room and start to write the book but instead, 20 minutes later I came out the room with a poem....

The sad truth a poem by Robyn Travis

There's no such thing as EQUAL OPPORTUNITIES, life's not fair, that's why there's so many you's and me's!!

Some had their MUMS but didn't have a DAD, some had both parents but the LOVE was still DEAD.

Then some have no CARERS and grow up in CARE! And hated the world because their parents left them there!!

My truth is the STREETS the STREETS that I knew, the place where I LOVED but I HATED it too!!

I had many of bredrins from HACKNEY AND TOTTENHAM, AND I never thought one youth's death would start a war that got so rotten!!

MANY in prison, and MANY are DEAD, but I still see my dead friends, but THAT'S IN MY HEAD!!

And it feels like nobody cares – ESPECIALLY THE FEDS.

But maybe I'm the fool for CARING too MUCH!

I preach to these youngers who CLAIM to be tough!

There's TALENT on our STREETS, these brothers are SKILLED, BUT when you live for the STREET that talent gets KILLED!!

I was filled with TALENT but also FILLED with RAGE – then I got STABBED and SHOT after, then locked up in a CAGE!

Now I've tried to change my life around, to prove that I'm HUMAN, but the SYSTEM don't make SPACE for genuine a NEW

MAN!!

MOTHERS against GUNS, a campaign that's new, but would you REALLY CARE, if the DEATHS of our young children didn't happen to you!!!

After that day I started to go in. I began writing down notes of the things I could remember. Then I hit a memory block so I decided to go to the doctors to find out when I first got stabbed. Then I went to the Hackney Gazette Archives to find out what the article had to say about that incident. While I was refreshing my memory reading it I saw headlines saying something about *'Gang or Thugs from Pembury and London Fields Attack Boy Outside His House'*. My first thought was, *'Here we go again with the gang stuff.'* Even though this group of boys stabbed me, I never saw them as a gang. But when I read the rest of it and the article wasn't talking about me. I started thinking *'that's strange, why isn't my name in here?'* Then I remembered why. It was because after I got stabbed I discharged myself from the hospital so they couldn't get a statement from me.

I went home after researching the past. Then I started thinking about what my real frustration was with all these British films depicting what the streets of England are about. And then I thought of the film 'Bullet Boy'. I watched that film when I was on a plane to Barbados in 2006 and what was weird was even though the film was shot in Hackney and was about the streets I didn't feel any real connection to it. Don't get me wrong, I thought some of the actors were really talented. But the narrative was only falling into the stereotypes of what was already being built about us in this country. My frustrations started to become clearer. I found it frustrating that the whole country and parts of the world were going to be learning from this film. And it didn't represent the Hackney I grew up in. It lacked substance in the sense of explaining why a young person may engage in violence. I had a whole heap of other thoughts. Then I came to realise that this film and others that came after it were counterproductive. Why? Well in my view, none of them were able to give an authentic portrayal of life on the streets. So instead of those films using the platform to give an honest example of the street experience I believed it did the opposite. I believe it created less awareness and more fear and stereotypes were produced.

Around the same time someone sent me a book called 'Guns and Gangs'. This book triggered me off even more than the films did. From what I understood, most of its information came mostly from court reports. And those court reports were then interpreted by the author and turned into a story about life on the streets of the UK. Operation Trident also helped out with the book by giving misleading information to the author about the issues we face in the community. To me this wasn't fair representation. It was like people were criminalising our experiences to the world without hearing from the people caught up in it. I'll never forget what the book said about the Holly Street and London Fields beef. It was so over sensationalised that if I didn't know better even I would've thought this was a gang issue. But I knew it was an inaccurate description because I grew up with both sides and was present when the kindergarten argument started the problems. My frustrations were broad. But at the root of my frustration was the fact that others were telling our story without having lived our experiences. And they were not only getting praised for it but they were getting paid too. I thought to myself, *'How can people be profiting off our pain whilst burying our images further in the dirt?'* I couldn't find any answers to my own questions. So I used all my frustration and emotion to write the book I was working on. And that's when the title came to me,

'Freedom from the womb - Prisoner to the streets.'

Between 2010 and 2011 I managed to get stopped and searched by the police 20 odd times. Out of those twenty odd stop and searches I was wrongly arrested a few times. It wouldn't have bothered me if I was still on the street but I wasn't. I was working for a safer London myself but not by police tactics. My aim was to teach, not criminalise. Every time the police stopped me the reason was the same: *'There's a lot of gang activity going on in this area so we have to stop and search.'* my response the same each time, *'So what does this mean? Because I'm a black male in Hackney I'm going to get stopped and searched because I fit your description of what a gang member looks like?'*

Obviously, there were days I got fed up of the harassment, so I spent some nights in a cell for not complying with the search. All of these experiences added to the fuel that birthed the concept of the book I was writing.

In this same year I took another blow of discouragement when I was made redundant from my position as a youth worker. I was back to square one. I started applying for other positions in the youth field only to be knocked by my criminal record. And that's when I made a conscious decision. I promised myself regardless of my financial position I would never do youth work again. I made that decision when I came to the realisation that these youth positions are not made to fix the problem; their purpose is simply to intervene. And in knowing that, I knew I couldn't be a part of a system which doesn't want to provide a solution.

Also in 2011 my fellow class mates graduated with a Bachelor of Arts degree in Youth Justice and Criminology. I was thinking I wasted two years of my life by leaving the course. Then I got a call from one of the lectures Anthony Goodman. Anthony was definitely a good man who persuaded me to come back and complete the course. So instead of having to be the college drop out again. Anthony agreed that the year I missed could be considered as a gap year. I still had a lot of work to catch up on and I was in the middle of writing a book. But in the end it all worked out in my favour. Instead of having to write a 10,000 dissertation on youth crime PTTS the book, ended up being my dissertation. I'll never forget this part of the journey when I was called in to the criminology department office to speak to lecturer Robin Fletcher. Robin Fletcher was an ex-police man with over 30 years' experience on the beat in areas like mine. After reading the book he said he couldn't help but cry. When I asked him why that was, he said he'd never seen it from that side of the law before. After deciding to go back to uni to finish off my course I got a phone call from Neville Watson. He said, *'Rob, I've found the perfect person to edit book.'*

And this is what the editor said:

In June 2011 I was attending an event at Tottenham Green Leisure Centre. I bumped into Neville Watson, a community worker and activist. He told me there was a young man who has written a book and is looking for an editor. I hesitated at first and told Neville that I had a lot going on and didn't really have the time to edit a book. Then Neville said, 'At least, have a look at it and then make your decision.' So he sent it to me immediately to my Blueberry phone.

I remember getting home and taking a look at the manuscript. I saw the beginning and the way it started I thought, 'Ok, very dramatic!' But as I read further I became much more intrigued by the young man's journey. I saw the highs, the lows, the dilemmas and the challenges. I saw it was multifaceted. There were lots of different angles, issues and themes. He explored single parenthood, fatherhood, education, racism, social exclusion, loyalty, community, the misrepresentation of young black boys and men, policing and social services. He also discussed growing up as a young man and shaping what it means to be a young black man in British society. I mean there were so many different aspects there that I couldn't really control my intrigue.

I then contacted Neville and told him I will make time to edit the book. I was further intrigued by the proposed name of the book, 'Freedom from the Womb - Prisoner to the Streets'. A meeting was then arranged and I met Robin for the first time. I was impressed by him when he began to explain his intentions for the book. He didn't see it as a book about him. It was more than that. The book had a mission; he explained how this was the first part of the solution. He was quite emphatic about that.

Throughout the editing process we had our difference of opinions and mature exchanges in some topic areas. But overall it was a learning curve for me. I got to understand life on the street from a different perspective. Quite often, I would allow my information to be shaped by what I saw or heard in the media. Or even by people who were 'on the streets' but who would give a more glamorised view of what street life was like. However, Robin gave me a different and deeper insight; one for which I'm grateful. It was also the interesting and critical way that he thought about things. He had, developed and owned his perspective. Robin even had his own terminologies. So whenever he articulated a situation or a topic he would use his own terms of reference. During the editing process I never heard Robin use the word gang in the pejorative context - just a group of friends caught up in society. The editing process was a good one for me at least. I met the mother of his children; his family and friends involved in the stories and situations in the book. They assisted in those areas and that helped to bring the characters to life. Sometimes, whilst editing, we had a good laugh. And at the end of every session Robin would say, 'Becks, come lemme get you a Guinness.' That was always my thing. It took us nine long months - from July 2011 – April 2012. That was the entire process.

Sometimes during the editing process, retelling and reliving the stories got too much for Robin. He would say to me, 'Becks, I need to take a break for a couple minutes.' He couldn't really deal with it mentally, then he would come back and we would tackle it. There were times when he would come back and still couldn't deal with that particular part of the manuscript. We would move on to something else until he was ready to deal with it.

For me this journey was more than just being an editor. For me this was an education, a nine month course to be exact. But like I said for Robin this was more than a book. It was about using his story as a solution for some of the pressing problems faced by young people on the streets. And his intention was to help free them. In fact I always thought there was a deeper meaning to the phrase 'prisoner to the streets'. And I've always felt that some people wouldn't get what he was trying to communicate.

I remember speaking to some people after the book was released. They had read the book and we had discussions about it. I felt many of them didn't get the message of the book, or what it was about. I also came to the conclusion that they were perhaps imposing their perceptions and predetermined views of street life on it. They kind of imposed that on the book. I felt they were already influenced by what the media had taught them about the streets, gangs and black boys. It was clear to me that people got caught up in that. They wanted to push the book in that direction, but that wasn't the purpose of the book. And that was strange because Robin never even mentioned the word gang in relation to himself in his book.

I remember just before the book was released Robin had an interview with a journalist from a major regional newspaper in the U.K. Robin asked me to come along. The journalist pro-

ceeded to ask Robin questions about guns, gangs and drugs. So Robin had to set the record straight and told him, 'I was never in a gang; I was a prisoner to the street.' Then he broke down the meaning. Once the interview was concluded and Robin had set the record straight about the concept of gang and the way society uses it for its own purpose, it was no surprise to me that the article was never published. The journalist wanted to portray and frame Robin as some ex-gang member or an ex gangster, which he wasn't. Or as an ex-gangster coming around and amending his ways, and that definitely was not the case. At least not the case for the person I sat down with for nine months to edit that book.'
James Beckles, editor.

I'll never forget the editing process with Jamesy. Those long days and nights going over the same thing over and over; it was the most jarring experience of my life. It reminded me of the 90's film 'Groundhog Day'. We had to read the manuscript again and again, and again. It took so long, it started to mad me. I couldn't help but replay certain scenes in my head over and over again, let alone the things I didn't add. Somewhere within those 9 months I began to lose my mind, literally and psychologically.

It's hard to explain what I mean by that, but I'll try.

I once watched an interview with Will Smith talking about when he played the role of the late great Mohammed Ali. In that interview he spoke about his experience of getting into character. He explained how he had to watch hours of Mohammed Ali boxing tapes. He said he had to wake up 6am every morning to train. And not only train like a boxer but train like the champ, Ali himself. He had to mirror Ali's life and his religious beliefs. And he mentioned that after playing Ali a part of Ali would always live with him. During the interview Will Smith was asked the question,

'Did you keep some attitude of Ali in your life?' Will Smith, 'Oh God yes! I mean you can't do that level of work and not, some parts of it stay with you. Like right now, I could drop you right now! I mean, if you got out of line right now!'

He joked about it but there was some seriousness about his statement that rings true to my experience.

I spent so much time editing the damn book that I got stuck in the 90s. All the people I forgave for doing me wrong in the past were now back on trial in my mind. And every single wrong I done as a youth had come back to haunt me. I started to think and feel like the old me. I didn't go as far as repping the block again but I had the block mind-set on standby. I picked up some of the old temperament and trust issues I buried. But this time it was on a complete different level. Unfortunately I picked up a few old habits to numb the pain and sped up the editing process. A day didn't go past without a spliff and a Guinness. And a day didn't go by where I didn't think to myself,

'Rob what are you doing? This is long.'

I don't know how Jamesy did it. Seriously, I've never drank that much water in my life let alone Guinness. At times I had emotional outburst, I became a threat to myself. A guy was running his mouth to me on the roads and the beating I gave him was quick. I hadn't had a fight for years. Straight after the fight I could see he didn't want it no more so I shouted at him, *'Why start what you can't finish?'* It was crazy. My people saw how I was going on, but not what I was going through. So they couldn't help me. I began to have second thoughts like, *'I'm not ready to do this being woke stuff.'*

A part of me regretted letting Lyndon and others talk me into taking 'the red pill'.
'I mean how can a scab ever heal if you keep picking at it?'
Although I had these thoughts I continued on the journey. In my head it was like I was escaping prison and on the way out I was bussing open the other cell doors. It started to feel like I was running out of time to escape trying to free the others. Even with that thought in mind I couldn't stop editing the book. When James met me he never knew how deep I was in battle with the demons of my past mind-set. I tried to hold it down and keep it to myself. I thought it was just a phase anyway. Then there was one time where I couldn't hold it down.
In July 2011 I nearly breached parole and became a prisoner to the streets again. This was when I first starting the editing process. At the time I had just uploaded a video on YouTube with my poem, *The Sad Truth*. This was before I wrote the first draft. I wanted peace so much that I sent the video to everyone I knew from Hackney, Tottenham, Holly Street and Fields. This was my way to get people from road to support the mission for peace and I made that clear in the video. I also let people know that the book was coming out soon.

At the time, rumour was circulating back to me that my old mates didn't like what I was doing. And my name was being used in a negative context. When I first heard that I was baffled. Because before I even started to write I confronted them about it. I didn't ask for anyone's permission but I promised to use fake names. All of the mandem seemed cool with it. Some of them even helped me remember things I forgot, so that's why I was baffled. The funny thing about the ends though is that most people can be really two-faced. They might nod their head and say one thing to your face but behind your back, those same people will chat you. So when I heard the rumours I never wrote them off. But it was petty, it wasn't a reason to breach my parole and become a prisoner again.

Strange to say this but I think the old me took it personal. The old prisoner in me felt hurt that the same people I showed the upmost loyalty and love to were playing Chinese whispers. The old me thought, *'I've backed these boys way more than they've ever backed me. I even did the decent thing and spoke to those involved in the story. And this is how the mandem repay me?'*
I was fuming when I started thinking like this. I kept thinking these guys are acting up. Whenever they saw me one on one they would be quick to *'show love'*. I started thinking how funny it would be to see them all at the same time. That way, we could pin point out who the two-faced donkey was.

I was with my bredrin one day when he showed me a watsapp message saying something about, *'Fuck London Fields'*. When he showed me the message it triggered me off for some reason. I thought, *'These man can't be serious we're grown men. How can the mandem my age be spreading hate in*

the ends when they weren't on the beef back in the days?'
I was pissed but it wasn't over the message. I was pissed that they were fuelling the beef I was trying so hard to stop. It wasn't even that deep. But because of the mission I was on I felt slyly disrespected. It's like something snapped in me that day. I got a phone call and someone had told me my old mates were shooting a rap video on the block. The prisoner in me thought, *'Great, now we can see who is saying what.'*
I didn't have intentions of hurting anyone. Call it ego but I wanted to set a few things straight.

I pulled up to Holly Street and got out my car. I told myself whoever doesn't say hello is the one who is chatting me. *Sounds stupid right?* But the prisoner in me thought it made sense. When I got out a couple of the youngers who only knew me through youth work said, *'Wah gwarn'.* And the olders didn't say nothing. I was vex. All the old feelings came back of the time when these guys ran and left me for dead. And that's because I was stuck in the story. I walked back in my car and put a CD in the player. Then I turned the volume up and opened the windows and the boot. It took a few seconds but after that I got the reaction I was looking for. My old mate Marcus and Risky Talent put their thumbs down in the direction of my music. So I shouted,

'I hope those thumbs down are for Margz and not me.'
You see I was playing a tune by a rapper who was from Fields just to piss them off. I don't know why it bothered them so much Margz wasn't even involved in our beef like that. He was just a good rapper who happened to be from Fields. They continued with the thumbs down business. And

I couldn't distinguish if it was directed at me or the music. So I went inside one house where my car was parked and brought out a kitchen knife. Why? Just in case it got messy. I was outnumbered by a lot to one and I had my prisoner's principal to defend.

When I was outside Risky asked me, *'Why you going on like that?'* Then Marcus shouted, *'Yeah we spoke the other day.'* Then I shouted, *'So why the fuck are you man acting so funny then? And who's got a problem with me writing this book?'* After voicing my frustration I started to walk towards them. Then Risky talent came over like he came to talk to me. But the way he went about it I wasn't feeling it. So I just said, *'I'll knock out anyone here who's chatting me or this book. And if a man wants to use weapons we can do that too.'* Long story short no one owned up to whatever they said behind my back. Then a fight broke out between my old friend Marcus and Darker. The fight was dead then a younger gave a shank to Marcus and that's when I switched on the younger. They were having a fair fight and Marcus was not losing, so I thought why give Marcus a knife? After all the foolish commotion I started, the police came round and everything cooled off. All of the older Holly Street boys my age walked away from the police and we had a grown up conversation. And that's when I learned the problem wasn't entirely with me or my book. The problem was with Darker and the book of lies that he wrote about us.

When I got home I felt like a bit of an idiot but that's what happens when you keep picking the scab. It takes much longer to heal.

A week later my friend from uni called me and said she heard what had happened. She had a tone of disappointment in her voice. She said that one of the youngers who was her cousin said, *'How can Robin be talking about peace and then come round and do that?'*

I thought to myself, *'Aint that a bitch. When I was preaching as the youth worker he never listened. But the second I get vex he pays attention.'* He was absolutely right, but it felt like I had to make noise to get them to listen. They didn't hear me speak as a youth worker. And they were still heavily influenced and young minded. They respected the street mindset, rappers, and people who do road. I didn't pre-plan it but I was trying to show them through my erratic behaviour that the streets were fake. Though I seriously doubt I got the message through that day. I thought,
'Dammed if you do, dammed if you don't.'

It was at this point of the journey where I got lost. I was having an identity crisis between the old and new me. In other words what I'm saying is I think I had a temporary breakdown. I don't know if it was a mental one or an emotional one but I'm 99.9% sure I had one. It's only looking back years later that I realised I was losing it. And that's how it goes sometimes. Most of us don't know we've lost our mind until we've found it again. And looking back I can see I was definitely a sandwich short of a picnic there. Why? Cos a few weeks after behaving like a mad man with a knife I found myself begging Mr Levi to let me read my poem on stage at Hackney Empire.

So imagine it was the upcoming memorial for Robert Levy my old mates little brother who lost his life to this destructive mind-set. For some reason I was on one. I was desperate to share the message I had, because I believed the book would bring fourth truth and change the youth game forever. So when I heard about the memorial I wanted to be a part of it to share this message of hope.

When I told Mr Levi about my book and poem he seemed interested. He was a genuine man wanting to see a change after losing his son. But without being arrogant I felt I had something more solution based to bring to the table. I asked him if I could perform the poem to get my message out there and he said no. At first I was confused. Then he said he heard about my little commotion in Holly Street and he wasn't convinced I was the man for the job. He also said he didn't want the violence to escalate at the event. At this point I responded like a child would when it is begging its mum to let it go outside and play. I was like, *'Nah Mr Levi I promise I'm not that guy. It was a minor thing, just a glitch in the matrix. There won't be any trouble I promise.'*

It almost felt degrading like I was trying to prove to him I'm changed. But I felt he saw the character of the guy who killed his son rather than the guy who could possibly bring forth change. I can't blame him for that if that was true. But I continued to plead with him,
'Let me do it.'

Not because I cared about his opinion of me but for the sake of greater good I needed this man to see the good in me. I wanted him to keep hope and know that a real solution was in the pipeline. I agree I wasn't the best example of a messenger, but I knew I had the best message so I pleaded just to get my voice heard. In the end Mr Levi gave me a chance, but the deal was I had to be part of the play.

Now if you know me you would know I had to be losing my mind to say yes to this. I mean really, me act in a play?
The same introverted child who always refused to be in school plays his whole schooling life? And the same guy who never wrote a poem before this one? And there I was acting a small role in some random play just to say my piece. Method in the madness I suppose.

It's 2019 and I still find it hard to believe I actually did that. Talk about acting out of character. And it wasn't just that. I was having emotional switches on a daily. It must have made it hard to be around me when all I was talking about was the past. This process made me switch on friends and loved ones. While writing I found myself pushing people away because of old trust issues. Some of my people thought I was just being defensive about my story but that wasn't the case entirely. Most of the time when I snapped in conversation with my people it was because I couldn't express my point without getting angry. My passion got confused for anger knowing I was doing something they didn't overstand. People thought I was dismissive of their opinion but I wasn't. I'm a fan of everyone having a voice and an opinion. But that doesn't mean the facts don't override there opinion.

While I was in the midst of my journey tragedy struck for the family of Mark Duggan. And when I say midst I mean just that I couldn't see clearly. Mark Duggan was killed in August of 2011, during the same time I was losing my mind. It was only the month before I took out a knife around Holly Street. And you heard what one of the young men thought about me as a messenger. Now when Mark Duggan got killed, it affected me. He wasn't my friend but I could put the name to his face. Worse still, he was from Tottenham so as a PTTS I'm not supposed to care right? Well I did and many other people did hence the riots. Why? Because the incident with Mark was a reminder of the injustices we receive from the police on a daily basis for years.

Anyway, Neville Watson called me one day in early October 2011 and said he wanted me to go on BBC Radio 5 and discuss the matter. I told him I wasn't interested because the media doesn't care about the truth. If they did they wouldn't have called him a gang member. Neville said that's irrelevant and he explained how I could use it as a platform to express my point and be a voice. I still wasn't convinced because I wasn't trying to come across as an activist. My focus was solely in reaching the people on the roads, see the way I viewed things was simple. If we found a way to squash the beef between ourselves then we wouldn't need platforms to voice our opinions; people wouldn't be able to label us gang members if we squashed the beef. Police wouldn't be able to easily stop and search us because with peace we kill the stereotypes.

I was on the Dotun Adebayo show and it felt strange being there. Some people get gassed when in these places but I was scared. I had heard many Rasta men use the phrase Babylon Broadcasting Corporation in my childhood. So I was scared I wouldn't be able to articulate myself without getting defensive. I wasn't in the right frame of mind, but when the interview started I held my point. I made the point that Mark Duggan wasn't a gang member. I said none of us are we are prisoners to the streets. I said it's not fair to label a dead man as a gang member to justify his killing. Then I said even though I wasn't there I know for a fact he didn't shoot at the police first, that's even if he had a gun on him. Then Dotun cut me and said you can't say that. And I said yes I can, I come from the same place. I know how we think. If I was getting chased by armed police for a strap I'm not shooting unless... You have to be a mad man to shoot at police. This isn't yard or the states. This is London - CCTV central. Any man from the road would prefer to go to jail for a strap than get into a shoot-out with armed police once cornered. Then Dotun cut me again and said I can't say that because the evidence hasn't been presented. Soon after I got frustrated with Dotun cutting me, so I silenced myself.

After the interview I didn't want to shake Dotun's hand. He said great interview. I said, *'For you maybe, but you never let me talk.'* Then he explained his job is to do that. But because I was new to it all I lacked the understanding that he had to play Devil's advocate during the interview. It's just the nature of the game he said. Then he said, *'Good luck with the book.'* After I spoke with Neville, he explained to me that Dotun was a publisher and that he would probably be a good person to publish the book after I finish the edit with James. But I wasn't feeling him at the time so I let it go over my head.

Four months later in February 2012 I was contacted by Ian, the founder of London gang's street website. Ian was a white brother, my age from West London. When we met he said he was intrigued by my perspective on the radio. He said he's never heard it put like that before. Anyway, we spoke about it and stayed in contact. I told him it's not a gang issue and most of the info on that web site was false. He agreed and said most of his info was taken from court reports etc. I told him to wait a few months and my book would be out. And that way he could get a better insight into what I was saying.

By April the same year me and James finally completed the book edit. I was drained. It took 9 months to edit that baby. After we finished I didn't want to hold it. I tried to distance my thoughts from it. I was ready to self-publish it and release the book straight away. I was so anxious to put it out there to transform the minds of my brothers. But I forgot Neville told me he had sent a copy of the manuscript to Dotun. After reading it Dotun decided he wanted to publish the book. This put things on hold a bit longer. It felt like round 11 of the journey and I wanted to throw in the white towel. I couldn't read that book again let alone edit it. But I kept my focus and carried on fighting, I mean editing. It was a real unexpected honour to work with Dotun. I mean I never knew who he was from the radio but he was a cool guy and a great writer. He taught me a lot of what I know

today. One day we were editing and he stopped suddenly,
'Robin you don't need me to edit this book with you. Look at this!'
Basically he felt the penny had dropped for me. He said I found my writers voice, then he sent me home. A second editing process went on from 2012 April – July. Then the book was finally complete. By the end of the edit I asked Dotun if I could write the book without putting my name on it. He laughed and asked,
'What would be the point of that?'
I told him, *'That way people would hear the message rather than ignore it because of the messenger.'*

We debated the ghost author thing for a while and in the end Dotun won. A few days after accepting I would have to be the face of this; I decided it was time to promote.
I contacted media schools, PRU's, youth services, probation workers the full shebang. Then two months before the book was launched in August I decided to go to Notting hill Carnival to hand out flyers. I was starting to feel like a street evangelist. I never knew telling my story would involve this much work. But I knew if the message was to get heard I was going to have to go hard in promoting it. I'll never forget the biggest example of ignorance I came across while I was street evangelising. I gave an elder man my flyer and he said he doesn't need it. I said to him 'What do you mean you don't need it?' Then he said, *'My two sons go to university, I don't have to worry about all that.'*
Then I thought back to my poem 'The Sad Truth'. Then I challenged him, *'So what are you saying that because it hasn't affected you directly, you're saying it's not your problem?'*

He ignored the question, waved his hand and then walked away. The prisoner in me felt so frustrated I wanted to crush the flyer and dash it in the back of his head. Instead I shouted, *'I hope the streets don't affect your children's children.'* For me it was hard enough writing the book. I never knew promotion would raise its own challenges. I still continued as the journey was near an end.

It was now September 2012 one month before the book launch took place. I finally graduated with a degree in Youth Justice and Criminology. It's quite ironic that the only thing I learnt from studying Youth Justice and Criminology was that there isn't any Justice in judging the Youth as Criminals. Regardless of all that I was proud of myself. After the teenage life I lived I never saw myself being alive at 21 let alone graduating in front of my mum and children before 30. It was a surreal moment. But it was a bit deeper than just graduating. It felt like I began as a student and left as a teacher. Nothing could describe that feeling coming from the child who teachers claimed growing up was unteachable.

The end of the road had arrived. 17th October 2012, *Prisoner to the Streets* the book launch. The book was launched in Tottenham's Bernie Grant Centre. The media never turned up but the room was filled with an audience of people from Hackney and Tottenham. I thought that alone was an achievement within itself, forget the book. Even Les Ferdinand came down to support which I rated highly. It was a night of peace love and progress. I remember when I got home in the early hours of the night I looked out the window with a spliff in my hand. I stared in the sky and made the question statement,

'I made it through the journey. So that must mean my purpose is fulfilled. Right?'

In *December 2012* my mate from the London Street Gang's website came to see me. He had read the book and wanted to talk to me. He said he finally gets what I'm saying. He said he realises the problem isn't a gang one. He then said, *'I've decided to take down the Gangs website. It's not helpful. I'm only doing this after reading your book. I get it now; this isn't a gang issue, it's as a prisoner to the streets one. I get it bro; it's a mind-set not a gang issue.'*

At that moment I felt like Will Smith when he was in that pursuit of happiness film. You know the part where he gets the job after all the bull crap he went through? I smiled and thought to myself, *'Yes, I did it. Message delivered and received loud and clear, right?'*

Wrong. In the early parts of 2013, I received an email from an organisation called Words 4 Weapons. They said they had heard about all the amazing work I was doing and they wanted to present me with an award. At first I was sceptical about it because this wasn't the purpose. I still went to the ceremony with an open mind to find out what the award was about. Two of the mandem came with me. My frustration came when I was given the award for *most transformed life.* I was pissed about it. My worst nightmare was that people would make the book about me coming off the roads. But that wasn't the purpose so why would it be misunderstood? I went on stage and vented that they misunderstood the purpose but that didn't help. They just looked at me like I was crazy. That's when I first realised I may not have reached the masses.

Then the tables really turned. I thought I had done something positive. I thought all the doubters finally understood why I wrote it. I thought I did the hood proud. That was up until my own family turned against me. They said they felt betrayed for the things I said. This was heartbreaking to hear. Especially, since they were the same family members who encouraged me to write it. One family member accused me of snitching on my brother and bad talking my mother. That was hurtful but funny at the same time. Because people didn't know my family sat down and read their parts in the book word for word. And when it was edited they were included in the process. But some of us can never do any good in some people's eyes. Whatever we do will never be good enough. And it hurts more when it comes from home base. The same people we love and try to make proud have a way of shooting down our achievements.

I started feeling like J Cole when he made 'Let Nas Down'. It was genuinely at this point where I regretted keeping it real. I wished I had kept it all to myself. I had all sorts of internal turmoil. I felt betrayed like I had been set up to fail. I felt betrayed and unheard. Yet I didn't give up I continued because I knew the message was bigger than me or any family members opinions. Some Black people have this view that none of our lives experiences should go in a book. And that's why we don't learn about our experiences through books. I over-stood that I didn't incriminate anyone or dishonour anyone so the story had to be pushed. That was with or without the support of my people.

Sometime after the book launch I was re-united with my girlfriend's older brother. He had come back out of jail since our last meeting. My girlfriend's little brother rightfully wanted peace between us. So he sneakily set me up to be in the same house as his brother, so we could talk. When I first saw him I was still vex. I didn't want to start nothing but I still hadn't come to a place of forgiveness. I sat down and told him I didn't rate him for bringing weapons into our argument. He responded with he thought I was dissing his mum. And he said he knew the odds of beating me in a fight were slim. From what he heard about me while he was in jail, so he instinctively drew for the knife. At that point his little brother came out the room laughing as if a joke was made. I didn't laugh. All I thought to myself, *'That's the realist talk I've ever heard coming from the streets.'*

But in the same breath that wasn't an acceptable reason to shake hands. I needed more. So I said,
'Nah bruv, you called me a Hackney boy. You didn't see me as the person who made you an uncle. You almost stabbed me cuz.'
Then he said something very profound which let me know we got more in common than I imagined. He said,
'Bruv, I'm not gonna lie, I've been in and out of jail my whole life. I can't say why I went to stab you. The truth is bro I think I'm institutionalised.'
In my head I shouted, *'Wow!'*
It was a wake up moment, almost like a reality check. I

knew I wasn't alone battling these demons. I knew someone else understood what it meant to be controlled by this mind-set. And at that second I forgave him because I understood it. And who am I not to forgive a fellow prisoner?

Years later I met Chris Eubank senior at Kiyan Prince's memorial. I was selling my books at the event when Chris senior came over and curiously looked at the books on the table. I always made it a thing to give certain celebrities the book for free. Not because I was a fan of them, but I knew through their platform the message could reach a much larger audience. So you could say in essence I was using their status for the greater good. I was never a fan of celebrities but there were always the few who I admired for their talent. Chris so happened to be one of them. So when I saw him looking curiously I started laughing because I had seen that look before. I never prejudged him like the rest of Britain did I thought Chris was a don.

As we spoke he asked me about the book and I told him I believed it was a solution to the madness. He didn't seem too impressed. And his body language reflected that. That day Mark Prince had asked me to do my poem at his son's memorial, and it was almost time to do so. Before Mark called me I signed a copy of the book while reasoning with Chris then I said,
'Chris, you can have that one King.'
He looked at it and kinda pushed it back on the table. I was bussing up at first. Because for a while this had been my tactic in promoting the message, but Chris weren't having it. Then while laughing I said,

'Alright cool, I can't force you to have the book but can I get a quick pic?'
He hesitated then said, 'Yes why not?'

I knew he wasn't going to hold the book for the picture, so I didn't bother ask. Instead I was a ginnal about it. I asked him to stand next to me behind the table where I was displaying the books. That way it would look like he was supporting the book. Then I gave my phone for a man to take the picture. Then I put the book up in the middle of the table between me and Chris. He gave me this side look before the picture was taken as if to say,
'You tink you're smart eh.'
I was grinning teeth.
After the picture Mark came in to call me. Then I thanked Chris because he didn't have to take the picture and although he didn't hold the book he was honest about it, and I respected that. As I was leaving he said something that left me baffled.
He said, 'Young man, your books there not a bad thing, but you've got to do more.'
The tables had turned, now I was looking at him curiously.
He continued, 'Well, what I'm saying is when I was champion everyone hated me. The people hated me. And through it all I triumphed. In life you have to do things which are big. You have to be courageous, you have to have teeth.'
At this point I got all in my feelings. Then Mark came over.
'Yo Rob, they want you on stage now.'
I looked at Chris completely lost for words.
'What do you mean have teeth?'
Then he said it again, 'You have to have teeth young man!'

The fan in me was eagerly looking for the wisdom to take from the great boxer's statement. But the boy in me was hurt by it. I wanted to tell him all I had been through but I was too caught in my feelings about the journey to even form a sentence.

'But you haven't even read it yet.'

As we were talking, Mark interrupted and pulled me to go on stage. Then Chris kind of pulled my other arm to insinuate to Mark he wasn't finished talking with me yet. But I had to go. And to be honest I didn't want to hear anymore of Chris's wisdom. He already made his judgement. I wasn't taking his comment personal like that. But instantly his comment made me think real hard about what I went through in writing that book.

Have teeth?

I stood on stage day dreaming.

'If only you knew brother, if only you knew you.... You think it was you alone getting death threats?

I fought a 15 month fight without my corner man, without my cut man.

'Have teeth?'

I didn't even have a gum-shield for this fight, let alone water to drink between rounds. I fought hard with a heavy heart, and I wore much heavier gloves than my opponent. I had much less time to train for this fight. And just as I thought I was winning the fight my close family members walked out of the stadium. They stopped supporting me, even though it was them who talked me into taking up boxing in the first place. When I started winning I thought the crowd was cheering for me. Only to find out most of the fans were cheering for the action. After the fight the journalist didn't even bother to interview me, even though I won this by KO. '

I think it's pretty safe to say that I had a mouth full of teeth when I wrote that book. And not only did I have teeth, it took brains, heart and balls too. No hard feelings though, Chris didn't know me or my journey. He actually did me a favour that day. He made me realise I had to do more to get the message across more precisely.

The journey and all its reasons had come to an end, but I didn't feel free anymore. I was still dealing with the past and the release of the book which made it hard to put behind me.

I spoke with the mental farmer and said,

'You know what Lyn I don't think the therapy worked for me. I feel worse now than I did before writing it.'

Mental farmer, *'Well, that's what happens when you mentally vomit son. You were holding all that sickness in and it had to come out. Tell me, how do you feel?'*

'I dunno Lyn, I can't explain it with words but I'll paint the picture. It's like I was in prison serving hard time. Then suddenly the alarm goes off and my cell door flew open. I couldn't believe it but I could see there was another way to get out of this prison, I saw freedom. So I jumped up and ran out of the cell door, I ran through the wing corridor I was on. It was surreal; I was on the verge of escaping. I put my right foot halfway across the prison gates at the front; I knew I was a free man. Then I stopped and hesitated. I thought to myself am I being selfish? What about the other prisoners who secretly

wanted to change their ways and get freedom? Enemies included. If I quickly run back and give them the master key then maybe they could get another chance to right their wrongs. But honestly speaking, I didn't want to risk it.

After putting my other foot out of the prison gate I stopped again. I couldn't do it. I ran back to the cells to unlock the doors of as many other Now I have to serve more time as a prisoner as punishment for trying to escape and for trying to set the others free.'

That's the only way I can explain it Lyn through visualising my feelings. When I went back to write that book I got lost in my past. Now my time is almost complete. It's time to get real freedom. The freedom we all deserve. Freedom is a must, Freedom from the Streets.

CHAPTER 2

THERE'S A MASTER KEY FOR EVERY LOCK'

*Prisoner to the Streets
workshop summary and
breakdown*

Question – What is a Prisoner?

Prisoner

(1) A person kept in prison. (2) A person captured and kept confined.

Synonyms –

convict, detainee, inmate.

What is a Street?

Street .n. a public road in a city, town.

What is a Gang?

Gang.n. an organised group, esp. of criminals or manual workers.

What is a Prisoner to the Streets?

A prisoner to the streets is a person who is imprisoned or trapped in a particular mind-set.

This mind-set is similar to the one of a prisoner who is serving time in prison. Most people who have been to prison can vouch for me when I say the prison mentality is a self-destructive kind of mind-set. One which seems to be based mostly on fear survival and misguided honour and misguided pride.

In prison there are rules and codes which most prisoners seem to follow without question. And I'm not referring to HMP'S behavioural policies. I'm talking about the prisoners rules themselves. That's right, where and when they can, prisoners live by their own rules and ideas of how they think the prison should be run. Most of these ideas are not original to us and most of them are self-destructive. And whether the prisoner realises it or not these rules are damaging to self. These rules made by whoever made them are making the prison time a lot harder than it needs to be.

Now a prisoner to the streets doesn't need to be physically locked up in an institution to have a prisoner's mind-set. And that's why I define the issue as PTTS one. Both the prisoner to the streets and the prisoner in prison are confined by invisible walls. Those invisible walls represent the mind-set. This mind-set keeps us divided by prison cells but equally imprisoned.

The same goes for the prisoner to the streets. The PTTS is lost in a mind-set where he feels the need to act out in a certain way to survive a mind-set that surrounds him or her. Like the prisoner in prison, the PTTS is unconsciously making life in their own community a lot harder than it needs to be.

Not too worry though because thankfully we have an anecdote for this ill mentality. We've found a cure that can treat this condition, but you can't just take the anecdote once and expect a miracle. The course of action needs to be taken at least three times a year to see the full effects. The anecdote is the 'Freedom from the streets Workshop'. We are fully aware that this workshop doesn't change the way the system works. So we are aware it doesn't create more jobs for the youth. We are also aware it doesn't cure poverty issues. And we are aware it doesn't get rid of all the drugs and the weapons, but that's the whole point of the medication. We have long discovered we don't have a decisive voice in what the system says or does. We know we don't control our environments but we also discovered we have the power to change the way we think and behave in those environments. Below is a sample of the Prisoner/Freedom from the Streets workshop.

The workshop is divided into 4 (x1 hour) sessions

Stage 1 – The Innocence before the Prisoner

(The child's innocence before the prisoner) this section looks at learnt behaviours. They say children are like sponges soaking up all the information around them. Well I agree, and a lot of boys I grew up with became PTTS partly because we didn't have the tools to deal with the stuff we soaked up. For example, things such as fear, conflict resolution, emotional maturity, childhood trauma, embarrassment and a range of other stuff. This section is all about the child before the change. The focus age of reflection here is 0 – 7 years.

LEARNT BEHAVIOUR (ALL BEHAVIOURS ARE LEARNT)

I learnt from a young age that if I misbehaved or did anything to vex my mother I would get licks. So in essence I was learning that if I was naughty or went against my mother's standards I would get pain as a form of punishment. Not the naughty step straight beats, discipline, licks, whatever you wanna call it. Some people would even call it abuse. However I don't believe that abuse would describe my personal experience. I don't feel I was abused, but I definitely got my fair share of licks whenever I acted up or lied about something serious. The point I'm making is, a child learns behaviours and I learnt certain behaviour from getting licks. I learnt that licks were a way of correcting someone's behaviour if they are doing wrong.

Then I may ask the class, *'Who can relate? How so?'*

I also learned from my mum that if one of us (Me or my older brother) got into a fight we both had to back each other to the end - Loyalty. I learned to have my brothers back from young. I'll always remember my brother fighting an older boy in Tiverton estate. I was about 7 years old. And I was on this older guy's back, hitting him in the head to help my brother. What I'm saying is we didn't learn to defend each other from no street code. These behaviours were learnt in house years before. And I didn't defend my brother out of an evil heart. In fact it was because I was scared he would get hurt.

I then turn to the class, *'Who can relate? How so?'*

By the age of 5 I learnt about conflict Resolution as explained in PTTS. I had permission from my mother and encouragement from my brother to defend myself against bullies. Her exact words, *'I gave birth to you and I didn't do that so that other people can beat you, now go outside and don't come back until you win that fight I'll be watching from the balcony.'*

Question for the class, *'Who can relate to this form of learning? How so? Another Question was my Mothers teaching Good or Bad? Was there another way she could have taught me about how to resolve Conflict?'*

Childhood Trauma

In life we are almost guaranteed tragedy at some point, and we learn ways to deal with it. But how do young children learn to deal with such trauma? Here are just a few examples of trauma that took place in my childhood and shaped the teenager I later became.

Racial Harassment - At the age of 2 I have a vague memory of my mother screaming and shouting late at night and stamping out the fire by the door. You see what had happened was a racial group called the National Front NF had petrol bombed the front door to our house.

Why?

The truth is being black in England hasn't ever really been easy and racial harassment was semi active back then. However we look at it racial harassment is a form of rejection. It's saying you are not good enough to be here you don't belong. Having experienced that type of childhood trauma I learned that I could be at risk to violence because of the shade of my skin. However, in saying that, I didn't feel threatened by all white people. My primary school teacher Miss Leonard treated me like I was her own son and she was a white lady.

As a child I was learning through no faults of my own that my kind (black people) were not wanted. Think about what that can do to a child's mind growing up. So imagine my childhood fear in 1993 when I overheard my mum cussing the TV because a man called Stephen Lawrence was murdered by a gang who hated the colour of his skin.

Added Trauma and **Fear** – News of father's death

Mum's words, *'My children grew so scared that on some nights I found them sleeping in the cupboard. I felt I had to be harsher on them to make them tougher. I didn't want them to be afraid of anything.'*

I then ask the class, *'Who can relate to racial harassment? Who can relate to this level of childhood fear? How do you feel this type of fear can impact a child growing up?'*

Another question for the class, *'My mum said she was tougher on us because she didn't want us to be scared of anything. Was she right to be tougher on us? And was she right to tell me to hit someone back if they hit me?'*

My opinion is her teachings came from a place of love and fear. She did the best she could with the tools she had. She didn't know that what she was teaching me was going to further shape me to think and behave like a PTTS.

Question for the class, *'What do you think I mean by that?'*

Well what I mean is that I was subconsciously learning how to use violence as a way of dealing with conflict and my fears. I don't believe my mother's intentions were to make me violent as she always encouraged me to write down how I was feeling. So violence definitely wasn't what she was trying to teach. However as a young boy I was too ashamed or scared to say when I was experiencing fear, so nobody ever knew. I just kept it to myself and it later turned into anger and violence.

Let me use a number of analogies to make it clearer as to how I explain the concept of anger and fear to a fellow PTTS. Volcano analogy - I was like a volcano that had the potential to explode. All the fire was in my belly and my mind was waiting to erupt. And when I did, I was very much afraid of what I had the potential to do. My rage erupted and overflowed in my defence as devastating as the lava from the eruption. © (Mental Farmer)

Fizzy drink analogy - Through fear, the mentality of the roadman is similar to fizzy drinks. One of the things about fizzy drinks is that it has an ingredient called aspartame. Two side effects of aspartame are depression and ADHD, which visits the mind-set of the typical road man. This is typical of the lifestyle which is as sweet, addictive and toxic as the fizzy drinks, which when shaken up is as explosive as a hand grenade. © (Mental Farmer)

After explaining the analogies I go back and ask the class my initial question, *'My mum said she was tougher on me and my brother because she didn't want us to be scared of anything! Was she wrong to be tougher on us? '*

Well, like I said previously, her teachings came from a place of love and fear. Fear that the world would eat us alive if we allowed it to. And love because every loving parent cares about their child's safety. She didn't know what she was teaching me would have taught me a behaviour which would contribute to me having a PTTS mentality. That behaviour was violence. I was learning and embracing the concept that violence resolves violence or that violence resolves disrespect. And violence will deal with my fears. These are all false statements. But most importantly, I feel that violence and fear are two things that shouldn't mix, which is an ironic thing to say because I feel most prisoners to the streets mix violence with fear daily. Most prisoners to the streets I know will never be honest about being scared. They prefer to act up front basically give the impression that they're not scared of anything.

I then ask the class, *'What are you scared of? Better yet what was you scared of as a child? To open up the conversation I discuss my childhood fears.'*

BULLYING

I then go on to discuss bullying and how this mentality we learnt starts early on in life. In primary school I knew of many children who were prisoners to the playground. The cure is in preventing that way of behaving in a holistic way, before they become too programmed. I also discuss childhood trauma not only from my perspective growing up but from the perspective of the so called bad child 'the bully' I continue to use my experience as an example by mentioning the character Mohammed. I explain how he was a bully but he wasn't the bad child. Some get thrown off by that. But it is the truth. How can Mohammed be the bad guy when he came here from war driven Somalia? He came here to seek refuge. I think it's safe to say he had way more childhood trauma than I could imagine. My childhood traumas are probably peaceful thoughts to him. This doesn't justify his prisoner behaviours by any means. At the same it's important not to label a bully a bad child based on his behaviours. You know the saying, *Hurting people hurt people.*

We also cover Environment, Adapting, Emotional Triggers, Emotional Maturity and Emotional Intelligence. Self-esteem and everything else relevant you can think of.

By the time I get to this part of the workshop the prisoners start to let their guards down. Not because I'm the so called chosen one. It's not about that it's because the medication is pure. And that helps it to be more effective because everyone in the conversation can be honest about their behaviours. 'If the truth is told the youth can grow' (Nas). This is just a snippet of what stage one looks like.

STAGE – 2.1

The Unconscious Prisoner

(REMAND TIME)

When a person is on remand in jail depending on the weight of evidence against them that individual has some form of hope. A prisoner on remand believes he has a chance of freedom – regardless of how slim. A prisoner on remand time can accept the fact that the prison he or she is in may only be as temporary as the upcoming court date. That court date will determine whether this temporary prison becomes more than temporary.

And if it so happens that the remanded prisoner gets convicted and has to serve a longer sentence than expected then that prisoner can begin to lose hope. That prisoner can become hopeless. And when a person realises they are going to be a prisoner for some time they can react in different ways.

1.   The prisoner may go into shock and find it hard to adjust. Feeling distressed maybe crying not wanting to accept the situation.

The prisoner may do what most prisoners do. Forget how they're feeling inside and say, *'Eff it, it is what it is.'* Then adapt to prison life.

The reason I mention this analogy is to explain that I see this part of my life as when I was a PTTS on remand. And looking at my lifestyle previous to this age of 14, 'the evidence' seems to suggest that I'm almost guaranteed a life on the streets. What I'm saying is that is not true? There is always hope. And it's not true for a lot of young men at this unconscious prisoner stage.

Question for the class, *'What hope can we show a young person who's falling into this mind-set before they become long-term prisoners? And what would you say to the younger you at this unconscious prisoner stage?*

Do you believe it's possible to show these young people there is much more to life than being a prisoner?'

You see, a lot of people have given up hope on the youth, but to me giving up on the youth would mean to give up on the younger me. I genuinely believe any prisoner to the streets can change we just have to find out what it is that makes them say F it and give up hope in the first place. This is what they would call intervention.

THE CONCIOUS PRISONER – REMAND TIME STAGE – 2.2

The Conscious Prisoner

(RIDING MY SENTENCE)

This is the stage where the individual has finally realised he is a prisoner to the streets, and although deep down he doesn't want this prison life, he's willing to say, 'fuck it' and role with the (prisoners mentality) and do his sentence. This can happen from any age, but I feel this takes place more often from 16-18. In some individuals it happens earlier and in some cases it happens much later. But from my observation, ages 16-18 is when most young people give in or disregard this mind-set. During the workshop I use (PTTS) the book to highlight the examples of what a conscious prisoner looks like.

First example of PTTS mentality – Using the book I describe how one minute I was running from police because of the fear of going to jail. Then an hour later the fear of getting caught slipping on the streets became greater than my fear of going to jail. I went right back to where the police chase started just to go pick up my gun.

'Can you see what I mean when I say this is an example of conscious PTTS behaviour?'

Another example of PTTS mentality – My old bredrin got a phone call from some guys in Tottenham about beef. Not only was I backing beef that wasn't mine, but I was willing to ride out for people who had tried to set me up in the past. For people I didn't even like I was willing to risk my life and freedom.

'Do you understand what I mean when I say this is an example of PTTS behaviour?'

Another example of PTTS mentality – In that book I explained how I was rolling with my gun or knife some days both almost 24/7. I wouldn't consider myself a gunman by want, but I was living like one. Feeling like I was on the verge of life, death or prison every day. And that was like a sentence within itself. The mentality I was trapped in attracted a lot of violence in my teenage life, at the price of what?

'Can you relate? Do you understand what I mean when I say this is an example of PTTS behaviour? Can we really justify living with this mind-set? Other than saying, 'It is what it is?'

Another example of PTTS mentality – In PTTS the book I wrote a chapter called, Six Months of Madness filled with stabbings and shootings. In that particular chapter the conscious prisoner is evident throughout. Then I ask the class is this gangster or a self-destructive way of living, is it really worth it?

Keeping it real? Ride or Die? Or mad man? On page 131 of PTTS I explain an incident where I could have gotten killed. I explain a scene when over 25 guys had knives and weapons targeted at me. At the time I just saw them jump a boy. The two guys I was with suggested we run but my pride would not let me. That misguided pride nearly got me killed. Most people would run away, but I did the opposite. I ran and attacked them first! Just like the first time when I got stabbed. I was willing to fight to the death over my chain and my name sake. Even when shots were fired at me I didn't run in fact the team doing the shooting backed off.

Question for the class, *'So were the actions of the younger me that night Gangster? Did I keep it real? Or was it suicidal?'*

After the class answer, I give my explanation of how I perceive my past actions. One might say I was suicidal based on my reaction that night, but that wouldn't be an accurate description. I believe my trigger was with people who, in general acted wicked in numbers. A combination of misguided pride, ego, anger, confused sense of self-worth, lack of self-worth and other learnt behaviours allowed this behaviour to manifest. I didn't keep it real or suicidal I was simply an A cat prisoner to the street mind-set.

My Pride - it wouldn't allow me to run. Even when gun shots were fired – I didn't want to be a victim of fear (Just like school days with Mohammed)

My Ego – as they got closer I turned and said, 'You lot don't want it with me.' Basically I wanted them to know this wasn't going to be a simple battle and there would be repercussions if they didn't kill me.

Anger – I remember being angry thinking I wish the numbers were even. I remember feeling angry that these guys were going to try to rob me for my chain. And we didn't even know each other. (Prison tactics)

Confused sense of self-worth – I was willing to risk my teenage life over a gold chain and pride. I was willing to die if need be, but I was not going to go out as a coward. This is another prime example of the mind-set of the conscious prisoner.

Lack of self-worth – The simple fact the younger me was behaving like that shows deep down somewhere I didn't truly value my life back then. Childhood depression-maybe? Continued Learnt Behaviour – Learnt to attack first in any situation – even when outnumbered.

Desensitized to trauma – that night I was stabbed in the head – CS gassed – shot at and robbed for my chain. But as it says on page 132/133 of my book *Prisoner to the Streets*, after the incident I went home, got my gun, then circled around looking for the guys. Then after I came to my senses I went to the hospital. Then when they refused to see me at the hospital, I went home to sleep with my gun under the pillow. And even when I saw my face and pillow covered in blood I still never went to the hospital. What I'm saying is at the time I never saw the incident as a traumatic experience. I was becoming one with the madness. I was becoming desensitized to the trauma. This is what I mean by 'conscious prisoner'. He or she is now aware at this stage and has accepted this nonsense as a way of life. And not the way we make it by converting to this mind-set.

STAGE - 3

Prisoner up for Parole

(EXIT STRATEGIES/STREET REHABILITATION)

Before a prisoner is granted his parole he needs to prove he is a changed man. The same process goes for a PTTS. Before a PTTS gets their freedom they have to prove they can change their ways of behaving and thinking like one. The only difference between the two prisoners up for parole is that the convicted prisoner can lie to the parole board about the changes they have made and cheat his or her way to freedom. As for the PTTS, he/she can't cheat their way to freedom. The PTTS literally has to make the changes to get free. The parole panel for the PTTS is one's self. He or she has to make the effort to rehabilitate their own mind to become free from the street prison.

Another important question for the class,

'How does someone rehabilitate themselves from the street prison?'

The main answer is the individual has to be committed and dedicated to growth and change.

Again, in using PTTS the book I describe how I had to make a risky life changing decision to move back to London to be around and raise my new-born son. I knew coming back to London would make it even harder to change but I stepped out on faith and came back to raise my son.

Back To Basics

Temper – in order for me to change my way of thinking I had to first work on managing my temper. I had to figure out what my triggers were.

CONFLICT RESOLUTION – RESOLVING CONFLICT

New responsibilities – On page 167 in PTTS I wrote about the birth of my son. When he was born I thought to myself I needed to become more responsible for my actions. I began to think - how could I teach him about the rights and wrongs in life if I hadn't practiced it much myself?

Finding a Purpose – I think it's sad that it takes another life to be born before a person sees the value in their own. However I can't lie, my son's life gave me a sense of purpose and direction. His birth gave me a reason to care about my own life.

Promises Made – before I returned to London I vowed to make some promises which I thought would help me change for the better. I believed these changes would enable me to have a better quality of life.

The two hardest promises I made were to give up my weed habits and to get rid of my weapons. They say that a promise is a comfort to a fool. So although the intentions of my younger self were good - saying it and doing it were two different things. Time itself would tell if my new method would stop me from getting drawn out into old habits.

On the road to change you're always going to find speed humps and traffic lights. Sometimes you're going to go down the wrong road, breakdown or even reverse back down the road you're coming from, but you will reach your destination if you stay committed to making the changes. This section is a snippet of the 'Prisoner up for Parole' stage. In this part of the workshop I also discuss forgiveness and how to achieve it. I also discuss the effects of karma, past ghost, and how to break negative cycles. Facing tests, temper issues, and how to find peace while having mental flashbacks.

STAGE - 4

Post Traumatic Street Syndrome

(DEPROGRAMMING THE MIND)

Post traumatic street syndrome is the final stage of the workshop. It looks at mental flashbacks, closing/healing mental wounds and psychological issues. This is for those of us who have seen too much coming up and are now looking for freedom in the mind. These people need to seek professional help which may help them to overcome some of the stuff they've faced.

I will go into this Post Traumatic Street Syndrome theory in more detail at a later stage of this book.

CHAPTER 3

POSITIVELY CRITIQUING THE CRITIQUES

'The Many Messages Missed in 'Prisoner to the Streets'

Nobody likes the sound of criticism which is another reason why I was so hesitant to write my first book. Because once you've put something out there to the public eye, you give people the right to pass judgement, which is ok. In fact it's more than ok. The right type of criticism can allow us to improve and grow. That's if we aren't defensive about a critic's opinion and listen wholeheartedly with an open mind. In that way we can actually learn something from the critic. That type of criticism could be exactly the thing we need to hear to reach the place we are aiming to reach. This type of criticism is what I like to call 'positive criticism' which I learned about from the Mental Farmer.

On the flipside to positive criticism, sometimes in life we find criticism can be just that – criticism. This is when the feedback is negative without reason. It's when the critic has no constructive feedback to give. It's like when someone posts a positive video on YouTube and the video gets millions of views and likes. Then you get that one person who decides to click the thumbs down icon. Not because they didn't like the content for any particular reason but because they don't like being the same as everybody else. Or because they don't like the artist or sometimes they don't even like themselves. Anyway the point I'm getting at is I want to reverse the roles of the critique now. Not in a petty way of getting back at them, but to highlight the damage of what 'senseless criticism' can do. You see my thing is if you are going to critique something or someone, the very least you can do is make sense in your statement otherwise its best you say nothing. I once read a quote that said, *'Before you speak, ask yourself. Is it kind? Is it true, and is it necessary? Does it improve upon the silence?' As much as I like that quote I have another one for the negative critiques of this world and it goes like this, 'Before you criticise or assume, learn the facts. Before you criticise or judge, understand why. Before you criticise, think about what the last quote said. Is it kind, is it true, is it necessary, and does it improve upon the silence?'*

If the answer is no to any of those questions you really shouldn't be in such a hurry to voice your opinion. Why? Because you're misinformed opinion may prevent others from wanting to look into it. Your misinformed opinion may be so damaging that people may take your opinion as gospel and then spread your opinion like it was a fact. Your senseless criticism can be counterproductive in so many ways. So please I beg you take heed before your criticise. Obviously, I know my quote isn't going to change the way people criticise but it felt good to write it anyway.

Now it's time for me to critique the critique positively.
To give you a better understanding of what I am talking about, here are some examples.

1 star review

'I have lived and worked with inner city gangs for many many years.... I passed the sympathy phase a long time ago. This is indicative of the 'don't blame me' society and the atrocious parenting that happens in some urban areas. Many of these parents need to learn humility, compassion and basic parenting skills including attachment and atonement issues that are clearly evident within these dysfunctional families. The 'rep and respect' vibe needs to go........it's naive, crude and destructive. It takes a lot more courage to walk away from a fight than to engage in one. I have absolutely no sympathy for the author. He mentions justice many times, but because of his unrealistic and emotional simplistic take on the world, expects justice to be fairly meted out each time something goes wrong. This doesn't always happen in the real world **** happens.

There are believe it or not still many peaceful communities in the world....check them out on Google and reflect instead of respect.'

5 people found this review helpful.

This critic here is a special one. He claims to have worked with gangs for many years and passed the sympathy stage. Well I'm happy you past that sympathy stage sir. Do you know what time you will be arriving at the empathy stage? Or at least the stage where you learn that Prisoner to the streets had nothing to with gangs it was about prisoners to the streets? You say the story came across as blaming society and not myself. Read it again sir. Most of the childhood trauma I experienced was from the hands of what society threw at me. Racial harassment is the very reason why my family moved to Holly Street in the first place. I witnessed that harassment from before the age of five. They say a child's experiences between birth and age five have a major impact on their future life chances. And you dare say society has nothing to answer for? You sound like you've been gang working for far too long and have lost all empathy for children. Maybe you should research childhood trauma? It might help you out at work. This gang expert goes on to criticise the poor parenting and what parents need to learn. Well Mr gang expert, why do you think I wrote about the experience with my parents if parenting wasn't an issue? He is what I would call a senseless critic.

This critic is so senseless, it's actually hard to critique him. I mean, did he really say, *'The 'rep and respect' vibe needs to go........it's naive, crude and destructive. It takes a lot more courage to walk away from a fight than to engage in one. I have absolutely no sympathy for the author.'*

He sounds like one of those parents who can't connect with his children because he doesn't listen to them. I clearly mentioned in my book *Prisoner to the Streets* how naïve and destructive my experiences were. I highlighted the price we had to pay for holding on to this road mentality. And you sat on your high horse preaching about it takes more courage to walk away from a fight than engage in one? Isn't that what the book teaches, Mr Gang expert? Seriously, I didn't write that book to deal with this level of stupidity. The saddest thing about this misinformed review is that 5 people read it and thought it was helpful. I hope this didn't discourage them from getting it. I won't even respond to what he said about my unrealistic views of justice. All I can say is – Wow! Your lack of empathy for what a child goes through is astonishing. And I think you should reconsider your profession.

1 star review

Here we have a one line reviewer, a no nonsense sort a guy.
'Straight in the charity bag. I still don't care about these hard done by violent kids.'
1 person found this review helpful.

When I first read this one I was in stitches. I read it the second time in a cockney accent and just laughed. Here we have another senseless critic, someone who doesn't care about all these hard done by violent kids. Well I'm glad you've acknowledged some of these violent children are hard done by. That is unless you were being sarcastic about them being hard done by, in this case you've have learnt nothing. And it's absolutely fine that you don't care. When most children feel hard done by they won't care about robing people like you who don't care about people like them.

2 star review

'I do a lot of work in prisons and was interested to learn more about the gang culture from someone who has lived through it and survived.

It's a very authentic read with the language being pitched at a level which could be understood by most but still feels very real.

He has lived through the worse experiences that society can throw at someone but seems to have come out eventually in a state of mind to be able to now tackle his issues head on by writing the book.

Personally, I never felt any attachment to Robin and struggled with feeling any emotion about what he saw and did.

I understand that this book has been good therapy for the author but I'm not convinced that it is a good book. Tries to be an insight into a closed world but I'm not convinced it achieves that.'

2 people found this review helpful.

At no point did I try to make this story an insight into a closed world, this isn't a Ross Kemp does gangs book. I am concerned how all these gang workers feel no attachment. It makes me wonder - is that because you still view this street stuff as gang activity? I really don't have much more to say about this senseless critic except to say, 'If you can't understand why as a child I or we did the things we did, then you also should ask yourself if you should be working with children.'

3 star review

'A very troubling portrayal of life on the streets... Coming from Tottenham AND knowing a key person in this story, I'm quite amazed at the level of poverty and crime taking place within my proximity and I truly fear for young black boys within my neighbourhood who are losing their lives over what is seemingly nonsense. All in all it is an interesting insight into how cheap young African lives are in London. However the most troubling aspect for me was the absence of an empathetic adult figure; there is a welfare state in the UK and it weighed on my mind a lot how in the 1990's, a single mother (who would have had housing and would have been entitled to benefits) managed to raise two sons who were so 'hungry' and I began to wonder if there was not a lot more behind the story of the mother and why Travis had to live with his grandmother and was constantly so hungry (there was only three of them in the house). To me this aspect overshadowed the entire book as I felt he may have been 'protecting' sensitive familial issues as a way of preserving the dignity of his mother.
Insightful read, but left many unanswered questions.'
4 people found this helpful

So here we have a man who can't understand why a single parent in the 90s could be struggling so much with finances because she gets benefits. Well I spoke to a few single mothers about this and this is what they had to say.

Mother number 1

'In the 90s as a single mother there were times when things were really hard. Me and my children had to share a tin of soup and some hardough bread for dinner.'

Mother number 2

'In the 90s it wasn't easy for a single parent to find work without having childcare. And when a single parent went out to look for work in the 90s they had to have somebody to watch the children. This wouldn't have been easy unless you had a strong support network. A lot of absent fathers use to have the view that their children's mother should be ok when they leave because they're getting benefits, which is ignorance at its finest.'

Mother number 3

It wasn't really a struggle for me because I had support financially. Well, it was a struggle until I asked from support from the children's grandparents. It was more of an emotional struggle. While I'm here trying to raise these children, the fathers were out there living there best life. Without a thought of the children - how their living, how they're eating, and even where there living. Sometimes I felt like I let the children down because there is only so much I could do with one income. And there's only so much one woman can do raising a child on her own.

It wasn't as easy as you think Mr Critique. A single parent in the 90s on benefits had it hard. They had to keep up with school trips, school dinners, and activities after school. As well as food at home, rent, birthdays and pocket money when that child comes of age. This was part of the working class single mothers experience in the 90s and you my brother say you struggled to understand that? You say it overshadowed the whole story? Like I, said I'm not taking any of this senseless criticism personal. The reality is that 4 people found this review helpful and there is nothing helpful about it.

Here's some more senseless criticism.

3 star review.

'I started hating this; it was written from a very victim per-spective and didn't seem to address the problems of macho culture and poor parenting. It grew on me, I found it interest-ing and depressing. I was glad the author extricated himself from this nihilistic culture. It gets a bit maudlin at the end. An important look into black gang culture and its drivers at a time when youth violence is escalating again in Hackney and Tottenham Worth a read.'
One person' found this helpful.

This is the second reviewer who felt the book was written from a victim perspective. I don't get it - is it not possible that before I became a street guy I may have been the victim first? Have you never heard of the victim becoming the ag-gressor? And of course, I addressed the macho culture and poor parenting. But why am I even wasting my time critiquing a guy who thinks the book is a look into black gang culture? It's funny how these critiques say I'm playing the victim but they overlook the beginning of the book. The part where white gang culture caused my family trauma as a child. Some of these reviewers give me joke. They only see it how they want to see it, not for what it is.

4 star review

'I found this quite well written and really rather interesting not really anything new to learn in relation to gangs and street violence... but well written. Sad and humorous in places... It is unfortunate that many youngsters find this their reality in the 21st century.'

This critic states they haven't learnt nothing new in terms to gang and street violence? Well even though this is a 4 star review, it's clear that this critique has missed the teachings of the book. If this reviewer's eyes were opened he or she would have learned from the title alone. It projects the message that street violence isn't gang connected. So obviously, there would be nothing to learn about gangs and street violence in *Prisoner to the Streets*. This present book challenges the gang theory and the street violence. But like I said in the introduction, maybe I'm part to blame. Maybe I failed to get the message across clearly because I wrote it in story format. So I can't take any of it personal. I just think it's a shame that this critic never gained from their experience of reading my book, *Prisoner to the Streets*.

Critics come in many shapes and forms and you don't always get to see people's criticism on your work. So I'm thankful for the Amazon reviews and all the feedback given by the people whether it was positive or senseless. I wish there was a section where the maker of the product could challenge the reviewer to balance out whether the product is worthy. That would be interesting to sit down and watch. I didn't only get reviews by Amazon though. Some of my one star reviews came from the streets.

The little street criticism that came back to me was disappointing to digest as I wrote that book specifically for the streets. I stopped being disappointed once I found out what was being said. Their criticism became irrelevant once I found out most of those same street critics didn't even read a page. At the same time I remember getting a lot of positive feedback from the streets critics who did read it. And that gave me so much encouragement.

I remember being told that a few senseless street critics were calling my book a snitch book. Which I never got to reply to - so I'll do so now. How can it be a snitch book when the only person I told on was myself? Even the murder I spoke of in the book, the people involved had already been convicted for the crimes way before I wrote the book. So for the negative street critics, your opinions are counterproductive, and other man in the hood might dismiss the book because of your ignorant statement. But I over stand that those opinions come from the mind-set of somebody who is still a prisoner to the streets. And I would have probably thought and said the same thing up to the age of 16. So

I really can't hold any feelings towards this older like that. Like 2Pac said, *'I aint mad atcha.'*

After dealing with that criticism I had to deal with hearing strangers critiquing the book based on my so called 'street credentials.' Some people who think they know this street life can be so ignorant. It's like watching a debate on social media about boxing. Almost everyone is commenting that a particular boxer is no good. They may not even know his fight record but because someone else said it they repeat it. The boxer could be a champion in different weight categories but because these copycat critiques don't know what they're talking about they will say he's the crap boxer. I say that to say this: I remember one girl telling me she heard I was lying about my story and that I wasn't about that life. That senseless criticism pissed me right off. That senseless statement could also prevent certain people from wanting to read into it and gain knowledge themselves. And since I'm being honest; it damaged my ego too. The prisoner in me wanted to prove otherwise. Then I calmed down after speaking with the Mental Farmer. He reminded me about something which he had taught me years before. He said, *'Remember Robin, you can't control what people think say or do. You only have control over how you react to it.'*
And after that I felt free of the opinions of senseless critics.

The worst critique I got came from close to home. Somebody I considered as family said something they knew they shouldn't have. The worst thing was how the criticism came to me. It didn't come first hand; it came through the grapevine and totally out of the blue. At first I didn't know how to take it. One of the children in my family was over at my house and randomly said,

'My daddy saw me reading your book and said I shouldn't read your book anymore because it's full of lies.'

I wasn't even vex, I was genuinely upset because I knew why the child's dad had said it. We weren't seeing eye to eye. I felt hurt because the child was like my own son. At first I wanted to reply to my friend's son and say,

'Your dad's just a bitter waste-man.'

But I couldn't say that to a child. And it wasn't true that his Dad was a bitter waste-man. He was just talking from a bitter place when he told his son what he did about my book. I struggled, holding back my tongue. Not about the criticism but because his dad knows he shouldn't have said what he said to his child as he knows the child looks up to me as an uncle.

It took me about a minute or so to digest what my friend's son had said to me. I looked at the young boy and my eldest daughter who was playing in my front room together before the statement was made. They were both eagerly waiting for my response. I looked out of the front room window to buy some time and I saw some guys cutting down trees in the garden. So I called the children to the window.

First I asked my daughter, *'How many people can you see through the window cutting trees?'*

My daughter responded, *'I see three people cutting trees Dad.'*

Then I asked my friends little son, *'How many people can you see through the window cutting trees?'*

He responded, *'I don't think it's three. I can see four people cutting trees.'*

At this point my daughter came closer to see the fourth person who she had missed. In a surprising voice of discovery, my daughter shouted, *'Oh yeah! There are four.'*

Then I said, *'Well, I can see seven men in the garden cutting down trees. It all depends from which angle of the window you are looking.'*

They both came over to the part of the window where I was standing. Then the young boy said, *'Oh yeah! There are seven of them, I got it wrong?'*

I then told him, *'You didn't get it wrong son; it's all about perspective. It's not your fault; you couldn't see the other three men because you weren't looking from the same angle I was looking from.'*

Then I added, *'And this is what your dad did when he said my book was full of lies. He's just not looking at it from the same angle as me. Your dad sees four men and I see seven, that's all.'*

CHAPTER 4

STEREOTYPED INTO YOUR PSYCHE

*Media games and society's
perception of those games*

*'To free yourself from the
streets, you have to know about
the mind-set which is keeping
you entrapped to the streets...'*

First of all, let's start with the power of words and the power of images. When you look at some of the images the media produce, do you ever ask yourself - *What is the purpose? What is the end goal? What is it supposed to serve? Who is it supposed to serve?* A lot of people from different ethnic backgrounds live in London. And because of this, some people who live here in London might get the false impression that a lot of ethnic people live in England. Well this isn't the case for Afro-Caribbean's and Africans. The last time I checked I think we made up like three per cent of the UK's population. As a minority in this country, we have to deal with the media constantly pumping images of negative headlines to the rest of the country about us. Well, over 90% of the country's population don't live around black people and some of them hardly come into contact with black people. It can't be constructive having these negative images pushed out about black people which are subliminally giving other individuals a false stereotype. The worst thing about having this constant negative image of self-programmed into our psyche is that eventually a lot of black people begin to believe and accept these false messages and stereotypes about themselves.

In some cases, we are further reinforcing these negative stereotypes, which I will discuss in a later chapter. The main point I'm making here is the media aren't playing fair in terms of representation. And because these unconscious bias stereotypical images are consistently being programmed into our psyches, a lot of black men are now beginning to fulfil the prophecy of what the messages are projecting. You can call that self-fulfilling prophecy.

I was with my friend and we were reasoning about this same thing. I said to him,

'Let me ask you something. What is the first thing you think of when you see a picture of a black face on the news?'

He replied, 'Honestly, the first thing I think when I see a brother on the news is that he's a criminal, a gang member, it's something to do with violence he's on the run, etc. Basically, nothing positive comes to mind.'

We ended that conversation with the same sentiment - *The programming is real.*

It's sad to say that I don't know a single black man from my estate that hasn't experienced a white woman grabbing her handbag that bit tighter when they walk past us. I'm not saying it happens every day but it happens enough to make it resonate in the psyche. But like I said, worse than that black people are beginning to believe these stereotypes about self and fulfil the prophecy. Emeka Egonbu, a fellow author and a friend of mine was reasoning with me about this same subject. In that conversation Emeka presented me with a scenario which supports the same self-fulfilling prophecy I talked about in *Prisoner to the Streets.*
Emeka said:

'Picture this Rob. I was talking to a few youths back in the day about the same thing - stereotypes. I told them to imagine that same typical scenario of being a black man in Hackney or wherever it is. And you're walking down a back road and you see a white lady grab her bag tighter. Then I asked the youth – how do you define her reaction to the black man? And they

all replied, 'Yeah she's racist.' Why is she doing this? Why is she doing that and so on? So I gave them a similar scenario. I said imagine you are the one walking down the street. You're not in your so called ends. And you see another 10 black boys ahead of you. How do you react? You can act like the white woman and cross the road. Or you could turn back. Or if your one of those whatever guys then you will walk past being ready for whatever. Regardless of how you react it's like you see them as a threat. You still have a negative reaction to a group of young boys who haven't done anything negative.'

Then the young boys said, 'Fucking hell that's true, that's true.' Then I said: *'Pause, but why do you think that is?' And they basically answered but not in those same words. Exactly what you are describing as stereotyped into your psyche.'*

Sadly, these images aren't new. In fact they've been going on since slavery. Black people were seen as three fifths of a man. For years negative images have indicated that black people are a threat or not equal to their peers. Even here in Great Britain Enoch Powell expressed how he felt with his 'Rivers of Blood' speech. And that was in 1968. Not to mention the additional disrespect of the recent Windrush scandal in 2018. The narrative about the black man has already been sold to people. And it's time for everyone to get a refund from that narrative, because it's not true. We are not a threat to the system; we are an investment to it. After the war we helped rebuild Britain, and during the war we helped them win it. We can't blame people of any nationality who bought into this lie - the promotion was great.

At times I've been a massive consumer of the lies being sold. Even on my journey as a writer I've felt reduced to less than. I'm rarely ever recognised as just a good author. They always label me as a BAME writer, ex-gang member, IC3, or anything that portrays me in a bad light. Nor am I ever considered to be a theorist with credible ideas to address the problem and provide solutions. My work tends to get reduced to that of an ex-gang member who has turned the other cheek. To those who know me best I may be perceived as a strong black man. But if I'm honest, there have been many of nights I've gone to sleep believing the lie. I thought to myself,

'You know what Trav, it doesn't matter what you achieve out here, you know you're just another nigga, right? A small fish in a big pond.'

And that should let you know the impact it has had upon the psyche over the years.

Imagine seeing years of the same negative images of your image, over and over again. Sooner or later you may start to believe what you see, no?

This might not ring true for everyone but that's my take on it. In the first chapter *Journey Within The Reason*, James explained a time when we met a journalist prior to the book being released. In that meeting, James said I stated

that I wasn't a gang member. James explained that the journalist didn't want to hear me chat about no prisoner to the streets term. Well - that was just one of the many experiences I've had with the media. I won't name call but I want to share some of the other experiences which I had in trying to promote the book and the term *'prisoner to the streets'*

Just before *Prisoner to the Streets* came out I was anti-media but I felt I needed their platforms to get to the masses. I did many of the local stations and it was great to be able to elaborate, but unfortunately those platforms weren't big enough. When the book first came out I thought it would be easier to get interviewed on those bigger platforms about the real pressing issues. After about a month reality kicked in and all the optimism was kicked out of me. If you only knew how many media interviews I turned down because of this ex-gang member bollocks you wouldn't believe. Every so often a journalist would call me and say they heard I was an ex-gang member who was involved in knife crime and they wanted to do a piece. And I would always set the record straight. My rules for using the media's platform have always been simple.

Rule number one - *I do not consent to being introduced as an ex-gang-member. And rule number two - I have to be allowed to promote and discuss the book, regardless of what topic the news wants to focus on.*

Well those rules were made in 2011 when I first started talking my truth. Since then I had to amend those rules because I wasn't getting any interviews. And at the time I still believed I needed those platforms to get heard. So I slightly lowered the bar of my own rules to get in there. Instead of only doing live interviews, I decided I would consider doing pre-recorded interviews too. Under the condition that I got to see the final edit before it was aired live.

After doing my first pre-recorded show I realised that you can't win by meeting these people halfway. A journalist would make all the promises in advance. They act like they are as serious as you are about getting the truth out. Then at the last minute they claim that they can't get the permission to show you the final edit. Then they add that they have seen the final edited piece. In that conversation they tell you how thrilled they are about the outcome of it. They see my disapproval and distrust but they still try to sell me their enthusiasm by suggesting that I will be happy with it. And because of wanting to make a difference at times I've bought into the bullshit they were selling. It's like when you buy something at the market without a receipt. You take the risk of losing out. The product might be faulty or a replica and the stool holder will still refuse to exchange it.

My media rules have changed again - *I don't shop at the market now. My thinking nowadays is - I don't care what the terms of an interview are, because a journalist has never kept to their part of the bargain. Now, they have to meet me on all of my terms or were just not doing the interview. Simple!* Before you start to think I'm full of myself by that last statement, let me explain. I've had an extremely hard time in attempting to change the narrative. Over the years, it's almost been comical. Here is a quick summary of the experiences I've had along the journey:

One of the first interviews I ever did was for a French newspaper in 2012. It was a short article written in French. I never got to read it till years later because I didn't do well at French in school. After reading it I was disappointed with the whole thing. The journalist made out that things were still tensed between me and the Fields' boys from down the road. But that wasn't the case because I was telling him an old story. He made out like I couldn't cross the road, which wasn't true I lived in fields for years. The article wasn't the worst in the world but it was far from the best. They falsified things and made it look like a gang war. The whole article can be criticised but the worse part for me was the misinformation. It was written in French that my mother was a crack head and that being the reason why I ended up in care. That pissed me off again because it wasn't accurate. And my mother never smoked anything else other than the occasional cigarette. It's a good thing my Mum never saw that article because I would've never heard the end of it. Even though she didn't hear of it I was hurt about the way they described her. They made my story a typical hood one. And my mother didn't deserve that at the cost of me sharing my story.

Then in 2013 I did a live radio call in about the Luton Riots argument. I was being asked what we should do about the police and the incidents in Luton. I remember being very dismissive of whatever he was talking about. He kept saying,
'So Robin what is the solution to this situation with the police.'
And I kept saying, *'I don't know about all of that stuff all I know is that Prisoner to the Streets is the solution.'*
He asked me the question about five times in different ways and I gave him the same answer every time. Soon afterwards he got fed up with me and said,
'You're not answering the question we called you about.
Then I said, 'No, You're not asking the right questions.'

The focus of his questions was about gangs and police and what is news now. I was tired of that conversation from way back then. As far as I was concerned my concept made sense to the problems and solutions and all these media people wanted to talk about was the latter problems. Like I said he was getting fed up with me being unresponsive to his question so the conversation was brought to an abrupt end. I found it frustrating they were getting frustrated at me for wanting to get right to the point of solution. Soon afterwards I was told in secret by someone from the media that I wasn't going to be getting called back from that show ever again. In other words I got barred.

In 2015 another massive platform called me for a live interview. They said they've got a live show about knife crime and they wanted to talk to me about how dogs in gangs are a massive problem. I told them I wasn't interested in coming in from that angle because it isn't a story to focus on. Then I suggested proof of a real solution. I said that if they wanted a real show I could bring all the guys I mentioned in my book who had stabbed me and those who I stabbed. The journalist on the phone sounded keen. *'Oh really?'* Then he asked me a bunch of other questions as though they were on board. Then I made a few calls to the guys who stabbed me and they liked the idea but we didn't trust it. So I called my friends instead and asked them to pretend they were the ones who stabbed me, that way they couldn't be criminalised for it.

Finally I thought the doors were going to be open for fair representation. Later that night I got a call about a cab being sent to pick me up. The journalist seemed serious. I was one sleep away from being able to come on the TV and collectively show the solution as proof. But they weren't up for it. Not the mandem - the media that is. Before I went to sleep the journalist called and said, *'We've decided to interview a police officer and an ex-gang member on the subject. But we will contact you again; your story sounds interesting.'* After that day I had vowed to never fuck with the media again.

Then in 2017 another journalist called me to do a piece in a mainstream newspaper. When he called me he explained that a young boy who had killed another young boy outside his school was recently sentenced for the action. He then went on to explain the teenage boy on trial made reference to the book Prisoner to the Streets. That caught my intention. Then he explained how the young man was in jail on remand when he came in to contact with my story. He said that the book moved him to take responsibility for his actions and confess to it. He also mentioned that in court the young boy turned to the parents and said,
'I'm sorry for killing your son.'
Then supposedly he turned to the judge and said
'If I had read this book before I wouldn't have killed him.'
Sounds like a solution right?

When I heard that I told the journalist about my previous bad experiences with the media. I explained I was only willing to do this piece if we talked about the impact *Prisoner to the Streets* could have had on the young boy beforehand. After we spoke I was excited and angry at the same time. Excited that the power of the message could finally be heard, but angry that it took another young man to lose his life before the message became relevant.

Then a few weeks later I get a call from my agent telling me that he wasn't going to use me for the piece. When I asked why, I was told it was my fault. Apparently the journalist got the impression that I didn't want to do it because I said I've had bad experiences before. I told my agent this wasn't the case.

By chance, I bumped into the journalist in person sometime after the article was published. I explained to him that I never said I wasn't keen on doing the interview. I was just expressing my scepticism which was fuelled by my past experiences.

We put it down to 'miscommunication' and he said we would do another article one day, but that day hasn't come yet.

A few weeks later I decided to read the article to see what it ended up being about. It wasn't a bad article; it was just frustrating to read as usual. The piece focused more on systematic failures. In terms of how the young boy's mother was trying to get help for her son's behaviour prior to him killing someone. They spoke on a range of early intervention services which could have intervened like social services, child mental health. The journalist concluded in his article in reference to the young boy's mother, *'Her story is one that is rarely told, but, we think, important to be heard if we are going to find solutions to this problem.'*

I wasn't impressed by that statement. How can this possibly be a solution to the problem? So in understanding the mothers struggle with the lack of support from the system is where the solution is? I doubt it. The system still fails to treat this issue as a mind-set one. So how could these services teach this boy about freeing himself from the self-destructive mind-set of the streets? Days like that made me want to throw in the towel. The truth is the journalist didn't need my permission to write about what that young man said in court that day end of story.

Last year was the most I'd ever done for the media and the worst experience of my life. In 2018 I was persuaded by a clean hearted friend to do a short documentary on some US news programme. I went against my rules - the piece would be pre-recorded but I wouldn't see it before it was broadcast. By now I thought if I stick to my piece then they can't edit my points too much. Regardless of my plan at the time, it went against me and the media done me over again. The show sensationalised the issue as one of knife crime and made the headline, *How Social Media Is Being Used To Fuel The Violence* the focus and name of the show. At the end of the interview they made me look like a right mug. They ended the video by asking me a typical programming question, *'What are the common misconceptions about knife crime particularly with children stabbing each other?'* I cut into the interviewer's question. *'I don't know about knife crime. All I know about is being a prisoner to the street, and having that mind-set of wanting to hurt someone because you can't beat them. Fuck knife crime!'* They ended the interview with those being my last words.

Now if you don't know me personally, you might see that interview and label me an angry black man. Or I may be perceived me as someone who is illiterate and can't express his point. If they didn't edit the video people would have heard me elaborate on that point. They would have heard me say something of substance. After my comment on knife crime I also said, *'Fuck gun crime too. It's not about a weapon or crime it's about changing the mind-set. What you going to call it next year when the weapon changes - acid crime?'* But they edited it and most of the other crucial things I said which explain my message.

The worst thing is after people saw it they called me to say it was a good piece. Which further wound me up because anyone who knew what I set out to achieve knows I wouldn't have let the media in my life for that shit. I only had solutions but those parts never made the edit. The journalist who filmed this piece said he shared my anger that certain parts were edited. He said that because the US was new to our issues we couldn't say too much to confuse them. Which I found confusing - but cool whatever. I was promised a show about solutions but I ended up starring in another show that was creating more fear and problems. They used me to get to the young people on board. They made out like they wanted to help push my solution, but now I see the games that were played. I told them afterwards that one of the children was receiving some hate mail. I contacted the journalist; he acted really concerned and said he would get the video taken down. He never did. It is a good thing nothing happened to that young boy because that journalist would have had to deal with the prisoner in me if it did.

A month or so later in that same year Canada TV contacted me. Surprisingly though, this was the only show that showed me and my message some love. My main points didn't make the edit, but the power of what the work could do did. And my proposed solution made the commentary as well. I was really pleased about that. I wasn't totally satisfied though because I didn't like my interview being mixed with a police officer's solution. And the other solution came from a mother who is fighting against knife crime. Now don't get me wrong, it is admirable that a mother can give back like this. I just feel there are more long term solutions in place. Like I said in the introduction, I'm not fighting knife crime and I'm definitely not supporting this 'knife in the bin' idea as a solution. This was my main frustration with the show. Though it may seem miniscule to some; it is important to me. I'm not knocking other people's intentions either; I'm just saying we are not saying the same thing. So it is senseless throwing everyone on the same programme or news piece. But overall, I was 40 per cent pleased with the news piece, which is good. Canada TV wasn't perfect but Canada showed me love. I just hoped the UK would see the Canadian piece and become more open to my theory.

A month later, what I hoped for had come true. I got contacted by a prime time TV show in the UK. I won't say I was optimistic because I wasn't but I was hopeful. The first few minutes of the documentary were alright. They let me talk a bit about the mentality and they filmed me speaking live at a Pupil Referral Unit. The only thing is they edited out all the good parts. I remember halfway through my workshop when they were filming, the film crew kept on interrupting my flow. Every now and then they kept shouting, *'Cut!'* I think this was done so they could change the direction of my conversation. I smiled when one of the young boys got pissed off and shouted to the journalist, *'Oi! shut up and let him talk man.'*

I checked the young man about his manners but I was happy he spoke up before I had to.

None the less, after watching the first few minutes I saw how the show had changed. They made the focus of all the problems about the olders' influence, which again wasn't my focus. The show then shifted to the mother's pain that I was a part of causing. I know it wasn't intentional but her story wasn't accurate. She said there was a mob of boys who stabbed her son. But from what I saw, that was not the case; it was a self-defence situation. I then realised that the power in my message wasn't about a mother forgiving me. The power in my message was about me taking responsibility for a wrong I did and apologising for it. The power in my message was also about her son being super real enough to forgive me for my part. The pre-recorded documentary wasn't the worse I've been in but once again they wasted my time. They even had the cheek to do a 2 minute interview in the live studio without me. Instead they invited my friend's mother. They told me about it last minute and I wasn't happy. At first I said to cancel the show. I told my friend's mum that the TV documentary was going to be about her and her son. And the makers did just that. Don't get me wrong, what we did was an extremely powerful message but it wasn't all that I was trying to teach. I spent four long days recording with them and I had to watch that show from my yard. When my friend's mum was on the couch they kept on talking about the pain her son had to go through and how much trauma he must have endured. As a viewer I started to feel like the narrative was the same old cliché.

I saw it as yet another game the media dabbles in - they feel this violence among our youth is about the Good vs Bad tactic. This is another way to pull the heart strings of the people. And this is where they miss the point. I sat at home thinking - *Why wasn't my childhood trauma discussed? You never know, it might have helped explained why young people get stabbed or shot.* And by not having me on the show I never got the opportunity to explain my seven year old theory. Not to mention we filmed at a secondary school in Hampstead about the book being on the curriculum there. And how the school said it should be used as a tool for prevention all over the country. After all, that's the only reason I agreed to do the show. They made their own story out of my story. Other than tainting my image a bit and not showing that the book made it on the curriculum, the show was alright. I'll give it 3 out of 10.

This last experience I'll share with you happened in 2018. The online article piece had a massive picture of me. Underneath the picture was a headline that included the words *Knife Crime,* a phrase that I am well known for disliking. When I saw the headline, I hit the roof. The rest of the headline stated - *I first stabbed someone when I was 15.* I couldn't stay calm. How could they write that? Talk about stereotyped into your psyche? Now they want to use my face as part of the stereotyping? I was so hurt. Not surprised, just hurt. In that interview I brought the 'Mental Farmer' Lyndon Walters with me. And I recorded it secretly just in case the narrative was changed. And it was.

I couldn't believe the journalist did me like that. At least four times during the interview I stated, *'I got stabbed twice before I ever used a knife.'*

And I also mentioned that I witnessed my brother getting stabbed when I was 9. I explained to her how this led me to become a prisoner to that same behaviour. But instead she decided to go with the narrative of staining my past character online in a very foul manner. Imagine if my daughter Google's me and this shit comes up? These guys are cold; they had no right to degrade my character based on their lack of understanding. Although in some places the journalist wrote what I was trying to say, at the same time every paragraph was incorrect in some way. Shows how much she was listening. I really felt violated about this article. One of the most cringing lines she wrote that I was supposed to have said was, *'I was stabbed many times and I have the scars to prove it.'*

Even the way it is written doesn't sound like me. Who the hell would say,

'And I've got the scars to prove it?' All I know is - never again. I can't win; I'm done with the media games.

It's crazy to think that out of all of those past experiences on big platforms the only one over here which let me speak my truth was LBC radio. And of course, the church show 'Revelation TV'. Other than that it's been a complete myth.

I'll conclude this chapter with a little story. On June the 8th 2013 I was with my friend driving through London fields. Police decided to pull us over because they said they could smell weed, which I found funny because none of us smoked weed.

After the stop, I asked the police,
'And at what point did you smell this weed, was it after you pulled us over or while you were following us?'
Anyway one of the TSG police officers was going on like a bully. He tried to handcuff me for no reason. Then he kicked me in the shin.
At which point I lost control.

'If you do that again bruv you're going on your back.'
A few people in the community intervened. Then a DC jumped out of his unmarked car and defused the situation. The day after that commotion I had launched Prisoner to the Streets to a filled out audience at Hackney Empire. That was a big achievement on paper for an unknown author but it never made it to the papers. A few days after the launch I found myself thinking - *Why is it the media never focus on the positive things we do?* I started thinking deeper on it - *Imagine if I lost all control when that police man kicked me.* I bet if I punched him up for kicking me I would've got arrested and made front page. And I bet the headline in the papers would've said something foul like, *Ex-gang Member Beats up Policeman Day before His Book Launch: Maybe he should read his own book.*

I'm not blaming the media for all the problems we have. But as a black man I've found if I want to free myself from the negative stereotypes that fill my psyche then I can't watch or attach myself to the news anymore. That's shit's depressing.

CHAPTER 5

DISPELLING THE MYTHS OF THE STREETS

When I was an unconscious prisoner to the street, if you asked me I if I chose the street life I would've naively answered, 'yes'. But that wouldn't be the truth. And I believe most guys who act like they love the roads would say they chose the road too. The streets are a second choice, not a first. I don't believe we chose the streets; I believe we settled for it. It's like when a man has a girlfriend but he doesn't really want her. He just settles for her because he knows he might end up a lonely old man. So he fronts in public with her, pretends he loves her and shows her off to the world but he doesn't love that woman. It's just his ego leading him to settle. I know plenty road men who wish they could go back in time and do something else with the knowledge they have now. It's never been about going back to be a better road man. Brothers have told me that they thought they chose the road life until they realised otherwise. They realised they had an older cousin or dad on the road influencing them. Or they realised that peer pressure at a young age led them to the roads.

There is no street honour anymore. People seem to be respecting people for committing evil acts.

Just last year, a brother I know got stabbed for trying to protect a younger on his way to the shop. The younger was surrounded by five guys. Then the group of sheep chased the young father of two and one on the way around the corner. Then they stabbed him repeatedly. That's not real shit that's some real unnecessary evil shit. But yet if you speak about it on the block you might get that one brainwashed yute who says, 'That's the streets bro.' No it's not. That's not street life. That's just evil and senseless foolishness that's going on in the streets, because no one is schooling these youngers or challenging the olders. There is no street logic to five people stabbing up one man for protecting a youth. How can five man stab up one person and think that action isn't evil as well as cowardly? Is this what we celebrate as street life?

The streets are confusing. First of all, just because someone has gone to jail it doesn't make them street. I've got friends who have gone to jail, been shot, stabbed, sold drugs, all sorts. But to me, none of those guys were street. These guys were affected by the streets late, but they weren't street. I'm not bragging about being a young prisoner to the streets at all, but a lot of these so called street guys who came in, came into it really late. They started paring on street with the mandem from after the age of 16. By that time most of us were already brainwashed and institutionalised to the street life. It took me years to figure out that certain people chose to be on the roads. It's like they made an executive decision to be on road. I've seen all sorts. Some man chose the road late in their teens because it gets them more attention from girls. I never viewed those types of individuals as street yutes. I grew up in an estate where from the age of 9 I was witnessing stabbings and robberies. As I got older I began to realise that certain man would go out of their way to hang around areas like mine. I'm guessing it was because they knew our block had a reputation and respect for being street. I know so many young boys who didn't have to be street. It's like they forced it themselves. You know the ones that were great at school who always looked awkward talking street and trying to be street? Then you get the ones like me who were out on the street from early, but not entirely out of choice. Some of us were affected by other things out of our control. Unlike many others, we didn't want the street life as children; it was just on our doorstep or in the house. And it felt like violence and dream chasing was the only way to survive.

You always get that so called street guy who chooses to go from his area to another because his area doesn't have a rep. This type of character isn't street. Me and my mates once had a friend from Stoke Newington. He knew from the get go our estate Holly Street had a reputation for being street. So he would always come around to par with us. I suppose it was for the girls and the hype we had surrounding us. At raves, he would always be the first one to scream out, *'Holly Street'* . He said it more times than we did and we lived there. At the time it just seemed like he was a good friend who was down for the team. He would act like he was one of us. And at the time I never realised he had an agenda. But let's check the reality of it, when the real beef was kicking off the enemy would come back to our block Holly Street; they never went to his block in Stoke Newington. So while we had to go corner shop for our mums and live on an estate where gun shots were firing. And when we were beefing on our doorstep getting stabbed or doing the stabbings this friend of ours could always go home where it was safe. This friend could come and go whenever he felt like it. So he wasn't involved in our beef; he wasn't anywhere near front line. Funny enough, he lived by the police station in Stoke Newington. Either way, after these late comers came to spend time with us the sickness spreads. They eventually become infected by the same mentality that had us trapped at a much younger age.

There are different levels to the streets. The streets are so confusing I know a man who went to court and told on his enemies but he still gets respected as a street guy. I just don't get it, but like I said there are different levels to this mixed up street concept. Some people deal drugs on the streets and some are violent on the streets. To become a young prisoner to the street you have to be guilty of one of two things. One of the offences is having a material-istic mentality and the other is having a violent mental-ity. Having both of these mentalities from a young age will surely lead you down a path of becoming a prisoner to the street.

So let's dispel the myths about the streets. The main myth I want to dispel is that the streets are not filled with gang members; they are actually filled with prisoners and each 'ends' represents a different wing in that mental prison. People always roll their eyes at me when I say I don't do gang work. I get asked quite often by workers in the field who want me to accompany them to some form of gangs awareness talk. And every time I decline their offer the more our relationship deteriorated. They would always think I was being difficult just to make a point I wasn't though; I was just sticking to what I believe in. There have been numerous of well-paid jobs I have turned down because they kept advertising the position as a gang worker. Taking such jobs would only misrepresent what I stand for as well as promote the idea that the problems of the streets are gang related. I didn't believe I was cutting my nose to spite my face. I was just standing my ground so the young brothers coming up don't get criminalised like we did. If I'm not a part of the solution then I'm part of the problem, right?

Everybody seems to like the word gang, right? OK. Let's switch it up a bit. Let's look at the history of gangs in this country. Let's start off with the 1930s – 50s, who did we have? Well we had a famous gangster called Jack "Spot" Comer, Billy Hill, Mickey Green and a few other G's. Then from the 50s to 80s who did we have? We had the Kray brothers the Richardson gang and so on. Then by the mid-80s when I was born we didn't have any issues with black boys in gangs. The only gangs I heard of in the 80s were the Teddy Boys, National Front and the skinheads.

I read this on Wikipedia and thought, how interesting! In the 1970s and 1980s, black people in Britain were the victims of racist violence perpetrated by far- right groups such as the National Front. During this period, it was also common for Black footballers to be subjected to racist chanting from crowd members.

In the early 1980s, societal racism, discrimination and poverty alongside further perceptions of powerlessness and oppressive policing sparked a series of riots in areas with substantial African – Caribbean populations. These riots took place in St Pauls, Brixton, Toxeth and Moss Side in 1980. Then in 1981, Notting Hill then a year later it kicked off in Toxteth. The riots didn't stop there, in 1985 the same riots kicked off again this time it was in Handsworth, Brixton and Tottenham.

So with all this history I sometimes wonder why we get tainted for having a history of violence. Black people get la-belled so hard for all the so called 'knife/gun crime' going on in this country. When history clearly shows that gun culture isn't ours. In fact gun culture is what took us from Africa in chains. This same gun culture controlled my an-cestors to the point where they were afraid to fight back. I'm certain it wasn't the whips that kept them enslaved.

I've watched many news debates on what they call knife/gun crime. And there's always that one smart presenter whose job is to reinforce the stereotype in your psyche. On one of these TV debates, the male presenter in his ignorance states, *'Well statistically speaking, isn't it true in London right now that the vast majority of attackers and victims of knife murders happen to be black?'*

I don't know why certain individuals choose to highlight that statistic all the time. Even if it was true, why would it matter? I mean, young people are still dying at the end of the day, are they not? But to answer that question statement I would respond saying something like,

'Yes it might be true the statistics show that. But do the statistics explain how when black people first came to England they couldn't get housed in certain areas? Do they explain that because of things like racial harassment they chose to be housed around each other, like the Asians and the Jews did? Do those statistics highlight that in the 80's a lot of single mothers were getting housed in council flats in areas like Hackney, Tottenham, Brixton, Peckham, and Harlesden and so on? And do your statistics show that these areas had poverty issues and poor schooling? Do your statistics show that black people don't own any boats ships or planes over here? Which means black people can't be responsible for all the drugs and weapons that are coming into our communities, right? I mean these things don't just end up in the communities. They have to get into the country first, right? One thing I did learn about statistics in university is that areas with high poverty issues are more likely to have violence and higher crime rates. So can you please stop giving me a reason to use the race card? I grew up in a multi-cultural London and I have many of white friends from the same working class estates to know that this issue on the streets isn't a black issue. The focus shouldn't be on making

black people the focus of knife crime and street violence. If the focus was on fighting poverty then maybe you wouldn't need to be fighting 'knife crime.'

There has been a history of *'gang violence'* up north in places like Liverpool Manchester and Scotland. So please if you do already don't believe in the myth - it's not a black thing. As far as I know black people didn't have any gang problems in the Caribbean before we came to the UK. So I'll never understand why in the late 90s Operation Trident was always on the news. That operational myth gave the false impression that *'gun crime'* was solely a black problem. A stereotype which a lot of people brought into and still own till this day - *'Till this day!'* This so called gang culture is not ours. If it was, we wouldn't be at the bottom of the crime ladder selling drugs on the streets. We wouldn't be doing small stuff like county lines. We wouldn't need 'the connection' for the weapons, or *'the connection'* for the drugs. They say, *'When you point your finger at someone else you have three fingers pointing right back at yourself.'* So please, stop framing us.

Like I said in the chapter earlier, a lot of people think they are/were street. But they weren't street, they were prisoners to it. Sadly, these days there are a lot of innocent people dying on the streets who are not prisoners to it. They just got caught up in it by the people who are prisoners to that mind-set. If we weren't so caught up in that street mind-set then a street is nothing but a street with houses. How come the streets of Hackney aren't affecting the Jews? It's because they don't have a street mind-set like we do. That's why their kids can walk care free up and down the street by themselves near midnight by the age of six. I've seen it myself. You can only respect that type of community - that's true *freedom*. I once stated - *You can't be real in something that is fake.* And I was making reference to street life. What I don't like about this street stuff is that we put it on a platform above our own morals. We put the streets on this pedestal like it's something to be praised. It's nothing to be proud of and we're out here crediting each other for our evil acts. The streets are fake is what I'm saying. How can we be real living by these standards? Random example, we might see a street film where the actor is talking about a snitch, *'Yeah we gotta kill that n*gga man, he a dirty n*gga. We gotta kill that snitch. That dude is a rat.'*

But are we not rats for stabbing our own brothers? Are we not rats for robbing our own brothers? Are you not a rat for stabbing a man over his gold chain? Or stabbing him for the sake of your ends? There's no honour in being a snitch out here, but there's no honour in living by this self-destructive road code either. Either way we're all behaving like rats because it's inward hate.

Seriously though, if this is what street life has become then I don't want any part of it. We are trapped in the game but we promote the mentality like it's something we really want. When deep down we all know we're prisoners to this street life. We've restricted ourselves to the places we can walk safe, because we've fallen for the mind-set.

The British street culture is a funny one sometimes. It's heavily influenced by what we see in American films and Jamaican street culture. Prime example in England today you

might hear a British born youth greet his friend by saying,
'Yo, Wah gwarn my nigga? You good?'
Can you imagine how we would speak if we weren't so
heavily influenced by Jamerica's street culture? What would
it look like if we did a Brexit on using slang from abroad?
Imagine if we only used British terms when we spoke. Can
you picture how ridiculous we would sound? Brothers will
be walking up to each other on the street yelling,
*'You good, my Nig Nogg? How you doing fella? How's the little
Golly Wogs getting along?'*
Sounds mental right? In some places the influences of the
streets are crazy to watch. I remember a time I watched
a couple man from across the water claim to be repping
Bloods and Crips. That's when I knew I was done with the
streets. The streets weren't for me after that. I mean how
can you rep gangs that are over five thousand miles away?
That's a long way cuz. Their argument isn't yours to carry.
Worst still, most people don't overstand how black people in
LA went from being Black Panthers to Bloods and Crips. But
that's a story within itself. Another story which shows we
didn't create this gang street culture.

Like I stated previously the streets are fake because there
isn't any love on the streets. We usually find this out for ourselves when we get a big jail sentence and our friends forget
about us. After the first year the visits start getting fewer.
Or the same friends who scream ride or die leave us to die.
It's not real. Your real friend tells you when you're doing
something that doesn't make sense regardless of how the
streets see it. I've always liked the film *Boyz in the Hood*, but
I never got the message until I was grown. When the char-

acter Ricky got killed, Trey (played by Cuba Gooding) took his dad's gun in a plan to revenge his dead friend Ricky. It was obvious from the scene with his father that Cuba's character Trey didn't want to become a killer. He knew that wasn't who he was even though he lived in the hood. Trey tricked his dad and jumped in the car with Ricky's brother Doughboy (played by Ice Cube) to go and make some duppy. Then as they were in the car circling he gave it some more thought and shouted, *'Let me out!'* Doughboy knew Trey wasn't cut out for it and he never judged him for it. Where most people would have seen Cuba's character as a punk, he was actually quite the opposite. I know a few people who were in a drive by shooting in real life. A lot of them didn't even shoot. But they ended up snitching and going to jail because they were too scared to say,

'Yo, Dough Boy, let me out.'

Sometimes it's ok to learn from other peoples stories. That classic film taught me a hell of a lot about the street mentality. It taught me that the only way to win on the streets is by not playing it.

Another classic film I've always loved is *The Gladiator* starring Russell Crowe. This film reminded me that violence has always been a part of mankind's history. But this film also taught me something deeper in relation to the streets. In the last battle scene, Maximus the Gladiator is due to have a one on one fight with the emperor of Rome, Commodore. The thing is Commodore was shit scared to fight Maximus but he acted like he wasn't. Before the fight Maximus was tied up in chains. Then his opponent Commodore came to size him up. But like I said, Maximus was locked up in chains.

Just before the fight the emperor Commodore hugged Maximus and as he does so he sneakily plunges a knife in to his back. Then he gives him his armour and covers the wound so that people wouldn't know he had cheated. The advantage was all for the *'great emperor.'* Long story short, Maximus still done him over. He managed to kill Commodore but as a result of the pre stab wound he died himself. Now when I saw that film it made sense to me how fake these streets of today are. We praise the badness then complain how bad it is. What's that saying again?

'A coward dies a thousand deaths. A solider dies but once?

CHAPTER 6

DISPELLING THE MYTHS ABOUT THE PERCEIVED SOLUTIONS

*'When you can't
cope with change, you feel
overwhelmed, and you look for
a simple solution.'*
Klaus Schwab

I f you can't identify the issues of any particular problem, then should you be given the platform to talk on the possible solutions? I wrote a book about the problems and the solutions. Yet many people who have read it still ask me, *'Why is this happening? Or what is the solution?'* As frustrating as I find that line of questioning, over time I've come to learn I can't get mad with people for not getting it. It's not fair to do that. Over the years on this journey I have been contacted by various groups and individuals from different backgrounds. This included youth workers, charity organisations, church pastors, Nation of Islam, and people studying criminology. All sorts of people have contacted me in terms of seeking solutions.

When they first made contact, a lot of them assumed they already knew me based on the book. Some of them were open-minded and really down to earth. Then there were those who thought they had all the solutions to our problems. Those are the ones who would start the conversation by congratulating me for my work and seem very genuine about it. They begin to discuss my work and talk about how it raises a lot of issues but they never discuss the solutions my work offers. Then they would start to tell me about the work they were doing to create change and what they think the solution is. At first I would listen with an open mind because everyone has a vision. I would soon switch off once I realised they didn't get what the problems on the street were. I tried my hardest to listen again, but the more they talked the more patronising I found them.

Whenever I interjected and suggested that they might be overlooking the solutions in my book and theory. They usually responded in a very parent like way. As if to say, *'Well, what would you know about solutions? You're a younger from the street; you just come off the streets the other day so how could you know?'*

But they're not saying it out loud. I sensed they respected me as an author but not a messenger. The conversation usually ended with them saying,

'Keep doing what you're doing'

I would always respond respectfully but inside I would be thinking what I was thinking when I first joined the Mental Farmer's football team. I was thinking -

How have these people got me sitting on the bench small talking about the solutions? I didn't come here for this shit; I came here to bang in goals.

The truth is it doesn't matter what team I'm playing for when it comes to finding solutions. To use a football analogy, none of them wanted me to play the full 90 minutes. They only wanted to put me on to play when I said something that went in line with their beliefs. So I stopped playing for everyone and hanged my boots up.

Whilst writing this book, my fellow author and friend Emeka asked me,

'Is the character assassination of the young black male now being perpetuated with good intentions?'

That question has been on my mind from the start of my journey and it gave me food for thought for this chapter. Let me begin by addressing my brothers.

The Pan Africanism or Black history solution

While educating our youth about Black history addresses the issue of being a prisoner to self-hate, it doesn't necessarily prepare them for reality of life on the streets. The issue of the streets still has to be dealt with outside the context of Black history as its role is different. It is not a criticism; I am simply saying that Black history has a different function. As a concept, Pan Africanism has its role in the empowerment of Black people but unfortunately for the movement, it hasn't got wide reaching effect in the 'black' community, particularly among young people. Black History and Pan Africanism has become a-one-hat fits all response to the issues we face in the UK. The point I'm making is that every medicine has its purpose.

If you teach people against the reality of the environment in which they live, then you are preparing them for a life that does not exist. There are a few people who would argue that once the youth learn about their history then that would solve the problem of violence on the streets. If this is your argument, then you may find you are contradicting yourself. It means you are suggesting or promoting the idea that the problem on the streets is that of young black boys. As I said before, this solution suggests that if they learn about who they are then the killing would stop. Evidently, it won't stop anything because a young Caucasian 'lad' killed a black boy in early 2019. We can't ignore the fact that a lot of young boys on road today are white, Turkish and so on. So the solution to this street problem isn't just about reaching the black boys alone. The solution is in changing the mind-set of every skin colour in the country. They say to be a good problem solver you have to be able to identify the issues. Well the problems of the street are not that black and white.

My mate from Manhood Academy told me he was planning to take some young people to Gambia on a trip. At first I thought that would be great for them. It would really open there minds. Notice I said open not change. Because once they come back from Gambia they have to come back to their estates. So it's all good those young people flying back home to do a rites of passage, but they still have to face a different rites of passage over here. What happens when they get moved to on the streets and they're only educated about black history? We haven't given them the tools to deal with people of a prisoner's mind-set. Unless we're in the motherland educating them on how not to get caught up in the streets then I can't see that as a solution. If we're just taking them to Gambia to show them about black history and where Kunta Kinte came from, then that's not the solution. Think about how much more flights we would have to book to get everyone to change. Let's remember though it's not just the black boys doing the killing. So that's a lot more flights to book. Regardless of how I see it I got a lot of respect for my brothers doing this. I wrote a book called *Mama Can't Raise No Man* so it's clear that I know the importance of manhood and stand up father figures. So organisations like Manhood Academy are a part of the wider solution, but it doesn't directly address the PTTS mentality. To be fair I've never heard anyone from this Academy say it was a solution to the streets, but I have heard a few people suggest that.

Overall, I agree that if Black history is taught in the right way, it can be the solution for self-empowerment, self-love, and knowledge of self-etc. I also believe it has the power to help free a lot of brothers who are prisoners to self-hate, as it helped Brother Malcolm X. Though broadly speaking I don't think this is the best solution to fixing the street problem. As I said before, each medicine is designed to target a specific problem.

Fighting the Gangs Matrix system solution

As a community I notice how quick we are to shout,
'No justice! No peace!' as if saying it to the system is going to make a difference. Sometimes when I hear people shouting this I wonder if they are protesting or reading their affirmation cards out loud. What I mean is we affirm what we are shouting, with little action that will disturb the peace. Some people spend their time shouting outside police stations,
'No justice! No peace!'
They ain't lying, it's true. Because after shouting at the system for the day we realise we still didn't get any justice. Then we go back home and after a few weeks the brothers go right back to beefing each other. So in essence we are right.
'No justice! No peace!'
We get what we affirm because we are trying to solve this problem from the outside in by just shouting, which isn't the solution. But you can't tell some of our older community leaders that without an argument. I once asked an older activist in the community,
'Why are you guys so fixated on fighting against the police and this Gangs?
Matrix stuff?'
He replied,

'Because, you have to fight these people from the inside out. This Gangs Matrix is a threat to our young people.'
Then I said,
'Yeah, I hear that. But if we spent more energy in pushing the narrative of prisoner to the streets as the new description for the problem, then wouldn't that eradicate the whole Gangs Matrix issue?'
He gave me a look that suggested I didn't have a clue. In terms of creating change to that particular issue, I felt the same way about him. But I knew his heart was in the right place. And credit where credit is due this man has my respect. He's been standing up for the community from before I was even able to stand. But I just don't feel that method is the solution.

We have to adopt a new description of naming the problem (PTTS) correctly therefore qualifying its existence. It must also gain currency among prisoners to the streets, youth workers, youth leaders, social workers, schools, etc. In other words, change the mind-set and the perspective of people from the inside out. The point I am making is, if you change a situation like this from the outside by changing minds and actions, then there is no need to fight the Gangs Matrix. By accepting their language and working within the terms of the Gangs Matrix, then we are effectively accepting the criminalisation of our young people.

I love my people for stepping out against racial discrimination or police brutality, but the solution behind that has to make sense. In other words, we have to squash our beef and come together as a people first. So right now we couldn't do a Million Man March. Why? Because certain man would be beefing each other on the march. We've lost our way a bit but if we make peace first then we can talk about coming together afterwards. It serves us no purpose in having the same meetings with the same people and expecting change. It's a great incentive but let's ensure our house is clean before we take on the garden.

<u>Pupil Referral Units solution</u>

Pupil referral units and boxing academies are businesses; they are not a solution to anything. By isolating and excluding young people, you just fast track them quicker into that street mind-set. The reality is - some children will struggle at school because all children are not academic. Some children don't feel challenged enough by what they are learning so they become disruptive.

Whatever the reason be you need to find out why a child is being disruptive in school. Get to the root of his or her issues. Address it then deal with that individual. Excluding them and sending them to a PRU is not a solution; it is actually part of the problem. How are you elevating those young people you exclude? You're putting so called 'bad breed' children with other so called 'bad breeds' and instilling a self-fulfilling prophecy. It's almost like being in a youth offender's institution. A child is waking up every day to go and study in an environment with other children who are not allowed in main stream. Do you have any idea what that self-fulfilling prophecy can do to your psyche? I was in a PRU as a teen and it's not the place for a child to be progressive. Every one of us had issues. Most of us were either in care or didn't care. And the teachers didn't care that much either. But somehow we were all meant to be getting an education in that same environment. All I'm saying is that it's going to be harder for a youth in a PRU to excel than it would be if he was in mainstream school. Why, because putting youths around other youths who can't behave in schools isn't smart.

So what is the solution to alternative education? The solution is simple - it's prevention. Let us do the work early enough so we won't need to have PRUs. There shouldn't be any alternative provisions for education. The simple fact people talk about making alternative provisions for the children proves we are failing them. We need to change the mind-sets early and regularly so that we won't need an alternative. Keeping a child in mainstream school may be what they need to stay off the streets.

The Marching against Knife Crime solution

For me, marching is definitely not a solution. What's the purpose of marching? It makes some sense if you're marching against the system like others did in the past, but not when the march is against your own children. I mean, what message do you think you are sending to young prisoners to the streets by marching against them? Do you think they will see you marching on the news and decide to change their life around? Sounds crazy, right? But that's what you're doing. People that insist on marching in this fashion are clearly being reactive. The majority of them would never go up to a youth from the street directly and express their opinion. Then at the end of the march they start to preach to the others who marched with them about what we need to do to stop the violence.

So in essence, they end up talking to the converted. The people they should be talking to are probably at home, or otherwise occupied. I wouldn't knock the marching solution if they marched to the block and spoke to the mandem directly. Or even if the elders went to their old friends' houses along with their children to show them how small the world is. It's like people really can't see the harm they are causing by marching in this fashion.

What I hate about this so called *'stop the killing'* marches is that it looks like this is a good vs bad argument. On Monday you're joining the system to march against your children. Then on Tuesday you're complaining that your youths are being portrayed as the bad ones by the same system. That shit's confusing to me. *Try know* that when you march against your own youth, you make them look like there the bad ones. If the youth are the so called bad guys in this, then who do you think the so called good guys are? Well, it must be you lot. The same people voicing opinions, displaying placards and shouting, *'Stop the knife crime'* are made to look like the good guys in the community. You're out here marching chest high with the police and the media beside you, not knowing this doesn't help matters at all. The hard to reach prisoners you're trying to reach know something you don't. They know the police and media you're marching with don't care about what's going on. And those who march with them are indirectly supporting that criminalisation with their 'naïve' actions. Reactionary behaviours are not the solution to the problem.

A good problem solver once asked,
'Are you fire fighting, or are you going to the root of the fire?'
In other words, are you being reactive or proactive? A lot of us have good intentions, but it's not enough.

After the murder of a young girl in Tottenham, some guys created a group called GANG. Now if you know my stance then you would know why I didn't like the name alone. Don't get me wrong, the intentions were great and the title had a good meaning, but I don't like the word gang. The anagram for GANG in this case was Guiding a New Generation. I loved the anagram, but it didn't change my views on the word. I reserved my judgement because I love the idea of others stepping up to be a part of the solution. A couple of my mates were involved in it too, so I got an insight to what it was about. It was about marching through the areas on the block without police. A part of me liked the idea because it made more sense than watching others march with plac-ards. At the same time I still knew it was a reactive action. I thought to myself,
'How long are they gonna keep this marching up before they realise we need a real plan of action?'

I don't mean smart answers for the news; I mean a real plan of action - A long term plan of action. What outcomes are you setting to achieve? Have you identified the problem? The answer to those questions - no. That doesn't mean they failed; it simply means they failed to plan it out long term. No big deal - go back to the drawing board. I respect the brothers for their fire and intentions. But in order to imple-ment change we need to have a strategy in place, otherwise it is just another reactive action.

The Reactionary Platforms and Panels solution

When it comes to finding solutions in this field people tend to turn to panel meetings to hear answers. Some people from the community come to these meetings specifically to shout at the person representing the government or the local council. I've never understood that process myself. The first time I ever went to a panel I was confused. The panel had a Rasta man, a politician and a pan Africanist speaking on the problems and solutions on the street. What I didn't understand was why these people felt it necessary to discuss the issues we have with a person in politics. Most Rasta men I knew growing up said they don't deal with Babylon and *politricks.*

Then there was another panel which confused the hell out of me. I was in a South London borough and sadly there had been a number of knife related deaths there. So a panel of speakers was arranged to come and give the community some solutions. On the panel I saw one black local politician who was sitting next to a guy I knew that claimed to be an ex-gangster. The ex-gangster who worked with the police was sitting next to the local counsellor. And the local counsellor was sitting next to a police officer. I sat down for two hours and listened to people who work for a system which is based on intervention talk about solutions. The ex-gangster bragged about working with police for two years. Then years later he made claims that the same police were trying to assassinate his character.

The local politician gave some story about being able to relate because his son was a victim. The police man talked about working together and building relations to find a solution. And the councillor got booed each time he opened his mouth to speak.

After the panel spoke, the floor was opened for questions. The community was venting their anger and frustrations about what the community needed; they sat there and heard the same old answers. I got so bored, I had to leave. But before I left I said,

'So you guys have come here to talk to people who profit off crime about solutions? The same so-called professionals who have never solved any problems before? Why don't you guys as the community and the parents sit down and be your own panel and audience? It would make more sense than talking to a bunch of people who might not have a job if the violence stopped today.'

What I was trying to say was we have the answers among us. But the community wouldn't know that because we only come out to shout at panellist. We rarely come out in numbers to listen to each other's ideas.

The Youth Club solution

For me, more youth clubs are not the solution to this street mind-set. I agree that youth clubs give young people a place to go to and something to do. The activities can help them occupy their time more productively but it's not a solution to unlocking the chains of the prisoner to the street mentality. I hear so many people screaming,

'The reason why there is so much crime is because of the lack of youth clubs.'

Now this might be an additional reason but it isn't the main factor by far. In response to all the youth closures some people start saying,

'More youth clubs are the solution. The youth need a place to go.'

They do need a place to go but why are we giving them a place to go if we aren't teaching them how to carry themselves in the real world? Why should we spoil them with trips when they show no respect for the place or the people working there? I know how it goes in this day and age - your child could be at the youth club but sometimes you're thinking,

'Is my child even safe there?'

How do we know the young ones brainwashed by this mindset aren't carrying weapons to the youth club? And no, I'm not suggesting the solution is in searching them before entry. Ask yourself-

Do these youth clubs or youth workers challenge the mindset of children attending youth clubs? Or do most of these youth clubs enable a space that allows the *prisonerish* behaviours to spread and become normalised?

I say that because nowadays whenever I walk into a youth club for the first time all I hear is swearing and bad manners. Youth clubs would be a great addition to the solution if they had the right people working in them. If things were like they were in the early 90s, things would be different. But you can't get that anymore because it's become a business. Everyone has to tick those boxes before they can begin to work. The old days had a strong community feel you felt at home at the youth club and play centres. Imagine a team of youth workers bringing a Coach Carter mentality to work. Imagine a few sisters with the firmness of I don't know, let's say Inyanla Vazant added with the soft approach of Claire Huscktable. But why imagine? The solution to better youth clubs is bringing back that love and discipline and getting rid of all the politics. Unless we can do that, we don't need any more youth clubs. And if we do get more youth clubs we have to own them. Damon Dash says it best if you don't own it – it's not yours.

The Mentoring solution

Now mentoring can be a great thing to help support changing the mind-set. But it has to be the right type of mentoring. And it has to be consistent. The right type of mentor could help prevent a young child from getting excluded from school. So this is a good idea. However mentoring isn't the solution to identifying the problems on the streets. But it definitely can aid in the solution.

The Knife in Bins solution

This one is a no brainer to me. If I put my knife in the bin and my enemy doesn't put his one there, will I be safe? No, well that answers why this is not a solution.
If I hand my knife in to the police there is no guarantee that the same knife won't end up back out on the streets. There is no guarantee that the same knife I'm handing in won't be used against me. People seem to forget the obvious that

knives are a household utensil – we need them to prepare food. The solution isn't in taking knives off the street; it is stopping them from getting onto our streets.

In early 2019 there was a news story about a brother who was taking knives off the youths and giving them to the police. Supposedly, the young people who handed in a knife was rewarded a JD sports voucher. I was asked what my views were about it. I didn't want to comment on it because no matter what I say, some people would still think that it's a good thing. Plus I hate to sound like a pessimist but I struggled to see how this method could be effective. The story got massive media coverage and I was constantly asked by people in the youth field if I think this is a solution. My answer was simple - No! How can taking a knife off a child with the added gesture of a JD sports voucher possibly be the answer? Wasn't it a few months prior to this story that the social media activist had a problem with JD Sports? Did you guys forget that JD Sports were selling sport balaclavas to our children? How do we know that young person handing in the knife isn't going to give their mum's kitchen knife to him then buy a balaclava with the same voucher money? Then after he buys the balaclava from JD sports he goes and picks up his zombie sword from under his bed? And then he uses that same balaclava which he brought with the JD Sports voucher to protect his identity after he stabs or robs someone?

My point is, we don't know, so how can this possibly be a solution? I think the important factor we should focus on is why the media gave this story so much attention. They always give oxygen to stories that are considered 'sexy' and anything that isn't, they are not interested. Stay woke!

I can't vouch for everyone's heart in this field of work. But I like to believe that most people trying to make a difference genuinely have good intentions. Then I think about the word intentions and this quote from MLK comes to mind, 'People with good intentions but limited understanding are more dangerous than people with total ill will.'

The Building Relationships with Police solution

Why would I want to work with, train with or build relationships with the police? People are still getting killed by the police. I still get stopped and searched by the police. Their job is to arrest people not to understand why young people are breaking the law. The police are there to deal with crime and 'law and order' as they call it. What I'm saying is we are not dealing with criminals so how can I train the police to think differently from how they operate? What am I supposed to do, teach them how to arrest us in a more polite manner? The solution isn't more black people in police or politics either. Why? Well, other than Bernie Grant when have you known a black person in the police or politics to effect any major or lasting change? Working with the police is a Catch 22 situation because our objectives are different.

Looking at it in a wider sense, some people believe that more police presence, increased stop and search and curfews are the solution to youth violence. To be honest,

I find it hard to waste my time on this one. People who believe this is a solution have obviously given up hope on the youth. When I hear people asking the government to put our children on curfew it sounds like fear – not logic speaking. Remember the old saying, 'Children should be seen and not heard.' Well it became an old saying for a reason. If we put our children on curfew essentially we are saying they are a threat to us. And in that way we silence them. As well as reinforcing the impression that they are the root of the problem. If we punish all children by the actions of some then we have in essence gone back in time. But this time the Children won't be seen or heard because they'll be on curfew. And as for increasing stop and search as a solution, well again that's fear talking – not logic. We all know which ethnicity is most likely to get stopped and searched by police. So let's leave this solution alone please.

The Mothers Against Guns solution

As admirable as I think it is to see a parent who has lost a child going around doing talks. I still don't think that is a solution. How can somebody losing a child talking about stop the killing be the solution? It's bad to write this but I know a few prisoners to the streets that would kill your child in front of you *'the parents,'* if they had to. What I'm saying is I think parents against guns and knives may be good for dealing with the prevention stage of solution. This type of work will be better for young children who are not involved in the streets. Maybe hearing this from this angle might help raise their conscious levels while they still have a heart. But if you think it can change the mind-set of a prisoner to the street, then you don't know the mind-set. The mind-set doesn't care about the death of your child. That mind-set has no heart. I empathise with your pain. As I do with all of my dead friends parents. However I wouldn't turn to them for the solution.

The Send Them to the Army solution

Why is this so called solution even a conversation? Most of them are already traumatised by violence, but you want to send them to fight in war to get more trauma? Are you suggesting that these lost young people are better off dead? Or are you suggesting that you don't mind young people killing people as long as it's not in our country? Whatever you're suggesting I think it's safe to suggest it doesn't make sense.

The Church is the solution

My biggest support and frustration has been the church, in terms of getting support to the street problem. For years I've reached out to the church to get them to help me with my solution and I've felt rejected by them. When I say the church I don't mean the faith I mean the people who call the shots in the church.

I once asked a pastor why I couldn't have my book promoted in his church.

He responded, *'Robin there is a place for these things.'*

I then asked, *'Where is this place because I would love to know?'*

He continued, *'Your book has swearing in it.'*

I replied, *'True, but the Bible has Sodom and Gomorra. It talks about murderers and it mentions more violence and wicked-ness than I have seen in my book.'*

But because my book has swearing in it the pastor decided it's not worthy for the church? Now I believe in God the creator. I really do. But when I hear this line of talk coming from a pastor I don't believe it is God talking. I don't believe God was saying to him that the book shouldn't be in there, I believe that was the pastor's call. He was just telling me that from his perspective, my message shouldn't be heard in the church and that the church wasn't ready for a book like mine. What I found funny is that some of the godliest children later turned into prisoners to the streets. Look at me; I was in church singing too. I told pastors about my frustration at getting into the schools and the youth offending teams to do the work. I asked everyone who would listen. Nobody was letting me in so I turned to the church. I almost cried in anger when they rejected the message.

Why? Because at the end of the book a young man who got stabbed said it was down to God and my letter why he forgave me. This was a Christian believer who very much wanted to kill me in revenge. But I was able to reach him on a prisoner to the streets level. In his letter back to me, he stated,

'Brother Robin, you've helped convince me that I should never give up on my Lord and to take pride that I didn't fall under the sword of the devil.' Can I get an amen?

The theory that the most high has given me has helped to motivate one of your own believers to believe. Yet this pastor says it has no place in the church? What's crazy is I actually apologised to him because my faith in God moved me to check myself when I found out I was in the wrong. That in itself is actually a testimony according to the church's belief. So it did hurt to offer to work with this church on a joint solution and then have that pastor reject it.

Some Jehovah Witnesses came and knocked my door one hot Saturday morning. They told me they were here to preach the good word. I told them that based on what they said I don't think I was going to make it to heaven. Especially if only 144,000 people can make it into the pearly gates. We carried on speaking and they assumed I was still stuck on the streets. Then I showed them my book. The two elderly black women gave me a curious look. One took it, scanned through it and handed it right back to me. The other one also scanned through it. Afterwards, she said,

'I don't want to hear anything about your book because it has swearing in it.'

When I offered to give it to her she gave it right back. I felt a bit unappreciated like they was confirming I wasn't worthy of what they believed in unless I did things their way. Then I thought about the two times I did a talk in the church and the impact it had when I explained my theory.

I was invited to a church event in Wood Green called, *'Pray for the Youth,'* another reactive event, which was put on to create change in the community. A week before that event I had a disagreement with a pastor on Facebook. I told him online that praying for the youth doesn't make sense. I told him faith without works is dead. Off the back of our Facebook debate, we ended up being friends in real life. When I came down to the event, he asked me to speak. I felt frustrated because I didn't feel talking at one event was the solution. But I yearned for some consistent support to bring the solution into practice. So I went on stage and did my thing. Afterwards, the pastor said he needed people who wanted to invest in my work to come to the front.

All of a sudden people came to the front saying they will invest in me. Now I was moved by that. Then they promised to invest in books and so on. After the event all these people came up to me and said they worked in this prison or that prison and they could get me in to talk. But after that day I never heard from them. I can't say all the people who came to the front to invest in my books did because only a few did. And with their donations I felt super blessed. This enabled me to go around and give out over 300 books free to strangers on the street. I almost felt like a street evangelist again.

Although I was super grateful, that wasn't the reason why I went there. I went there to have my solution supported. I was very precise about what I needed to make the change. I needed support for the workshops to cover my finances while I go into the schools for free. I needed the financial support to give the young people free books after the free workshop. More importantly, I wanted them to help me get into all the youth church services around the country. However disappointed I am about it not manifesting into action, I'm still grateful for every single individual who was given a book off of the back of the church. That was the first time the church supported me and that meant a lot to me. I just wish we could have done more.

After that event, my friend the pastor continued to put on

'Pray for the Youth' events. He knows how much I respect him for his heart and desire. Pastor Junior is a very genuine man. However my point still remains - faith without the right works is dead. So no, I don't think church is the solution, but it can be if it is done with the right people. I believe that with the right works and the most high on side anything is possible.

The Prisoner to the Streets solution

The book alone is not the solution. Although many people have read the book and told me it has changed their life for the better. Still, I don't see the book as the entire solution. The book offers a powerful insight into getting people to see the trap they are in from an honest perspective. And it gives them the key for freedom. However, the individual trapped has to want to work for that freedom because freedom isn't for free. I strongly believe the book mixed with the workshop on a regular basis has the power to unlock the mindset of any prisoner. I don't believe it is the whole solution, there are no singular solutions but I'm certain that PTTS addresses the root. PTTS needs a lane of its own no doubt. But in saying that if it was mixed in the schools alongside things like Manhood Academy, Womanhood Academy, some top quality mentoring and empowering black history, then collectively these things can bring forth the changes we want to see. Add to that list motivational talkers like Action Jackson and Mark Prince. When it comes to motivating young people's minds those guys are like the black Anthony Robbins. If we had a dream team of workers who played their position managed by someone like the mental farmer, then I'm sure we would be effective in making change. But I can't see it happening because most of us are not team players. Most of us feel we have all the solutions for a problem we don't fully understand. For that reason alone - I'm ready to hang my boots up.

In closing this chapter, I want to add that I didn't write it to take shots at anyone or to hurt them in terms of the solutions they're offering. I'm just trying to navigate people through all the confusion. To reiterate what I said previously – Every medicine has its own purpose.

CHAPTER 7

BLAME PARENTS, SOCIAL MEDIA AND GRIME?

Every so often I'll go on to Facebook or watch the news to hear what's going on in the world. Mind you, these are two platforms that don't really deal with reality. Anyway when I do log in or switch on, a lot of the time the conversation seems to be about what is happening with our youth. A lot of the time I see people finger pointing. And it's always the same stuff. If it's not the olders getting blamed for grooming the young ones, it's the parents, social media or grime. So let's touch on that.

Parents - can we blame the parents? Well you can blame them if you like because that is the easy option. When it comes to blaming the parents there seems to be a lot of assumptions. Nobody knows from talking to a young person what type of house they live in. So to blame the parents is to already assume he has parents. When you say blame the parents, most of the children you are referring to don't have both parents, so it's dangerous to assume they have two people who care for them. Their parents could be mentally ill, drug addicts, or they could be in care for all we know, the truth is we don't know. So can we quickly acknowledge that first before we begin blaming the parents?

I'm aware some parents are a part of the problem but they are definitely not to blame for the problem. One thing we can all agree on about parenting is that it doesn't come with a manual book. And we all know that every child behaves differently. So I much prefer in holding some of these parents accountable for their actions over blaming them. A lot of the parents especially us young ones need guidance, not blame. Lyndon the (Mental farmer) and I were reasoning the other day about the word blame. He broke it right down to me. *'Blame is about a distortive way of thinking, so it's not clear. So on the computer you have bold text then you have italics. Well it's like taking normal letters and bending them, blame is a condition of the mind. This is based on the culture, beliefs and values of an individual. Somebody who blames somebody else does not realise that they're blaming themselves. Maybe that message is coming from a deeper place.'*

Me and the Mental Farmer have lot in common, because I couldn't agree more. Although I don't blame the parents, I do believe some of them aren't helping matters. A lot of them haven't set boundaries and their children think they are their parents' friends. This is not a good thing because we can't discipline our friends. If we look at what's happening, we can see that there a lot of children having children. That isn't necessarily a bad thing all the time. It only becomes a problem when we refuse to grow up. And right now it feels like we're in the Peter pan era of parenting. And were we've stopped aging our children are ageing faster because of what they are being exposed to.

My mate *'Leon Da Realist' broke it down to me one day, 'The internet is mad because it's keeping us at the same age. You're right. When you say 'our parents', the adults were the adults back then. But that's because there was boundaries when we were yutes. Like we didn't know all the stuff the adult's knew. That's what made them adults. That's what generated the respect. But now we have the internet the children don't need their parents. If they need to know something they can go and ask Google or Siri. They don't need to have any real interaction with the parents anymore. Because of that they're now exposed to adult material or things that would've once made an adult an adult. Now the children are on the same level as the adults. There's know generation gap, there's no boundaries. The children know exactly the same stuff to the point where they're telling us things. There are no more boundaries cos they're exposed to the same shit. So now we listen to the same music and we dress the same. Now there is no division or separation - were all the same now. It's mad. I agree with you were raising our children like they're our friends.'*

Sometimes we even do worse than make them our friends. Sometimes we ignorantly encourage our children to become prisoners to the streets because we are still prisoners ourselves. Sometimes it's not even the parent; it can be the partner they bring in the house. I remember when I was about 16 years old and I was at one of my friend's house who was a *dream chaser*. We were chilling in his room when his Mum came in and gave him the mobile phone. I thought it was his Nan or something on the phone. I don't remember exactly what words she said to him. But as a result of the call we had to go and run the errand. When we got to the house all I could see was fog. Then through the mist of that fog I saw people sitting parched out in the corner or stuck to the sofa. Then I clocked what happened. I clocked my friends Mum just gave him instructions to lick a shot.

That friend of mine later lost his life to the streets. So in that instance is the parent to blame? She might feel that she is but I don't believe that. As parents we don't always make the right choices for our children. But when someone is trapped in a prisoner's mind-set parent or child they can't make the right choices. They have already normalised the behaviours. For me, it's not about the blame game; it's about finding the reasons to why we are failing. I heard years later that my friend's mother became a qualified drugs councillor. She now helps drug users to get their life back together, which teaches me something valuable. It teaches me that parents are not perfect they are human. And they are capable of making mistakes too. My friends mum is not to blame for the loss of her son. She made a mistake when she was trapped in that mind-set. But evidently she's figured out that lifestyle isn't productive. And I'm sure her son is looking down on her from above with a great sense of pride. To know that she freed herself from the life she knew. I don't blame you Mum in fact I salute you.

While a lot of people are blaming the parents, a lot of them are forgetting the lack of power that these parents have over their own children. At the moment I see the government calling all the shots, over what our children can and can't get away with. And they control what they learn also. The government are the parents. And they're supposed to be the best parents in the world, right - but they still fail. So if the government can't get it right, the people that control society, then how the hell can the parents get it right? They've told the parents they can't discipline their children and if they discipline their children they'll be disciplined. My mate Jerome's Carer use to say, *'Blaming is not a good energy for a solution, because there is no responsibility. 'Blame or shame ends the game.' So if you blame anybody else for your problems or you feel shameful you end the game. Because there is no responsibility in blaming there's just finger pointing.'*

This is very true. And this is what people are doing now. Everybody is pointing fingers saying, 'it's your fault.' So where's your responsibility in this? Once we start to take responsibility we come to understand that everyone is drinking some type of poison. It's just a case of how much it has infected our body and our mind. So no - I don't generally blame any of the parents for where we are in the streets but some of the irresponsible ones are a big part of the problem.

Social media – can we blame social media for fuelling the violence? I don't know if social media is fuelling the violence. But I know the beef and mentality was there before social media. Social media might heighten an incident and bring crazy attention to a situation. That attention can cause somebody to feel an increased level of shame and humiliation. So for example, the brother that got caught on the stairs doing something he shouldn't have been doing. If that was back in the day only the people who were present that day could comment about it. But now that brother can't get a break. Every New Year's Eve someone has to post it to make him feel like shit again. It's so bad I can't even forget his name, but we can't keep shaming people like this. With all that being said I'm curious to know - is social media responsible for his humiliation or is it the people recording videos and uploading to social media?

Social media is just a platform and a lot of prisoners to the streets happen to use the platform. Occasionally some prisoners ignorantly use it to promote their beef or to stunt on someone they've robbed. So this can't be a good thing, but is social media to blame? Of course, it is, because we're playing the blame game. I don't blame social media. It is the mindset of the people using social media which is the reason why it's being fuelled. I refuse to participate in the blame game but I do wonder why strangers, mainly adults, always record incidences of youth violence without thinking. It's almost like strangers are the new modern day journalist. Just a few months ago, one of my little brothers aged 17 got stabbed in his face in Tottenham. Instead of the grown people in the bookies making an attempt to help break it up, they came out with their mobile phones to record it. Imagine Tottenham police station was just a few doors away from where the incident took place, and yet still nobody ran to get help. Nobody picked up their phone to call 999 they just picked it up to record. I just want to thank the person who called for an ambulance. Unfortunately, this is the mentality of a lot of the elders nowadays in the community, but I still don't blame them.

Social media is what it is - it is a gathering of individuals who are mixed up in their purpose for joining. Some join it because they are lonely and don't have many people to have a discussion with. Some join it for attention; some join it for spite. But social media itself without people with their warped type of mentality is harmless.
I'll leave it there.

Grime/Rap – can we blame the rappers? Well, the problems we have were here way before grime or rap. I believe that some songs can reinforce you to think with this prisoner's mind-set we deal with.
I once had an argument with a friend when I was 16. The argument wasn't even that deep to begin with. Things only got heated when that friend came to my Nan's house with a knife hidden up his sleeve for me, as I explained in *Prisoner to the Streets*. That day I was listening to a song from one of my favourite New York rappers called Nas. The song I was listening to was called *Ok You Wanna Play Rough?*

That song was on my mind all day, even more so when I saw my friend at my Nan's door with the knife. When I saw the knife in his hand, my mood changed swiftly. I swear I could hear that Nas song playing on repeat in my head. The lyrics to that one was quite some foul. Man was talking about *'put these ni@@as in boxes, where their moms and pops is'*. And something about running up in his house and letting the team tie up his lady friend and run game on her. The tune was foul and so was my mind state at the time.

Now it's obvious that Nas wasn't responsible for my actions that day. All I'm saying is, that tune was in my head vividly and it helped set the scene. Gangster rap mixed with the 16 year old prisoner to the street mentality who smoked skunk.

Once upon a time hip hop use to be about inspiring and uplifting the people. This era of hip hop was in the 80s. Rappers were pushing some real knowledge then. By the 90s when gangster rap came into play the game had changed dramatically. Now many people believe that the rap game didn't change by accident. Many people believe the rap game was infiltrated by those who didn't want rappers to be lifting up their community through lyrics. Which I'd like to think isn't true but it actually makes sense when I think about it.

I remember watching the film *'Straight outta Compton'* in 2015. In one of the scenes the young rap group were at a concert about to perform. Before they hit the stage the police reminded them that they weren't allowed to perform the song entitled *Fuck da Police.* Apparently the track was getting too much negative reaction from the fans. The police feared the song could be problematic and didn't like people rapping with that kind of hatred towards them, which is interesting to say the least. So what are they really saying about the rap game then? That it's ok to rap using the N word, the B word or talking about selling drugs and violence towards ourselves? But it's not OK to say, 'Fuck the police' in a place where police harassment was striving. That is why it is believable to me that the rap game was infiltrated. And if you say fuck the police the dance gets shut down.

I'm probably one of the biggest rap fans I know. I grew up in the middle of the gangsta rap era. The game shaped me as a teenager. But as of recent I found it hard to listen to some of these mumbo jumbo rappers talking about being in love with coke. And to be fair I feel like I've out grown most of the rap I once loved as a yute. These days when I try to listen to rap I find it hard. I'm in my early 30s now so I feel like I'm way too old for hearing about the streets. My first born is 15 years old. So when I hear man my age or older talking on the microphone to get my attention it has to have substance or be totally lit. Since the whole debate started with the system blaming grime music for 'knife crime' I've heard a lot of silly defences. I've heard some big grown rappers say some ridiculous things to defend the music their putting out there. One rapper I heard said something along the lines of this, 'It's not our responsibility to watch what we're saying in our lyrics; it's the parent's responsibility to watch what their children are listening to.'
I wish I was there at the debate to say,

'No brother, you're an adult nearly 40 years of age. Speak life into them'.

Learn to speak life into these children because they need to have life spoken into them. If you keep speaking death, violence and negativity, then their gonna gravitate to the same thing your projecting. What are you projecting? What do you want them to gravitate to? If you keep projecting this trap mind-set then they might end up getting trapped. Music isn't to blame we all know that, but music can affect the mood of a person, and we know that. We know the power of it.

Just remember how impressionable the rap game was to us when Biggie and Tupac died. Certain man knew the lyrics to ten crack commandments word for word. They didn't even know what crack was. I don't believe rappers are responsible for this mess but some rappers are adding to the fuel.

A know a lot of rappers who I grew with and are still friends with now. Sometimes we converse about the state of the rap game and I ask them,

'Why don't you speak more substance when you have the talent to?'

They usually respond by saying,

'The rap games hard cuz. If I talk too much positive I won't get through. I gotta do a street banger first then I gotta do a party tune, you gotta give the people what they want.'

As much as I hear all of that I still think outside the box,

'So why can't you be the first to change the game? Why can't you give the people what you want?'

Then they'll usually say,

'Ah Trav, you're getting old cuz, have you forgotten how the rap game works?'

I hear that argument a lot but it's not that I don't understand how the game works. It's just that I've always believed in changing the game. Let's remember Tupac died at 25 and he changed the game. He would have done a lot more had he been able to see up to the age of 30.

My friend might be right. Maybe I am getting old, because it was only this year that I heard of a young rapper called Cadet. Cadet was a brother who died in a car crash as his rap career was about to blow. I don't even know the brother but I got to salute the young king. I heard he was spitting some constructive fire. From what I hear this young king was about to change the game and set pace. I'm glad to know he got to shine his light before the sunset. Cadet's loved ones can only be proud of that type of legacy, may his soul rest in paradise.

CHAPTER 8

DEFINITION OF A SNITCH!

Snitches get stitches?

Ten years ago I was working as a project worker in Hackney. Me and another colleague got invited to do a few talks about our street experience. At the time it was two years of me being a freeman but I was still rough on the edges. I was in my early 20s at the time and some of the people I was talking to were aged 16-19. When I was in the middle of doing my talk one student in particular was acting up, like he was about that street life. I can't remember why he shouted,

'Nah man don't snitch, snitches get stitches.'

When he said it I laughed because that statement isn't true. They don't always get stiches. And worse still he said it like he believed he was that guy. So I made it my point to challenge him in front of the class.

'So what are you telling me bro? Snitches get stitches yeah?'
The student replied, 'Yeah that's right.'
I responded, *'Alright, what would you do if I robbed everyone's phone in this class and left out right now?'*
The student replied,
'Ah, man wouldn't have that; man would stab you up cuz!'
Honestly I had to grab myself when he said that. I was still a freshman to this trying to kick knowledge stuff. The hot headed prisoner in me wanted to stomp the little fucker out just for thinking he could stab me. I chose to smile instead and tried to remember the point I was trying to teach him.
Then I said, *'So you would stab me up yeah?'*
The student replied, *'Yeah.'*
'OK, so after you supposedly stab me up what do you think happens next?'
Student, *'Well I'm gonna get back my phone innit!'*
Then I said, *'Well, maybe you will, maybe you won't. But after you stab me up you're gonna get nicked innit?'*
The student looked confused and shrugged his shoulders.
So I said, *'OK, erm... what are you here for?'*
Student, *'What do you mean what am I here for? Man's here to get an education innit!'*
I replied, *'Ok then, so why let me draw you out by robbing your phone? Do you know what else you could've done in that scenario? You could have told the fucking police rude bwoy!'*
The student responds, *'Nah, nah that's snitching.'*

I paused for a second just to look at his ignorance then I went in.

'Why is it snitching and what are you here for? You're in college, four days a week. You're coming here with the aim of getting qualifications. Then with those same qualifications you plan to get employment. You're working towards paying taxes to these fuckers so you can not be a snitch. How the fuck can you be the snitch when I'm the draw out? You're just a student at college who got robbed. But because you thought you weren't allowed to 'snitch', you'd rather lose your focus and stab me up over a phone. So basically my actions just made you become a prisoner to the street over nothing. Well done bad man.'

After that he didn't have much else to say. I just hope the young brother got the message and completed the whole course.

So many people get it confused out here. They proper get it twisted. It's like people have put the law of the streets over the law of the land.

Quick example, if a conscious prisoner to the streets decides to go and stab up a man at the bottom of the road. Then a civilian see's him and they call police, the street prisoner cannot be mad with them. It's impossible for the street prisoner to be mad with them, because they're civilians; they're not on the streets. That's the misconception people keep getting over this snitch word. They're not on the road so you can't label them a snitch, they don't live by your values and beliefs. If a street guy rats on another street guy then that snitch is a rat in my eyes. And that rat is a snitch.

When I was on the roads I always kept it 100, I lived and was ready to die by this no snitching concept. What's funny is even at this age I would still much rather be called a son of a bitch, than a son of a snitch. That might sound weird to some but please let me land my trail of thought. A bitch is a lady dog, or someone described as an unpleasant person. Bitches are renowned for giving spiteful criticism and spreading rumours. Then a snitch on the other hand is described as a rat. A rat is otherwise known as a person who has absolutely no loyalty. Rats are renowned for spreading something worse than rumours, they spread vermin. So I'd rather be a son of a bitch than a son of a snitch. I prefer my parent spread rumours than spread vermin. If that went over your head don't worry about it, I'm just trying to get my word count up so I can finish this chapter.

Seriously though, let's look at a few so called *'snitch scenarios'* and see how we feel about this word once we over stand its meaning.

Scenario number one: Imagine you are 17 years old and you're still living at your mum's house. One minute you are in your house minding your business. Then one of your friends come round and knocks on the front door. You go and speak with him and he says he wants to borrow your car. Back then, most people only want to borrow sugar. But still you let you're not so close friend convince you into borrowing your car. The whole day goes past and your so called friend hasn't come back in the time promised. So basically he is taking the piss. Then while you're waiting for him to come back, you get distracted by a phone call telling you that someone who you're cool with has been killed. Soon after that phone call you fall asleep whilst waiting.

The next morning there is a knock at the door. You get up thinking,
'This better be my car.'
But it's not, instead it's the police who claims your car was involved in a shooting the night before. But how could that be? You borrowed your car to your friend, right? Anyway you get arrested and treated as a suspect for the murder. So what do you do in this position? If you tell the truth, you are considered a snitch, right? If you say no comment you very most likely will be held on remand. It's a catch 22; either way you lose right?
So would you (a) keep it *'so called real'* say no comment and go to jail for a friend who did a murder in your car? Or do you (b) tell the police who you borrowed your car to and be considered a snitch?
This scenario is a sticky one to be caught up in. But that's only because of the confusion of this snitch word. I don't know your answer but personally I know which one I'm going to choose. If the car is registered to me then it doesn't look that good. If my solicitor tells me it looks like I'm going on remand then I'm singing like Usher Raymond. I'll be on the tape recorder literally singing,
'They call him R-O-B-I-N... T-R-A... Then I'll hit some high notes, *This mother fucker lives at 54, that's his door, yes I'm sure... Maybe he can help you better than I caaaan.'*
Some wannabe street dude would read that and think,
'Nah, that's still snitching.'
How the hell is it snitching? I mean what the actual fuck. If my friend ever took my car and dusted out someone in my

vehicle then that's obviously not my friend. If friends do that then I'd much prefer having enemies. My so-called friend wouldn't have to worry about police catching him, he better pray I don't catch him first. So basically, my so called friend was trying to frame me for a murder he was a part of? A man selected me as the pawn and I'm meant to keep it real? My answer in this scenario is definitely (a). For those of you that chose (b) you're the reason the streets are confused.

Next scenario
You're 16 years of age... You're currently doing the road ting, your active in the street life. A situation sparks off with you and your friend. Some outta town guys chase you for being in *'their so called ends.'* Somehow you manage to get away safely. But sadly your friend doesn't. He loses his life. Now the police are involved and this has put you in a sticky predicament. You know you are on the roads so telling them would mean snitching, right? But then you are only 16 years old, and so was your friend when he got killed. In that scenario I can only assume the family members of the 16 year old want answers. If you are the friend who was there then you are their only hope for justice to prevail. So what do you do? Do you (a) go to court on behalf of your friend's family and possibly be labelled a snitch? Or do you (b) so called *'keep it real'* and deal with matters yourself?

Well if you don't mind me sharing my thoughts I know which one I'm choosing. I know most people won't get this or agree first time around. But it's simple for me if I go to court and snitch, then I know after that I can't do the road ting again. That is the only way I could do it. But I would know to myself I can't ever do road again. I might need to move far away after that, because my enemies would know I told. What I'm saying is my answer is never (a). I would never snitch in that situation regardless of my friend's family. I'm not encouraging young people to pick (b) I'm just saying that picking (a) is snitching. It's simple. There is no way around it unfortunately. Personally being a prisoner to the streets at 16 I would have opted for (b) it wouldn't be fair for me to snitch knowing my friend like me was no angel on road. I guess it's a hard position to be in at 16 years old. That's why we shouldn't play the road game in the first place. We can all pretend but none of us are really built for this life, and it shows.

Scenario number three: You are a 26 year old working man but some of your friends are not working. Your mates call you one day and say, *'Come we go out to a dance.'* But you tell them you're not really feeling it. You decide to go out anyway because you just got a new job at a secondary school. You've never been in trouble with the law before. On your way back from a good night out the police decide to pull you lot over in your car. Your friends ask you if you're legit and you reassure them you're good. After the police do their checks they see that you are clean. They then decide to search your car and your three bredrins in the back. Ok, so now police have found a gun in the back seat, but you don't know anything about it. They decide to arrest you guys for the gun and put you all on remand. You decided not to tell on your friends because as friends you expect them to come forward and confess to it. While on remand you realise your friends are not going to confess for the gun left in the car.

They haven't said they will take ownership of it. What do you do in this scenario?

Do you (a) tell him to confess to the strap so you can get on with your non-criminal record life? Or do you (b) do the so called street thing *'keep it real'* and hope we buss case together?

This is another sticky situation to be caught in. My first thoughts are: why are my friends bringing a strap in my car and not taking ownership of that? My answer is (a) from before we get to the police station a real friend would confess to that. I don't care if were in America and you're on your 3rd strike, you better own up to that shit. A lot of prisoners to the streets don't understand that the rest of the world doesn't live by the streets. Common sense would tell you if your friend is not on the road life you can't expect them to keep it real to the road. My answer is simple (a) and you got 24 hours to do it or I'll do it for you. How can you consider yourself a real human if you let someone do the time for the dirt you've done?

Scenario four: What is one of the main things gangster rappers preach against doing? The answer is snitching. Although this story isn't about a gangster rapper he was definitely in a gangster situation. American rapper Soulja Boy was in Atlanta in his apartment in his kitchen. The next thing he sees is five guys running through his house with ski mask on, and AK47 guns. Luckily for Soulja Boy in some parts of the US it is legal to carry fire arms. Soulja Boy said he saw the men running through his house so he reached for his Glock 45 handgun. Then he opened up the kitchen door and started shooting at all of them. He said the first guy ducked and ran out the house. The second guy he hit once and the third guy he hit five times. Then he came into the room to finish the guy off but instead he took off the guys mask, and saw it was one of his home-boys. From there on he knew it was an inside job.

After all the commotion the police showed up at his house. They asked him what happened and he told them he had to shoot some guys who tried to rob him. The officer explained that Atlanta gun laws are different from LA's. He said the officers told him he should have killed the guys, because it's not against the law here in Atlanta. Plus the firearm Soulja Boy was shooting from wasn't illegal, so he wasn't prosecuted. Anyway after all this commotion he had to go to the police station to formally explain the situation. He had to tell the officers why there was blood everywhere and why the door was kicked off. Not long after this incident the streets started talking and tried to label Soulja Boy a snitch.

So let's put ourselves in Soulja Boy's position. For one, he's not a gangster rapper. Two, he got attacked in his house by his own so-called friends. So if you were in his shoes and the police came to the scene after the shooting to ask you what happened, what would you do? Would you (a), run with the 'no snitching' word and go to jail for defending yourself? Or would you (b) tell the police you had to defend yourself against a robbery, an inside job at that? I don't know about anybody else but this one is easy for me, it's (b). How can a man be a snitch when he's not on the roads? Soulja Boy isn't on the road and the last time I checked he wasn't rapping for the streets. Not to mention he's own friends was trying to rob him with big guns. He had no choice but to tell the police in that situation. He had to explain to the police why there was blood all over or his house or he's going straight to jail. So for me this is simple. He's not on the road and his own friends tried to rob him, he defended himself and the police wanted answers. So no - there was no snitching here bro, none. On the other hand if he was a gangster rapper I wouldn't be able to defend it because that is the life you promote. That last point doesn't mean I'm right but it shows how much technicalities lie behind this word snitch. So we shouldn't be so quick to use it.

Outside of that scenario I noticed that over the years rappers talk a lot about snitching. But the funny thing is when you're rapping about your day to day life you as the rapper are already snitching, it's called self-snitching. There have been many cases at court where the judge can use your own lyrics to help convict you. Go and listen to your favourite rappers and tell me I'm lying. Haven't they snitched on themselves in some shape or form? Imagine your favourite gangster rapper calling the police after his house got robbed.

There are so many different scenarios to this snitching thing. That's why we shouldn't use the term so lightly. But one thing I've seen in the so called hood is that snitches don't actually get stitches. Some snitches are in rap videos dancing or spitting. Then some snitches get banned from the area and still come to the area to go to their aunt's house. My thing is who is the allocated snitch enforcer?

Whoever he is, he's not on his job, because I know many snitches in the ends that walk around safely attending funerals. So please guys let's stop acting like we are in the mafia. The reality is a lot of mandem are now working as snitches for the police, on and off the books. Corruption still exists in the police and that's another reason why I don't work with them. Or look to them for the solutions. Yet the streets like to act like some of their favourite guys aren't snitching off the books.

The worst kind of snitch for me is an informer (the king pin of snitching). When you're telling on everyone for everything but you're from the road. A guy I know once said to his brother, *'It's not snitching if they're not my friends.'*
Your right its worse; it's being an informant. This same guy supposedly came out of jail and gave police information on two of his *'not so close friends'* who were selling narcotics. Rumour was the police had repaid him with getting a flat for his help and a job. One of his jobs was to go to police stations and encourage people to snitch. After those individuals snitched they would be re-housed and put under witness protection. Now I wouldn't have anything to say if it was the victims he was helping to get witness protection, but it wasn't. These men were on the roads too.
So in essence this man didn't even see his new job as being a snitch. He actually thought he was teaching them something to help free them from the streets. In reality all he was teaching them was his own beliefs which is,
'It's not snitching if it's not your friends.'
Like I said, for me, this is the worst type of snitch I know.

What is dry snitching?

When you call yourself a gang member, try know that you're already dry snitching on yourself. What spins my head is that people who scream gang gang seem to be surprised to have snitches in their crew. It's because some of us are so programmed to believe in the street mind-set that we forget people are still human. My point is human beings in general are not honourable by nature. Mankind are wicked, the world has never been a bad place, the people walking on it have made it that way.

We all know the world could live poverty free if we didn't live in a world controlled by greed. The people who run the world have power and live well, and they didn't get to that spot by being honourable. I say that to say this. The world we live in has been teaching us it's everyman for himself. The world lives by the concept of *'money talks bullshit walks,'* so why would the streets be any different? Is there more honour on the street? I don't get why people from the street act surprised by another street person's dishonourable act towards them. We seem surprised that people would go to the extent of snitching on us to survive. But why, we ask ourselves? We forget the main point I've been trying to make since day one. That we are not gang members we are simply prisoners to the streets, and most of these street prisoners find it easy to snitch, because they never wanted or had the heart for the prison in the first place.

CHAPTER 9

STREET DREAMS

'A place where death doesn't reside,
just thugs who collide

Not to start beef but spark trees, no cops
rollin' by No policemen, no homicide, no
chalk on the street No reason for nobody's
momma to cry See, I'm a good guy, I'm
tryin' to stick around for my daughter...'

©*Nas*

'...Every corner, every city There's a place
where life's a little easy

Little Hennessy, laid back and cool Every hour, 'cause it's all good,

Leave all the stress from the world outside, Every wrong done will be alright

Nothing but peace, love, and street passion

Every ghetto needs a thug mansion.'
©*Nas and 2Pac*

' ...I got love for my brother but we can never go nowhere

Unless we share with each other

We gotta start makin' changes

Learn to see me as a brother instead of two distant strangers

And that's how it's supposed to be

How can the Devil take a brother if he's close to me?

I'd love to go back to when we played as kids

But things changed, and that's the way it is.'
©*2Pac*

'...We gotta make a change it's time for us as a people to start makin' some changes.

Let's change the way we eat, let's change the way we live and let's change the way we treat each other.

You see the old way wasn't working so it's on us to do what we gotta do, to survive.'
©2Pac

It seems as though these guys had street dreams of things being cool on their streets. These same rappers who made songs like *Hit em Up'* and *'Got Yourself a Gun* had street dreams. I often look at America and think why didn't we learn from their culture instead of following or falling into it? I remember a time when the streets of England were far less violent than the streets of America. Now it seems as though we are just as violent but with much less firepower. I can't pin point at what stage of my life it was when I stopped feeling safe on the estate. But I believe it's when I witnessed my brother get robbed at knife point for his bike. I think that was the point when I realised how crazy my estate could get. A part of my innocence died that day. When that innocence died, the prisoner was born. Although there are some things I hated my estate for, I loved it. I had a love hate relationship with my block. I've always felt that a child has the right to feel safe at home or in his community. If a child doesn't feel safe at home then where can they feel safe?

Since becoming a father I've been compelled to mature in various ways. When you have a child you instinctively think to yourself,

'I want my child to have a better childhood than me; I don't want them to want for nothing.'

Then as they age you start wanting to make the world a better place for them to live in. And if you're broad minded enough you don't only dream about your own child. You begin to dream for the future generation on a whole. You become semi-conscious of the things that could help make those changes in the community. But a lot of the times those thoughts will stay as just thoughts. It becomes wishful thinking because this community dream is too big a problem for us to solve on our own. Your child's dream is your number one priority, right? I fully understand that - I get it. A lot of people have stopped dreaming for the youth of today. Some of us are tired and have given up hope. I don't mean given up on the youth, I mean given up on the dream for a safer community. It happens to me every other week. One minute I'm dreaming for the streets to be a better place. Then the next minute I'm reliving a nightmare cos I heard someone else I know has lost their life to violence. I know how disheartening that can be, we all do. However, I've always believed that a big part of the solution lies within the street dreams. Well, if those dreams could become a reality that is.

Not too long ago I was having one of my Pinky and the Brain moments with my bredrin Emeka. We had a conversation about what we would do if our dreams for the street could come true. Emeka shared his idea of the street dream with me,

'I've got this idea something called Community Investors for young business minds. When I say this, I want to use whatever small platform we have to create a lot more positive outcomes for young people. That is not inherently down to the gatekeepers or funders. How can I make a young man believe that the community is behind him? And I came up with this concept, you know about Dragons Den, Rob?

So obviously in Dragons Den they go and they pitch their idea to the panel. Think of the same set up for this but focused on young people. Let's just say young people aged 16 – 24. And we create this online series but not based on any one person that has money like Alan Sugar.

So we get these 8 young people, we follow their lifestyles. In terms of where they've come up from the whole back story type of thing. All they have to do to apply for the show is have a business idea and a very basic business plan. Explaining why they need five grand to start their business. The show is like an alternative for people who can't get a loan or can't get funding to kick start their dreams. We then have a panel of entrepreneurs who have already made it in the business world, but here's the thing those people on the panel won't be giving any of that five grand to the young person who wins. It don't work like that, the panel are just there to ask the questions to see who is ready for this business world. The panel won't even get to decide who stays and who goes the public will. But the catch is we don't have five grand to give them. This five grand has to be raised and come from the community. And this is what will change the mentality of how a young person views his community. This is what builds the community again, because the community is now going to be investing in their future. I don't want one person from the community to invest two grand or *a large amount, it won't work like that. All I'm asking for is a thousand people to give five pounds. Not six pounds, not seven pounds just five pounds, and that will give us the 5k. And then that makes us all equal share holders in his or her dream. Can we do that please?*

The message is the fact that this young man can then say if he's business becomes successful that the people in my community believed in me. And I'm working on making that dream a street reality.'

I replied, *'Nah that's dope.'*

Then I told him about one of my street dreams. As a young teen after I got stabbed I realised the streets didn't have any values – things changed. I tried to understand how a man could come back and stab me after we already had a fair fight. As a yute man back then I realised this is where the morals in the street were going wrong. But more so I use to wonder how much better life could be if we kept certain morals in place. Like Dr King said, I have a dream. The dream is that we bring the morals back to the block.

'Thou shalt not shot in the hood.

Furthermore thou shalt not reduce his God given talent and genius to such a low level of destruction as a means to survive.

Thou shalt not screw-face his own brother on the street especially if he's black.

Thou shalt not call his brother the N word or his sister the B word.

Thou shalt admit when he's in the wrong instead of being wrong and strong

Thou shalt not raise his hand to strike another person but if a person strikes you, not only are you allowed to strike him back, but the whole community is allowed to strike him once on his way home.

Thou shalt not encourage violence. But if two parties agree for a one on one fight to settle a dispute thou shalt not accept or respect the brothers who jump one guy during a one on one fight.

Thou shalt not accept or respect the brothers who jump one guy and stab him to death.

Thou shalt not kill. But if a person is forced to kill in self-defence that person shalt not boast about catching a body. For evil acts are not celebrated in our home.

Thou shalt not call my child his younger and give him drugs to sell. Thou shalt let the children be children and allow them to be free of such sin.

Thou shalt not praise, respect nor look up to the person who is using his tongue to promote wickedness in his community thou shalt not look up to them or revere them as gods.

Thou shalt not rob from their brothers; thou shalt not steal from their brothers

Thou shalt never kill their brother for the gain of money.

Thou should treat their neighbour how they want to be treated.

Thou should not compete, thou shalt not hate.

Thou shalt not be red eye or green eye.'

Can you imagine what life would be like if we kept these basic kind of commandments in the community? There's one big problem I see with the street dreams of Emeka and mine. Which is - we don't have a community. Well not any more we don't. It's not like back in the day. I'm not saying back in the day was perfect but back then the essence of what makes a community existed.

I can't see these dreams coming to fruition while we are still at war. That's why I wrote *Prisoner to the Streets* because the first step to building a community is peace. You can't build a community without that. Who or what are you going to build in the community if you don't have one? At the moment we live in fear of one another. People rarely say hello to each other. And because there are so much new buildings popping up, the community has become further divided. Sometimes I wonder if today's youth community workers feel satisfied at work. I personally didn't feel satisfied in that field because there was no community to work with. Just boxes to tick.

People need to bring back part of that 90s community vibe again. Although on the outside it looked like the ghetto. It was actually really community based back then. We had cook-outs. Families would come together. Mothers would check in on you to make sure you're good. You could be on the block and everyone's front door was half open. Children were running up and down playing run outs, 40/40 water fights the lot. And there was no reason to fear you just felt safe. Although there was madness going on in the area, it was still safe. The negative didn't always overshadow that community feel. What I'm saying is that we shouldn't have allowed those unwritten hood commandments to slip away. They should have been maintained to keep that community spirit alive which has evidently gone wrong. We had a community but we didn't fight for the do's and the don'ts of that community. Like I said, I witnessed a stabbing at 9 years old and I watched teenagers rob someone of their bike and that's the same sinful nature that messes up a community.

We need to let the children be children again. Let's take away the phones and I-pads and bring back creativity time. As much as I hated it as I child I'm fully grateful for Saturday school and being sent to my aunts to improve on my writing and reading. I miss the days when we could knock on someone's door and ask to wash their car for a little sweet money. The community can rebuild that vibe but we need to stop dreaming and start taking action.

I had my last book launch for *Mama Can't Raise No Man* at Hackney Empire in 2016. At the time I knew I had to ask my brother George, the outstanding poet to bless the stage for me. The reason why I asked King George to perform this specific poem is because when I first heard it, it resonated with a lot of the street dreams I envisioned over the years.

George the Poet:

'The first thing to acknowledge is we need our own colleges, scholarships, politics governing systems, to prioritise our own brother and sisters.

Secondly, we need intellectual weaponry. Research institutes, employers and friends in high places, cuz, Judges and lawyers in ends.

Thirdly, education is very certy. Our youth need to be leading by at least 2030.

Fourthly, let's look out for each other everywhere,
North East West and South, let's test it out, bredrin that's how
it's gotta be.
And number five, one word - property.
Our community's in need of this, if you want I'll get Akala to
leave you lot a reading list.
Cos I rather he's the one providing the word for you lot to con-
sider when you're riding your bird. And that's my five point
plan do you understand?
For now it might sound a bit strange, but if you're down for the
change then it's you that I'm giving it out to.
But at the same time it isn't about you. It's the youth will
be living it out through. And it's gonna happen with or
without you.'

Street dreams...

CHAPTER 10

EMANCIPATE YOURSELF FROM MENTAL SLAVERY

'I have decided to stick with love. Hate is too great a burden to bear.'

Martin Luther King Jnr

Mental slavery – This phrase sounds as though we have accepted that we've been designed to be slaves. I'm not sure about mental slavery but mental enslavement might be something we can free ourselves of. We can't free ourselves from mental slavery, because slavery is the act of being the slave. In other words if you're a street cleaner it means you clean the street. Enslavement is getting into your psyche and training you, programming you to be what I want you to be - that's the difference between enslavement and slavery.

The first step to freeing yourself from mental enslavement is to acknowledge you were in some type of bondage in the first place. You have to be able to assess and evaluate what it is you are a slave to. You have to assess how you've been programmed, and who's been doing the programming, then after that we can begin to de-programme. You won't be able to free yourself unless you do these things first. Another key step to freeing yourself is that the person enslaved has to want to free themselves. You have to ask yourself - do you think you are going to gain from being mentally enslaved? And if the answer is no, then you have to be a rebel towards status quo. You have to accept and acknowledge that mental enslavement exists, that's the first thing you have to do.

There are lots of things I had to do and still have to do to emancipate myself from this street mentality. It wasn't an overnight thing as you saw from the journey I had to implement the switch concept a lot.
Unlearning and relearning isn't an easy thing to do but it is necessary to make the changes we want to see. You have to learn to unlearn your old behaviours that kept you enslaved. I had to learn not to have a heart of stone and start feeling again. Because once we lose feeling on the streets it's more or less whatever goes. And that way of being never brings any true happiness or freedom.

You have to learn what the triggers were which kept you so reactive; my answer to the temper trigger was to start boxing and let the rage out.

The mental famer helped me a lot along the way to emancipating myself. He sowed a seed which motivated me to write prisoner to the streets. And as much as a hated doing it I can see it was part of the therapy. Now I'm not suggesting people write a book to get that freedom, I'm just saying that by expressing myself it helped me to mentally vomit. And we all know after vomiting we slowly start feeling better again. As though vomiting was necessary to get over the bug.

I had to think of the things that were important in my life. I had to come to a place where I didn't want to be a prisoner anymore.

I had to change the places I went to chill. I had to check the people around me to see if we were thinking like minded. You can't think freely being surrounded by prisoners.

Before I met the mental farmer I tried to free myself from the street plantation. I tried all sorts. I put down the guns and knives as was one way I thought I could free myself. Then soon after I stopped hanging around certain mandem, which was another way. I tried to stop thinking the way I used to think every time I made eye contact with a man on the street. I stopped going raving, I stopped smoking skunk. I stopped being in places I didn't need to be in to avoid drama. I stopped doing so much but I wasn't feeling free, in fact I was feeling anti-social. I became an isolated individual and some say a granddad. The transition was rapid. Almost like I was speed driving on the M1, then the traffic ahead came to a sudden halt. And instead of me slowing down correctly I reacted erratically. I swerved and went straight from 5th gear to the 1st whilst burning out the clutch. Imagine switching lanes from the fast to the slow lane without indicating. Well my change was rapid like that. What I'm saying is you can't drop all you know and expect to be free. I found out the hard way it doesn't work like that. Freedom isn't for free you can't just run away and live happily ever after. Once you get free from the plantation what do you do next?

I had to learn to let things go and not be so bitter about the past. I was bitter about all the losses I took on the street. And the unfinished business I wanted to finish. I turned my pain in to hate and it showed at boxing. All the bitterness I had didn't do me good internally. Nelson Mandela said something like, *'You can't drink poison and expect the other person to get sick.'* This falls in line with what Brother Martin also said. *'Hate is much too great a burden to bear.'* They are both a hundred per cent right. The burden is heavy and the bitterness self-damaging. We have to heal and we can't heal by picking the scabs or carrying hate.

A lot of us have been enslaved to be attracted to the streets and street life. What some call street culture but I don't perceive it as that. Looking back I can see how I had an active part of being a mental slave by my behaviours on the street. The enslaver even got me to own my behaviours rather than be responsible for them. The reason why I am now becoming free of the enslavement is because I have decided to be

responsible for my past behaviours instead of taking ownership of them. This is part of the process of freeing yourself.
We are not our behaviours.

Enslavement – when slavery was first abolished people
were still waiting for their *'Massa'* to tell them what to do.
Imagine being a slave for your whole life and then one day
you're told you can go free, what would you do? You'll probably get up the next morning waiting for the 'Massa' to tell
you what to do. I know that would freak me out. I wouldn't
even want to come out my yard in case it was a set up. Like
they wanted to see how we would react if they said we was
free. Then the second we back talk the chains and whips
come back out and man get sent to another slave owner for
being disloyal.

Or if it was true I still wouldn't want to come out my yard
without my shank just in case. You never know the KKK
might be rolling around heavy with the *shotty* looking for
some N words. What I'm saying is I wouldn't know how to
act as a free slave. It would be a complete shock to my brains
configuration. Imagine being a slave for so long, you genuinely don't know how to be free. You've probably dreamed
about this in the hut when you were a slave. You and your
bredrin stayed up late discussing about what you would do
if you was free, and you boasted, *'Yeah, imma eat food when
I want, and massa aint gone tell me what to do no more, he
aint gone beat me no more.'* All of that good stuff, then you
ran away like you said. You run away from the physical environment but you run right into the slavery mentality.
Because we still have the plantation mentality or the street

mentality. The Jim Crow laws still exist or if you like the street code still exists. So the truth of the matter is you can run all you like but where can you hide? Because the land isn't yours so you have no place to go. So that makes me mentally enslaved.

To emancipate yourself from mental enslavement you have to be a rebel. Now even before I write this I have to say I've got the most ratings for this guy. In some ways he's kind of an unsung hero. He may have had the blood of a slave but he definitely had the heart of a king. My man Kunte Kinte - I remember when I first watched the film *Roots*. In one particular scene the slave master was trying to force a new name on Kunte Kinte, but Kunte weren't having it. Kunte was tied up in front of all the other slaves to be made an example of. But also it was put on show to further instil fear into the other slaves. Just in case they got inspired by Kunte's rebellious ways. Though the slave master got the overseer to whip Kunte Kinte, he wasn't backing down. Every time the overseer whopped him the slave master shouted, *'I want to hear you say your name, your name is Tobi, what's your name?'* *Then he would respond in agony, 'Kunte!'* Then he would get another lash for not conforming. He took as much lashes as he could take before he decided to play the game. At the end he couldn't take no more so when the master asked him what his name was he responded, *'Tobi, my names Tobi.'*

Some people might have viewed that scene differently to me. They might have seen a slave who was eventually defeated but I didn't see that. Do you know how hard that must have been to make that stand? Each one of those whips had a sharp stone on the end of it to ensure it left them physically scarred with welds. It cut through the skin to leave a scar. Kunte was standing up for what he believed in while other slaves had stopped believing in believing. While a few other slaves viewed him as a rebellious fool, he fought to secure the belly – which was his identity. He didn't want to lose sight of where he came from. For that, he knew would have made him mentally enslaved. He didn't let them break his spirit, he knew he couldn't say it out loud but deep down he knew he was Kunte. And I thought that was so gangster. He was a top runaway slave too. He ran away so many times that they got fed up whipping him for it. They got wickeder and decided to cut off his foot. And even after that he made sure to pass on tradition to his children and their children's children about who they are. He wanted them to know that they weren't slaves. And if it wasn't for people like Kunte how many of you black folk would know you weren't always slaves? What I learned here is you have to be rebellious to the programming if you want to free yourself from the mental enslavement.

'I freed a 100 slaves I could have freed 1000 more if they knew they were slaves'. ©Harriet Tubman

While in isolation trying to free myself I discovered that the key thing I struggled with on this road of redemption was forgiveness. The struggle wasn't so much with forgiving others but I struggled to forgive myself. The truth is you have to learn to forgive yourself to emancipate yourself from mental enslavement.

Forgiveness – I remember I was struggling with this and the mental farmer picked up on it. We were just chilling at his house one day and he asked me to do what he called a timeline thing. He asked me to stand up and visualise myself in a timeline. And in that line it was different versions of the younger me, from age five to 20. When we started he asked me to stand at the beginning of the line by the 5 year old Robin. At first it was all fun and jokes, I wasn't even taking it serious at age 5. But the mental farmer kept asking me questions about how I felt towards the younger versions of me. And I found that shit funny. Until we got to about age 15, 16 - I wasn't smiling anymore.

I stood in front of the younger version of myself at that age and I couldn't even look at him. The mental farmer could see I was agitated standing in front of the 16 year old Robin. So he asked me to do the same thing with the other versions of myself. He asked me to talk to the younger version of me. But I couldn't. I wasn't responding to the Robin at this age the way I responded to him at the other ages. Then the mental farmer said, *'Can you talk to the Robin at this age? What do you have to say to him?'* At this point shit got real. I actually started to visualise the younger me, so I responded, *'Nah, I aint got nothing to say to him.'* The mental farmer asked, *'No? Why is that?'* After pausing and swallowing that lump in my throat so the tears didn't come, I responded, *'Cos he's too far gone, and I aint got nothing to say to him.'*
The mental farmer said, *'You seem angry with him.'* And I nodded trying to remain calm and said, *'Yeah, a little bit.'* He responded, *'But why?'* I nearly broke down crying whilst responding. *'Because he stabbed a man on his doorstep and his*

Nan died a few weeks after so he's to blame for it.'
After that, the mental farmer explained how important it was that I forgave myself. And I have to admit he was right. There are still a few things I haven't forgiven myself for because at the time I feel I could have done better. In saying that though, using the mental farmer's timeline method really helped me see where I was enslaved. It also enabled me to go back and find forgiveness, which really helped me look at myself differently. Using this method has really helped me get closer to true freedom. What I'm saying is - forgiving yourself is another way to free yourself. We haven't learned how to forgive ourselves from the things that we've done. So we keep ourselves enchained by our past actions. Because we think that ID makes us. Not realising that our behaviour is a thing, it's not who we are. We are not our behaviours. So we need to free ourselves from the attachment of our things we've done to emancipate ourselves from this mental slavery.

A friend of mine once said to me, *'If as humans we were to lose the ability to walk right now, it would be mad. It would be mad to rehabilitate and learn how to walk again. But if it was a toddler they would rehabilitate much quicker than us, because they've just learnt to walk. They remember the process, but because we're much older, walking has become automated in us. Almost like second nature - a part the normal process. As adults we don't think about walking at this age we just do it. So there are a lot of things we would need to revisit and refresh over and over to be able to walk freely again.'*

And that's how I feel about the issues in the UK, in comparison to a LA or a New York. What I'm saying is - in terms of being prisoners to the streets they have been imprisoned longer. The beef with the Bloods and the Crips dates back to the 70s. Prisoners to the streets in England have been mentally enslaved since the 90s. That's 20 years longer. That's 20 years more bitterness, 20 more years more hatred, murder pain and jail time. Recently we have seen places where the Crips and the Bloods have united to set an example to the young bucks of this world. So please, let's stop talking like freedom isn't achievable. There were four words that I held on to which kept me free from the enslavement of jail time in Jamaica. Those four words where written in chalk on the board just outside my cell door. Every morning I woke up I would read those four words to keep me going. *'Freedom Is A Must!'*

If you don't believe that in your heart and mind then you will never be freed.

There are many greats who freed themselves from a prisoner's mind-set. Study the likes of Malcolm X, Tookie Williams. You can learn from those who were almost free but still kicked mad knowledge like 2 Pac Shakur. If you're black you may find it useful to study people who emancipated themselves and other black people from mental enslavement. Those like Marcus Garvey, Malcolm X, MLK, Black Panthers, Umar Johnson, Maya Angelou and Inyanla Vazant. Not forgetting those who inspired the liberation of the mind through musicians like Bob Marley Marvin Gaye, Sam Cook, and Lauryn Hill.

Emancipate yourself from mental enslavement none but ourselves can free our mind.'© Bob Marley

CHAPTER 11

POST TRAUMATIC STREET SYNDROME

It was 2004 and I was in Clarence Road Hackney. It was only a few months before I had been found not guilty of an attempted murder charge, which I was relieved about. Anyway I was walking through Pembury estate when I saw 30 plus of my enemies. They gave me the look so I knew it was on. I wanted to shout, *'I'm not on the foolishness; I want a better life now'* But I didn't because I knew that wouldn't stop me from getting jumped. Plus I didn't want to go out like no punk.

The crew of 30 started running towards me and I stood still ready to get it on. Then at the last second I did something I haven't ever done before, I started running. They were close behind chasing me through the estate. Then as I was running I started thinking, *'Why the hell am I running for? I don't run from nobody, I'm not a punk.'* So I stopped running and I did what I always do when I'm getting jumped by people I clenched my fist and threw the first punch. After that punch was thrown everything slowed right down. I looked at my fist and it was shaking. My knuckles were bleeding through the cracks of my fingers then I realised the 30 boys chasing me were gone. Not because the punch was that special to knock out 30 people, but because the 30 people weren't there in the first place. It never happened I wasn't even in Hackney that day. I was in Tottenham in my bed. My pregnant girlfriend was sleeping right next to me. She turned around and just gave me this look of confusion and asked, *'What happened?'* At the time I was still trying to register what was going on myself. It appears it was all a dream. All I was thinking was if that punch was thrown any lower I could have hit my unborn child. That shit spooked me out.

A few years later I spoke to the mental farmer and told him about that strange experience. I told him how I got chased in my dream. The mental farmer said, *'I think you were getting chased by your own mind. I think that's what was happening to you.'* I can't even argue with that because I remember this was the time when I was trying to emancipate myself from the streets. So, all the thoughts on my mind of the streets were still fresh. At the time I was having problems sleeping anyway. If it wasn't for the weed I doubt I would've got any sleep back then. All these thoughts were coming into my mind from my unconscious mind.

The central nervous system works strangely, but I under-stand why I threw the punches. I mean I've been rushed countless times and every occasion I fight. I fully knew the guys in my dream because I moved to them before on the same street, just two years before. I believe my unconscious mind was keeping these things in and released them every so often at random times. It just so happened to manifest itself in a dream.

I hope this chapter deters young people from creating neg-ative memories that stay with us. The crazy thing is ten years or so after having that dream I spoke about it ran-domly with one of my girlfriends. She said that she's seen it all before. She said she's been in bed with her boyfriend and the mans jumped out of the bed in cold sweats thinking he was in a situation. She told me that I'm not alone in dealing with this type of trauma, and that most women she knows have told her the same things have happened to their part-ners. And how some of them have hit or grabbed their girl-friends by their neck in their sleep. It just goes to show how deeply affected some of us are subconsciously.

Police sirens can trigger off something in me. I can't explain it, I won't call it trauma but there is a connection there. Whenever I see police rough up somebody the flashbacks come back flooding. And that's what's crazy about it. I don't need to be the one getting apprehended for those memo-ries to surface. It's not all the time I'm triggered and it's not that I can remember all of the flashbacks but certain things trigger certain things. That's just the way it goes.

Sometimes seeing the scars on my body can trigger off a memory. It's quite crazy - the different angles at where the trauma comes from, not to mention trauma from our homes as children.

Even in my adult life I've had a couple youth who have taken out a knife on me. And what's weird is I have no emotion or fear towards it. I've been stabbed too often and been in front of a man with a knife or gun too many times to freeze. To me this is an example of being desensitised to violent behaviour when threaten by it. Some of us have this in them because of a result of the past trauma. It's crazy but I know a lot of prisoners to the streets that are just like me. Even as an adult in my house I'm always on game. I sleep with one eye open and the slightest sound out of place and I'm ready for whatever. I'm always ready. I can go from sleep to war and war to sleep. So in essence your mind is never really switched off, no peace of mind.

I witnessed a lot of trauma back in prison in Jamaica. But at the time I didn't realise I found a coping mechanism to deal with the trauma, and that was sleep. Yeah, I loved a good sleep whenever I saw too much. I remember I was in Spanish Town prison South block near the front of the building. I remember hearing what sounded like gun shots being fired in the middle of the night. I turned to my cell mate and said, '*What's that noise; it's not what I think it is it?*' Then the cell mate confirmed my suspicions that it was the sound of gun war. He added that the police were shooting at the mandem.

At the time I was thinking – isn't the sight of the prison a deterrent for the mandem? Then I remembered the police over there aren't too interested in making arrest. If they can make a body then it's just as good in their eyes. After hours of gunshots that night I just went back to sleep as normal. What was strange was, after the first night of hearing it whenever it happened; I managed to sleep through it without noticing.

I suppose I couldn't sleep on the first night of shooting because it was the fear of the unknown. Had I not known what it was I probably would have continued to at least be curious and listen out for the noise. It gets trapped in the unconscious mind. Trauma never discriminates, it will just keep it in there, it leaks out and then the conscious mind tries to make sense of the trauma.

Trauma is a huge thing. I could be in a situation with the police and hear the sirens go off. And when they stop me I go into a mode that says anything can happen. It's so deep in my psyche that I know where the police are, even when I'm not doing nothing wrong, I see the undercover cars early it's just a natural reaction now.

I get all types of flashbacks - times of when I've stabbed people and times of when I've been stabbed. Flashbacks of whenever I've been shot at, had a gun to my head, or had a gun in my hand standing at someone's door ready to shoot. It's chaos at times, you can't escape it.

Trauma is not a made up thing. Even now I still live in Hackney. I could be driving or walking through the borough, and the trauma comes back to haunt me. You see, I'm not exaggerating when I say nearly every street I go down I have another memory triggered of extreme violence, whether it was my trauma or I just witnessed it. At times there's no escape from it. I can't help but visualise the madness. Walking past places where friends were killed or friends were shot and stabbed multiple times.

Or it could be I'm on social media or watching the news and I see a picture of a youth who's been killed and it does me over. Then it takes me back to when I got stabbed as a youth - it replays in my head again. Or when I hear another friend I know has been killed. Or a friends son, nephew or cousin has been stabbed it brings the trauma back home.

Sometimes those traumas don't always resurface because of the things I see. From time to time they are simply trigged by what I hear. I could be walking anywhere in the borough and I might see an old face. And they might bring up a name to me which reminds me of a negative time. Or they might remind me of the trauma I caused them by something they witnessed me do in front of them back in the day. Whatever it is it brings up the past and I'm trying to get away from it. Or I might see my dead friends Mum when I'm going to the market. I'll never forget the day I was in Mare Street and I saw two of my dead friends' mothers in the space of five minutes. When I got home I tried to get on with my day as normal but thinking about it triggered off some mad thoughts. After that I had to go and take a quick nap to escape from those thoughts. I wondered if the mothers I saw that knew day their sons' deaths were connected. Its things like this I'm left to go home to and deal with alone.

The biggest post trauma came from writing *Prisoner to the Street* but it didn't stop there. Like I said before, I didn't put everything in the book. I've never had to live with killing anybody, and I'm so thankful for that. I just believe some of us have seen way too much violence to be working in the youth field. We need to seek support for ourselves.

They say when a soldier gets sent off to war he never returns home the same way. They might see their friends get blown away, step on a mine anything. They might get kidnapped tortured, lose a limb lose their mind in some cases, but they never come back the same. Now I'm not saying we go through what a soldier at war goes through, but the two worlds are not far apart. One of the clear differences I see between the soldiers on the streets and the soldiers at war is that some of those soldiers get to come home from the battleground. They come home with the trauma. Whereas the soldiers on the street don't get to return from the war field, the war field is where they live, so the trauma can always be triggered off.

So how do we get freedom from this post trauma? What's the solution? You have to face your demons. You have to mentally vomit because if you hold in all the madness it might mad you. But eventually after you vomit you feel better cos you've got rid of it.

I remember when I was writing my first book trying to mentally vomit but it wouldn't come out. The writing wasn't slow but the sickness just wouldn't come up. I remember I called the Mental Farmer around this time because I kept getting these headaches, and he said,

'Robin, it's called a busy mind you're thinking too much. This is to be expected because you are writing a book about your past.'

Then he said, *'Let's look at it like junk food. If you eat enough junk food and you wasn't going to the toilet it will cease up your system. Have you ever seen the effects of putting diesel oil into an unleaded car?'*

I responded, 'Yeah, I've seen that.'

He continued, 'What happens is it clogs up the engine in the car. And the car can't operate properly until all of that fuel is flushed out. So imagine you had traumas that could be represented by the diesel oil in your engine. You have a full tank of diesel. But in your case Robin all those trauma's where in your head, and that's what gave you so many headaches. You need to stop overthinking son.'

The Mental Farmer was right I had to stop overthinking. But this was needed in order to write the book. And I needed to overthink to get the full mental wash out.

So again what is the solution? Therapy and prayer. What type of therapy? I don't know, probably an advanced course. What I'm saying is I'm still in need of this therapy myself. I'm not exempt from post-traumatic street syndrome. I know a lot of man around me who would laugh at the thought of therapy. They view it as a weakness in their armour and many of them won't seek out this step. I'm not knocking them but smoking skunk at funerals isn't going to erase the problem, it just numbs the pain for a while. I call that escapism and any form of it whether it be alcohol sex or drugs won't eradicate the trauma. There has to be a better healthier way of dealing with it. I haven't done therapy myself, I went for one session but I needed someone who was in touch with the world I'm from. But after writing this book I plan to get the right therapy. I just hope my people who can relate to this madness consider therapy as part of the healing to freeing themselves from the streets for good. And I'm praying that between the most high and therapy I will get the peace of mind I need.

I want to thank Joy DeGruy for writing such an amazing book in *Post Traumatic Slave Syndrome*. That amazing book is where I got the inspiration to explain this section.

CHAPTER 12

THE OPTIMIST, THE REALIST AND THE PESSIMIST

Freedom is a must

Optimistic – being hopeful and confident about the future.

An optimistic person thinks the best possible thing will happen, and hopes for it even if it's not likely. Someone who's a tad too confident this way is also sometimes called optimistic.

Realist - a person who accepts a situation as it is and is prepared to deal with it accordingly.

'I am a realist; with no time for your world of make believe.'

Realist... Some may say you never expect good things to happen, but maybe you're just a **realist,** a person who uses facts and past events, rather than hopeful feelings and wishes, to predict the future.

Pessimistic - tending to see the worst aspect of things or believe that the worst will happen.
'He was pessimistic about the prospects.'

The definition of pessimistic is constantly expecting the worst. An example of pessimistic is a person who always believes that something is going to fail.

Before I started youth work I was very optimistic about doing youth work. When I first came in the game I was still optimistic. And then I started working in the youth field and I saw what was really going on. I realised within the youth field we couldn't make the changes, so I became a pessimist. Shortly after that, I got made redundant which only reinforced the pessimism. Then I had a light bulb moment and became a realist, realising we could make the changes ourselves. After deciding to write a book with some 'enemy inclusion' I felt a strong sense of change and became optimist again. Then after putting in so much work heart and soul I became tired. After the book came out I was overwhelmed at first, then I realised people weren't getting it, so I became pessimistic again.

I tried to fight that pessimism with optimistic thoughts but I struggled. More so, when I heard other pessimistic people negatively stating that the book wasn't going to change anything. Although I didn't agree with people's pessimist statements sometimes their words permitted me to think more pessimistic.

Then I had to get out of my own head, be a realist and go back to the drawing board. And that's when I decided to break down the book's meaning through a series of workshops. And through this I became optimistic again. Because I could see the feedback from the workshops was life changing. I bubbled with optimism knowing the potential of this being done nationwide. I could finally explain my work in a way they could understand it. Even if they weren't from that life or they were pessimistic about it beforehand.

I stayed optimistic through delivering the workshops and sent emails to figure heads all over London, but the response was next to none. I tried to fight the feeling but I couldn't, I became pessimistic minded again. I lost the motivation knowing that I was coming against blockages that would prevent me from executing the strategy. The irregularity of it and getting into the schools and prisons created many stumbling blocks, so the work couldn't be done effectively. Then I became a realist again when I heard my mum's and Nan's voice saying,

'There's more than one way to cut down a tree.'

Now it's 2019 and I'm back to being myself again – a realist. I'm optimistic about this book *Freedom from the Streets* but the realist in me is aware my words won't guarantee the prisoners their freedom. In saying that, I am still optimistic. I can almost hear Sam Cooke singing, *'Change gone come.'* I'm not a naïve realist though I'm fully aware freedom isn't for free but freedom is a must.

The fastest way I feel this freedom is going to be achieved is if the gate-keepers open the gates. As well as being open to the new idea of PTTS rather than addressing the problems with a cops and robbers mentality. Once we decriminalise the mind-set then we can begin undressing what really matters. Then the PTTS workshop needs to be introduced in the schools from an early age. I'm optimistic if we can get to the root of the issue early enough, with the right nurture and guidance, we can watch those roots blossom. I'm pessimistic about other projects or ideas that don't deal with the root. Again - I'm not saying that *Prisoner to the Streets* workshops is the only solution. I'm saying that *Prisoner to the Streets* is the streets. And if you want to influence change on the street mind-set, you have to start there.

I'm not dissing or trying to undermine other workshops - everything has its purpose. But ask yourself - would you use a hammer to drive a screw through the wall? Or would you use a screwdriver and save the hammer for hitting nails? That's all I'm really saying. This workshop has the potential to deal with the preventative stage of this problem and can shift a lot of mind-sets at the intervention stage. But I'm still a realist about how my own workshop would work. If it can be delivered a few times yearly then I'm optimistic about the mind-sets changing. But if it isn't done in this way then I'm pessimistic about the whole thing. And that's why I'm leaving the game for good, because it's taking too long for the message to get into those places. It's become too draining, and I'm a realist about that.

Although I'm not overly optimistic at this time in life, I must admit I do get fed up of being in the hood hearing people's pessimism. You know the ones who have never tried to help the problem but are the most negative? They're always the first to say things will never change. I don't believe things can't change not even in my most negative state. Things don't change because most prisoners act like the streets is the way it is and not the way we make it. I'm not saying we made the streets like this but simply by contributing to it means we're accepting it for what it is. So they remain pessimistic based on their view of the world. They stay grounded in their street values and beliefs because their belief comes from a pessimistic perspective. This perspective has allowed them to be blinded of reality and that's why they lack optimism.

Other strategies for prevention such as motivational workshops or black empowerment and women empowerment will go a long way but this comes alongside addressing the root. I'm not here to criticise or compete with any one or organisation. Some of them do some really positive work. It's all good, but the root of the solution is to get them to stop thinking like prisoners to the streets. There's no point in doing all the other stuff without that. We can have all our motivational talks but if we're still killing each other, then what's the point? A lot of those motivated children aren't going to live long enough to see that dream manifest. I didn't come in this field to argue with other people who think this is about me wanting to prove I'm right and they're wrong. I don't care about all of that, I care for the solutions. Bottom line - the reason why achieving freedom is a problem is that a lot of people are stuck in a pessimistic state. And the ones who are optimistic don't know much about the streets or its solutions. That's a problem. Having done the optimism and the pessimism more than once, I now sit in the middle as a realist, learning from optimism and pessimism. I've learned from both sides so now I'm in the middle. I can be optimistic when I need to be. And be pessimistic when I need to be. I'm not perfect; I have times when I think about things in a pessimistic way.

The idea of having the workshops in the schools and other establishments was just one way of executing the preventative stage. But preventing would only mean stopping people from becoming prisoners to the streets. You can't prevent without intervention and expect to get a solution. That's why I've always been stuck on both. At the end of 2018, I delivered a few workshops to some prisoners in Cookham Wood, Belmarsh and Aylesbury prisons. The feedback was out of this world. I realised the lifers I spoke to both young and old were coming to grips with this *PTTS* concept.

I realised I could be much more effective if I stopped going to the prisons. So after one workshop in Aylesbury prison I suggested a solution to the prison warden. I asked him what could be put in place for me to come in and train the prisoners to be PTTS workshop facilitators. My line of thinking is that I came and trained prisoners who understood the concept and wanted to do the work themselves. So for example, if a man's doing double figures and he wants to give back while he's reforming himself, then why not train those individuals to deliver the workshops? That way the prisoner can travel to other prisons around the country and really influence the changes of younger juveniles. And that would reinforce the message without the prisons having to pay me money they can't afford. Not only that, the prisoner doing double figures can get his time reduced if he manages to stay out of substantial trouble while delivering the work. As optimistic as I am about this prison reform idea I'm very pessimistic that it will happen. But the realist in me is a fan of - *you never know, anything can happen.*

I've had another solution for years that I've only ever shared with a few people. The truth is, in this industry, let's just say it's like the streets - you can't trust no one. Even your closest friend will take your ideas. It's a good thing I don't have to worry about those trust issues no more, because I'm leaving this field of work for good. But before I go let me ask you something solution related. Can we please shut down every single youth offenders institute in the country, please? Why? Well like I told you, these children are not criminals; they're prisoners to the streets, who happen to be breaking the law. Do you remember how I explained earlier in the chapter, *Dispelling the Myths of the Streets* how people become prisoners to the streets? I said to become a prisoner you have to be guilty of one or two things. I said, *'Some people deal drugs on the streets. And some people are violent on the streets. To become a young prisoner to the street you have to be guilty of one of these two things. One offence is having a materialistic mentality and the other offence is having a violent mentality. Having both of these mentalities from a young age will surely lead you down a path of to becoming a prisoner to the street.'*

So why are we quick to criminalise these young children if they are not criminal minded? So the child who has a materialistic mentality, is he criminal minded? No! Most of these children want the latest clothes computers etc. Nobody likes to feel like they're missing out. I know a lot of children's motivation to getting money by any means came from peer pressure. The pressure to fit in at school when your mum's buying you Dunlop and you really wanted a pair of Nike. Or your Mum' buys you Adidas trainers but they got two more stripes than they're supposed to have. Or schools finished and everyone is in the shops buying sweets but you gotta pretend you don't want that because you don't have that. Eventually your school friend's start cracking joke and you feel worthless. You're twelve years old going to school in some trainers that you resent having to wear you think the crep' are dead. Really, we should be grateful just to have shoes on our feet, but a child doesn't always think like that. The child then decides - *'I've had enough of feeling like a waste-man I want money now so he begins dream chasing. By robbing or selling drugs.'*

Then we turn around and call that child a criminal. But hold on, if he is under the age of 16 can he or she work? Nope. He or she cannot work because he or she is only permitted to work by law at the age of 16. So what does a 14 year old do? He thinks like a 14 year old does and says to himself I want it here and now. They don't wanna leave school and be remembered as the bummy looking brother, so they start breaking the law. To me, that's not criminal-minded that's infant-minded.

Let's look at the child with the violent mind-set. If a child learns violence as a means to survive, does that make the child a violent criminal? When I was 14 I was coming back from football practice and I was with one of my friends who I viewed a *dream chaser.* He started selling drugs because most of the children used to cuss him and say he was trampy looking. Anyway, as we were walking two police officers were walking head on in our direction. I looked at him and told him to act like he was saying goodbye to me and walk the other way. I only did this because I didn't want him to get arrested for his lack of self-esteem. Meantime, I'm still walking towards the officers with my football kit on and my *'bora'* in my boot-bag. When police saw me, obviously they searched me being black and that. Then they found the knife in my boot bag. The officer asked me, *'What have you got that for?'* I was honest about it. I told him I'd been stabbed before. I told him I needed the protection. I told him it was for me to survive. I wasn't bullshitting him, I meant it.

Every time I think about the younger me or the younger versions of the guys I grew up with (who have been criminalised) I think this isn't right. If a child is fearful of his environment and makes irrational choices within that environment we can't label him a criminal. It's just doesn't sit right with me. Out of all the times I've been stabbed I've never seen the motivation for those attacks to be criminal-minded. In fact, it comes from the fear of losing face of losing the fight. So I ask myself back then and now - were their actions criminal behaviour, bad-mind behaviour, or was it infant-minded actions taking place, at the cost of protecting some form of reputation? I know the answer even if it doesn't come from the horse's mouth. I know that a lot a children who are violent are scared to be the victims, so in their infant-minded logic, they decide to wild out more.

So to me, criminalising these children is counter-productive. I was on a tagged curfew when I was in Year 10. I remember going to probation after school feeling like a right criminal. I had friends going to Feltham for silly stuff before the age of 16. Then by the time they come out they're not thinking about getting a job because they already have stained records. Plus they want to make up for the time they've missed out on, so they tend to go even harder to fit in. So they go to prison infant-minded and come out criminal-minded and identified as criminals. And I think that is disgraceful. So that is why I'm screaming out that every youth prison should be shut around the world.

How about a real solution to so called youth crime?

Why don't we knock down those youth prisons and build them into little flats with a training ground? That way we can send children there who are breaking the law. Then we employ some real thoroughbred youth workers with that Coach Carter type work ethic, both male and female. While the youth are here we will reform their minds. We will train them, educate them discipline them and show them love. At six o'clock every morning, their beds have to be made and ready for inspection. No prison cells we can all share a massive space in one room. A child who is sent to one of these youth stations has to spend six months to a year there. If that child completes the course, whatever he was sentenced for gets removed from his criminal record. That way he isn't criminalised as a child. They'll spend a year with great influencers and their mind will be freed. There will be one on one mentoring daily, therapy, group workshops, everything. People are allowed to come and visit them but that's only if they are staying on target with the goals we've set in place – Coach Carter style. If a child wants out of it then he can go to jail and get a criminal record. But remember, there won't be any more youth prisons about. So you would have to go to big man jail and most children wouldn't want that. If a child re-offends after going to one of the youth stations before 18 years old then that child has to have a seriously strong argument as to why we don't let the law take him to jail. It would have to be a serious situation to make us let that individual return to us. Because our belief is that we can help them change their mind-sets the first time round.

If you are over 18 then you are not considered for this type of reform because you are not a child. Your only option would be jail which isn't a solution in my eyes but there is only so much one can help. For those youth who do get sent to these youth stations they can't play reformed with us because our work station is intense. But if a child doesn't want to take the course seriously or they're using us to bide time, then we will have no other option but to contact the courts and say we can't work with him. The youth stations are not a life line for people on the way to becoming prisoners; it's a life line to stop them from becoming prisoners. And if these young children are already prisoner minded, then it's a great way to spend thorough time with them to help them free their minds and unlock their true potential. This youth station idea could be the very thing that helps change a child's mind-set before he starts thinking like a criminal.

So there you have it. I would be over optimistic for change if we were allowed to counter this problem with these solutions at the forefront. I hear professionals claiming that this problem would take ten years to fix. That isn't true. Based on what study, what findings? As drained out as I am over my time in this game. I'm very optimistic that change will happen in less than half that time if we get to working on what makes sense now and not later.

CHAPTER 13

PARENTING THE PARENTS

There is no book on how to be the perfect parent. If there was, I'm pretty sure you wouldn't see my name on the front cover. From generation to generation the world is forever changing. It's an age old thing that parents don't understand their children. There needs to be some sort of community class so that we the parents can be supported in better understand our children.

Sometimes as parents we might say to our children that they don't have it hard, but I've learned I don't have the right to say that to my children. Times have changed; our society is different from our parents' society, just like our children's society will be different to ours. In the 80s we had different drugs floating around so when we got older and lost our innocence. Our parents would always tell us that there is nothing new about drugs, they've seen and heard it all before. I hear that but there are always new things to learn about the world your child lives in. Like I said, times change. When I was younger the children weren't blazing home-made skunk, now they are learning through trial and error that this new type of weed is no good for them. I won't even mention spice.

As times change things change with it. Look how advanced technology has gotten in the last 20 years. We went from vinyl and tape cassettes to Mp3 players and Spotify. The way our parent's parented us then is different from the way we parent our children now. And it's going to be different from the way our children parent theirs.

Most parents from the 80s grew up in an era where every-body wanted designer clothes and the latest trainers. So now you find that none of the parents from that era want to send their children to school in Hi-Tec trainers, even if were signing on at the Job Centre we still want our chil-dren to have the best of everything. And a lot of that goes on because the parents know what it's like to not have because it happened to them, and they don't want that for their chil-dren. In some cases we try to do things better than our parents.

As a parent you have to ask yourself - *am I dressing my chil-dren for how other people might perceive them or am I dress-ing them beyond my means?* A lot of us break our backs to give our children what they want. But sometimes we have to ask ourselves - is this what they really want or is it what we want for them? What are we teaching them? We can't condition our children to have the latest of everything. Then act confused when they get older and there always asking us for things. Did we not programme them that way? Most children are calm; they don't care about designer clothes or jewellery unless you introduce it to them. A lot of the things that our children imitate comes from us their parents. There are children who see their parents being obsessed about the latest iPhone and they see them doing that so they want it too.

We're now in a society where children eight, nine, and ten have iPhones. What's mad as well is that most of those children who have iPhones their parents can't afford it. Some parents are breaking their backs to get them the phones. We break our backs to get them stuff but we fail to teach them about value and longer term ownership. It's all about immediate gratification there's no looking towards the future. As the parents we have to teach our children patience. But like I said if parenting came in a book I'm not the one with the answers. I can only share my experience and what I have learnt from other parents.

One of my friends who grew up in care told me about his experience with the different types of parents he had. He mentioned three different types of parents.

'In the first care home I had the abusive parent. She was someone who was lost in themselves completely, so she just beat us. And then I had a woman who was a lovely parent. She had good intentions but she didn't understand our needs. Then we had the parent who gave discipline, boundaries, love and

everything. She just never gave up. She was the parent that never gave up on us. One time, me and my brother smashed the front room window. And most parents would give you a beating for that but she did the opposite - she gave us permission to be little shits. But when she did that, it actually had the opposite effects for us. She came in the front room and shouted, 'Oi, y'all come 'ere right now! Listen you wanna break up window? And smash up me place, and do this and do that? Well, go ahead, cos me not going nowhere. Me ah stand right here.' I'll never forget that conversation. It was like she was unconsciously saying you can do all those things but I'm not going anywhere. We was surprised because in the care homes if you were bad they would get rid of you. But this was the parent that stuck through our stuff and said, 'I gotta help you grow through what you go through.' Out of the parents I had, she was the one I responded to the most because she never gave up on me. Two of the parents I had gave me boundaries and the other one never hit me, even when we did bad things. I would ask her why she didn't just hit us. She would say she didn't hit us because we would have missed the message and focused on the beating. I guess that's what you call unconditional love. I heard her messages loud and clear.'

In my line of work I've come across all types of young people. A lot of them young people I've worked with are not aware that I know their parents or I know of them. It's sad to say this but my expectations of reaching some of those children were not always high. Because I knew some of their parents had grown up on a mad one. And now they've become parents nothing's changed, they're still on a mad one. So now your child is more than likely going to grow up and be on a mad one too.

We're at a place and time where we got both dad and son on the road. I saw this coming years ago. When I first had my son I realised I had to come off the roads or he was going to follow the leader. But what would have happened if I stayed on the roads with the same mind-set as a parent? You never know, by the time it is my son's 18th birthday I could still be on the road getting into beef. But what if the person I get into beef with was my son's friend, and I had to take him out? Sounds crazy but we could face situations like that if we don't interject. Or what if a man's not in his son's life and he gets into beef with his own son? Anything can happen. So parenting is crucial to building the community. We need to ask ourselves what are we teaching our children by being on road as parents.

I see many problem solvers on social media giving advice or criticising parents with children on the streets. You hear people say stuff like, *'you should search your child before they leave the house. Or you should call the police on your child when they are acting up.'* And whatever else they may say.

My thing is - doing that type of stuff won't build a good relationship between you and your child. Those tactics sometimes break the trust. I know a woman who searched her son and found a knife on him. Then the next time she searched him she didn't find anything. After that I asked her if she found anything on him since. She said no, she thinks he's stopped carrying one. Now I'm not her son, but I'm pretty sure he hasn't stopped carrying it. He's just aware that his mum does random searches, so he knows he can't make the same mistake twice. Maybe now he leaves it by a parked car, or under the bin outside. I could never knock this parent for trying to save her son from himself. But I know the way to do that isn't by frisking him down. It's by investing quality time and love into him so he knows the king inside him exist. Parenting is hard because each child is unique and you have to recognise the patterns of your child or children.

The other day my friend told me he feels like he's let his children down. He said he felt he didn't set the best example. I didn't agree with him because personally I think he's a great dad. Then he explained it's not that he thinks he's a bad dad. He just realised that he has too many different women parenting his children. He said he feels like his behaviour in having children from all these different women might have taught the children the wrong things. I totally hear what he's saying. But I told him straight, *'At least you're doing your best to actively see those children.'* There are a lot of men out here hiding from their responsibilities. He said he realises the time factor becomes more of an issue when you have children all over the place.

He told me that after thinking about his past mistakes he now understands that when he was sleeping around he was still dealing with issues from his past. He explained how much he loves his children and how much more he wants to show them about life. He added that when his children get older and ask him why he had so many different children by so many different women he wants to be the one to tell them the truth. Then he gave me a wonderful analogy.

'Imagine you're in an abandoned building that's got a lot of pot holes in and traps. And you fall through every single one of them. You've taken the pain and the bruising but you deal with it. So what do you do next? If your child has to go through that building, surely you would point out all the pot holes and traps, so they can avoid it? You don't want your child to go make the same mistakes you made.'

Personally, I can only respect a man like that. And based on how I see him juggle time for his children, well dem man get an A for effort. Our prime job as parents is to protect our children and guide them into adulthood. So we must encourage each other on this journey of parenting.

When I was a younger, acting up on the streets, I always had in the back of my mind that my mum's people might see me. So I knew I had to act right. We need to bring that back. Nowadays most people would walk past a group of children acting up, even if they know that child's parent. I have chosen to take my parent's parenting and carry the same values where I can. So if I see my friends' child acting up, (I have already done this) I'll pull them up and talk to them or take them home. As a parent I can't walk past another friend's child misbehaving and pretend like I don't see it. If I see my friend's child is acting out in public I'm shutting that down and reminding them the last name their carrying or I'm reminding him what his mum would be telling him. They say it takes a village to raise a child. Well, let's start building the village again.

Some single mothers do a great job without a father present and some don't always make the best choices. But I don't blame them, I never have and I never will. I just believe that a woman or a man wasn't designed to do it alone. When I wrote *Mama Can't Raise No Man*, my biggest supporters happened to be women. In the reviews I read, the mothers said how much they learned about what they needed to do going forward in raising their boy children with the right balance. I didn't write that book with the intention of reinforcing the stereotype about single mothers. Quite the opposite, I wrote that book to enlighten them and empower them. I'm grateful that 65 five star reviews reflected what I set out to achieve. I'm not even going to focus on single mothers because I touched on it in my last book already. All I would say is that every child needs his father. If you are in a situation where you have no other choice but to parent alone, then do so with your head held high. But if you are the parent hurting because of a man's actions, then please get some support for healing. Because it's true what they say - one hand can't clap. And for the sisters forced to do it alone but open to love. Please, just be mindful about who you are letting come into your house. Sometimes the presence of the wrong type of man can be more damaging than having a man at all. To all my single mothers, please keep your crown on tight so you can raise those kings and queens coming after you.

Let's look at some stuff us the parents could do better to guide and equip our children through some of the times today. Parents shouldn't let their children stay out at ridiculous times at night, especially on a school night. We give our children everything they want but we don't give them what they need. Then they grow up being spoilt - what they needed was love, discipline and boundaries. When a child grows up without these things, what happens to them? Do they end up traumatised? Is this how the cycle continues?

As parents we need to know where our children are at all times. How many parents can say they know what their children are getting up to when they leave the house? Even down to our daughters. I know girls that leave their house with the longest of skirts and by the time they reach school that skirt is rolled up in the bag and they're rocking the mini-skirt. We invest in work. We invest in ourselves. We invest in the gym at times but where's the investment in our children? Parenting goes on beyond what just happens in your household.

Question for my brothers still on the road. If you're a parent who's been on the road, why would you let your child be on the road? Do you think that is good parenting? What type of parent doesn't mind their children being caught up in the street? Each to their own but I told my son the score from early in life. I told him straight that if he ever wants to be a road boy let me know. I said to him that if he ever made that mistake, he and his friends wouldn't have to worry about beef on the road or any ops rolling on them. They would have to worry about me coming for them. You must be mad, I didn't go through all of that foolishness on road so my son could follow suit. What's crazy is - I know 40 year old grand-dads still acting road. At this rate if we don't change the mind-set, certain man are gonna reach 70 years old and still be beefing on road. I can hear it now - stories on the news about elderly men pulling shanks on each other at Bingo. They won't call it youth violence again they'll call it pension-er violence.

Seriously though we have a massive influence on who our children are going to become. I think it's sad times that some parents don't strive to want better for their children. For some reason we became parents and forget to parent. I'm not saying we have to be the best parents in the world but the least we can do is want the best for our children. I personally have to respect any parent who works through their flaws to raise their offspring. To me those parents are the best; it shows a child that they matter.

A lot of parents fall off by the time their children reach the age of 11. They stop parenting and let the children raise themselves. We feel like because our children can half wash themselves and can walk to school by themselves that they are grown. We fall off. We stop checking their homework as often as we should. We ask them if they have homework but we don't always check to see what that homework is or if they have even completed the work. We leave the teaching up to the school. They spend most of the day there and when they come home we don't always have that time to give to them. As parents we have to try to find a balance.

Some parents are scared to challenge their kids. We need to be firm with them. If we don't challenge them in the home settings, they start thinking they can push boundaries out of the home. We need to find a balance. A lot of parents play the blind eye game too. I know when I'm tired and my son's doing something I don't like, I might occasionally let it go over my head. Reason being - my mind is otherwise occupied. But we must stay consistent in our parenting we need to find a balance.

Encourage your children to pray. I must say my children encourage me more to pray at times than I encourage them. But I feel this is important that our children see the thing we believe in. If you believe in anything that is, spiritually we need to find balance.

We need to aim to praise our child or children daily. We must speak life into them. We must try not to put our children down when correcting or disciplining them as this can dampen their confidence. We need to teach our children that they are here for a purpose. Even if we don't know what that purpose is, we must speak life into it.

As parents we're always teaching our children to stand up to bullies but how about we teach them that there's a good time to run? Why I say that is because sometimes it could save their life. I've told my son if anybody ever took out a weapon to rob him for his phone give it to them. We need to teach our children they are not cowards if they get robbed at knife point or by a group. We have to teach our children their lives are much more valuable than the cost of an iPhone. We need to teach them that the coward is the one using the knife or in numbers to rob them. If that day ever comes to them, it's our jobs to protect them not theirs. It's all about balance.

As parents we act like we're going to be here forever, the truth is we won't be. And for that reason we have to prepare our children for the world. A world without us, we have to teach them the basics from early. Teach them how to cook and clean - both our sons and daughters. We need to give them those basic survival skills; we need to give them balance.

We need to teach our children how to deal with emotions and not to bury them. We need to teach them that it's ok to cry. Anger is usually a disguise for something else. We need to find out what they truly feel when they are emotional. We need to know our children better, we need to find balance.

Let's teach them about their ethnicity. We all know that saying if you don't know where you're coming from. How do you know where you're going?
If we all teach our children to have better values then the future generation will have a lot more to offer this world. We can't be perfect parents, but we can find an imperfect balance. We can't let our children come in the house with new things and not question them about it. We need to know where our children are getting money from to be able to buy the things we didn't give them money for. As parents we need to become better observers. We need to learn to listen more in order to build the relationship between us and our children.

Outside of all this parenting the parent stuff. I feel it would be really solution based if there were work-shops suited for children to do with parents collec-tively. People who need support need to do a parent-ing club within our local community halls where parents can meet up every month or so to converse and seek advice. If the people in each different area were com-mitted to attending the monthly meetings with their children this might go a long way in bringing back the right balance between our parents and our children.

I'll leave this chapter on this note, it's the best piece of parenting advice I was given. If we the parents don't deal with our own issues and trauma's then how can we raise balanced children? We have to deal with our own past in order to be effective parents. The best way you can be the best parent is to be the best version of you. When we can look after ourselves then we can look after other people.

I'm not trying to tell people how to parent their children; I'm just sharing what I've heard a good parent looks like.

CHAPTER 14

PRODUCT OF MY ENVIRONMENT

'You sure?'

Personally I'm not a fan of this statement. I don't find this statement to ring true for me. And I refuse to accept that this statement is true for the youth of today. I feel like by saying that we are only perpetuating its ideology. It's almost like your taking ownership of some bad experiences or the bad area you live in. Don't get me wrong, I am fully aware that the things you see as a child can help shape and mould you to think in a certain mind-set. But at what point do we stop owning the hardships of our realities? And if we are products of our environment at what age, does this stop?

I was born and raised in the UK and lived in an environment where I witnessed a lot of crime. On my estate, there were a lot of single parent families. My borough was considered one of the poorest boroughs in London and had some of the worst secondary schools in the country. Drugs and violence was always around. All of this was happening in my environment so I need to know am I a product of that?

I can think of a few films where the characters didn't live by that statement. The first film that comes to mind and I mentioned it before, is John Singleton's *Boyz in Da Hood.* This film was filled with substance beyond belief. Laurence Fishbourne was a single parent raising his son in the hood. But he made a conscious decision not to raise his son to be hood. He didn't have the money to send his son to private school. He didn't have the money to take him away from where Bloods and Crips were banging daily. He didn't have the best of everything but he gave him the best of what he had. Laurence's character instilled so many morals, values and discipline into his son that he wasn't able to become a product of his environment.

Then there was that classic film of inspiration called *Coach Carter.* In this film Samuel L Jackson played a basketball coach in a school which was failing badly. Based on the environment, these children came from, most of the students weren't expected to pass the school exam and go on to college. The expectation for them was that most would end up dead or in prison. But Coach Carter just like Laurence Fishbourne in *Boyz in the Hood* were determined that these children didn't grow up to be products of their environments. And how did they do that? They didn't accept this as a reality for themselves and they didn't believe or teach the children around them that they were products of their environments.

One more film which is more on the jokey side and maybe not the best example for bringing home my point, but I see the same message. *Nough people say you know we don't believe Jamaica we have a bobsled team - Cool Runnings.* I mean come on, these man were from a hot environment but they excelled in the freezing cold. If they had attached that same 'product of my environment' to their belief system they would have never achieved what they did. It's funny when you think of it. My friend Jay who was in care said he doesn't like the statement either. Looking at his own experiences he said he should be a product of his environment but he's not. He grew up in care, he was mixed race and from the working class background. He also grew up having a lot of trauma on his mind. In my eyes Jay defined the odds. The odds were telling him he was bound to be a product of his environment.

I'm a massive fan of Tupac but I'm not a fan of the thug-life statement. I agree with the breakdown - the hate u give little infants fucks everybody! That aint a lie, but some people only took in the words thug–life. Meaning they accepted, wanted or liked the idea of living their lives as thugs. When you fail to breakdown the term thug-life as 2Pac did, then you are counteracting the meaning. So now the phrase 'thug-life' carries the same meaning as 'product of my environment'. In other words, we have accepted the circumstances of our situation. So I can't walk around anymore screaming out thug-life because of 'the hate you give...' No. 'The hate you give' is gonna motivate me to rise above that shit. Product of my environment, why? Why should I be a product of what you threw at me? Give me lemons and I'll make lemonades. That statement is defeatist, it's accepting things as the way they are. Then we go on microphone and rap about it, saying, *'I'm just a product of my environment.'* It's not empowering we love to rap about what we've been through, why don't we never rap about the good things? Things we are grateful for. Why is it always the bad things? Don't tell me because its reality rap, right? How about we rap our desired reality into existence? Maybe that would help change the mood a bit?

I think it's the same thing with life experiences. It's not about what you've gone through, it's the meaning you give to it. So most people who grew up in trauma will only talk about the negative side to it. They won't see the resilience and the strength in overcoming what they've been through. Like rah, you've been through all of that and your still here? Instead, they'll run with the belief that they are a victim of their circumstance. In other words, product of their trauma. It's the meaning of what they give to the product. Some people use it as fuel. So you have to ask yourself - are you a victim or victor to your circumstances? I bought into 'a product of my environment' statement until I realised that this is just an environment and I'm not a product. I believe that even if the roads don't change, every individual has got a choice. They can become a product of their environment or rise above it. Many people have risen above their environment. What makes them so different?

Why is it that a youth from Holly Street, the same environment where I grew is able to fly aeroplanes when certain man his age haven't even been on a plane? Man his age from the block are doing long flights in jail, why? What's the difference? What is it? Is it because he had his dad around? Ok, that definitely helps, but what's the difference? The difference is he had discipline; he had culture and family values. He kept his children in the yard. They weren't out past seven o'clock in the night on the block jamming. Parenting the parents again. If you know that there's madness going on outside then you got to keep an eye on your children. You got to know where they are at all times.

Educate them, give them dreams; this man's child had a dream. Teach them about work ethic, manners and focus. If the street is messy, keep your children inside. If you can't change the street, keep them inside. You're not teaching them fear - you're giving them tools to excel and become more than their environment. Like what Laurence Fishbourne did in the film *Boyz in Da Hood.* He kept his son in the hood knowing he could raise his son not to be a product of his environment. Both fathers knew with the right tutoring and guidance their sons wouldn't be out their screaming thug-life. Because their sons are kings who knew they're worth. They knew their children we're above thug-life. They knew their children we're above being a product of their environments. Because that statement is defeatist. It means that we've given up. We've accepted what they've thrown at us.

They say if someone gives you lemons make lemonade. We're not making the lemonades. Their giving us lemons and were proudly repping their lemons. And were getting a tattoo of the lemon on our stomach, and were screaming lemon life. I love Tupac I've learnt a lot from that brother genius, but I don't think thug-life is productive to us freeing ourselves of the mind-set we are trapped in. Thug-life is a great observation of the situation once broken down, but again does that mean you're going to stay in it? Because if you're saying you're going to stay in it then you are a prisoner to the street. You're saying that you can't get out of this prison. As much as I get what a young 2Pac was doing, I'm not down with taking ownership of that life. I'm grateful that 2pac broke down his meaning of thug-life. If it wasn't for this man's incredible genius I wouldn't have ever understood myself to be a prisoner to the street.

Can you imagine if after slavery was abolished and the slaves were saying we are a product of my environment? And instead of rising and fighting for our right to equality, they give up and accept being the product? I can imagine feeling like that after slavery. And without argument we were classified as products in a foreign environment. So naturally after years of slavery you might feel like a victim of your circumstance. Initially you might not see the resilience within you which enabled you to overcome slavery. Imagine all the ex-slaves who rose up to become something bigger than slavery; they didn't let their circumstances hold them back. Imagine if every ex-slave decided not to chase their dreams because they were waiting for their reparations to get them started. Then they would have become a product of slavery, and we wouldn't have the freedom that they fought for us. The 'product of your environment' statement is defeatist. I'm not saying we don't deserve our reparations because it goes without saying. For those of us who have ancestors who worked to build other peoples land. I get that, but to become dependent on receiving that pay-out is defeatist. It's almost saying we can't climb as a people until they pay us back what they stole from us.

Many people have adapted a mind-set that says, *'Ok, they stole from us and their throwing more lemons at us in the community.'* Let's not wait for the pay-out let's make a way out. It's ok to acknowledge when you've been hard done by oppression. But we can't let oppression turn into regression and this is the lesson. Some black people are still stuck in the mind-set of we are a product of slavery and it is what it is.

What I'm saying is - I'm not a believer of the phrase, 'it is what it is.' I don't believe that no more I more believe in, 'it is what we make of it.' In order to get people to free their mind you have to get them to look at their environment differently.

CHAPTER 15

FALSE PROPHETS

"Everybody from the street
aint street and it's not every
youth worker who knows how
to work with the youth."

L ast year I heard so many individuals in the youth field state,
'*We need to change the narrative for knife crime.*' I heard '*change the narrative*' so much last year that I started thinking to myself, '*Shit, maybe we need to change the narrative on using the phrase change the narrative.*' Seriously though, I found it so frustrating hearing people trying to sound smart by saying this when I clearly changed the narrative in 2011. The phrase '*prisoner to the streets*' is the new narrative.

My biggest frustration with false prophet youth workers is that they are getting in the way of the solution. Some of these false prophets speak very articulately on the news and are good at sounding like they know the solutions. When the truth is, what they're speaking about isn't even clear to them. I remember I was the first youth worker I know making a big deal about not wanting to be recognised as an ex-gang member. I fought that narrative single handily while being perceived as the delusion one.

Since 2007 this has been my stance, and I cemented that stance in 2011 with the new explanation for our issue as a prisoner to the street one, a mentality. Even though I claim to be the first one (I know of) doing that I've seen some false prophets who get more of a platform than me for saying the same thing I've taught them without paying reference to prisoner to the streets, or even myself. That's not genuine. That's some false prophet behaviour.

I wouldn't even mind if they understood the depth of what it was I was saying. When these people first came in to the youth field they were all using words like knife crime, gangs and postcode wars. Then I drop prisoner to the streets and all of a sudden these false prophets have fresh new ideas. Instead of their usual topic of discussion now I hear everyone saying it's a mind-set when years before they were campaigning against knife crime. Or years before they were working for the police but now it's a mind-set. Did I not teach you that? Years before, some of these false prophets had organisations which were registered under the name of gang something. Gang exit this or gang exit that group or

Gangs R us. They were obsessed with the word gang. Now all of a sudden I release PTTS and all of these youth worker prophet's start saying the problem is a mind-set. That's not genuine, that's stealing, that's verbal plagiarism. I've heard interviews were these prophets will go on the news and 'now' confidently say, *'The problem is that it's a mind-set. And we need to understand why they are involved in knife crime.'* Not realising that they just contradicting the whole point I'm making. It's like playing Chinese whispers and by the time the last person says it out loud the first person realises that they never really got what was said.

For example, how can it be a mind-set issue on one hand and a knife crime issue at the same time? Think about it for a second please. I can't keep explaining it but if you don't understand this question then you won't understand the meaning of the two descriptions. Knife crime and gang crime criminalise the behaviours while prisoner to the streets de-criminalises the behaviours while describing the type of mind-set it is. You can't just go around repeating it's a mind-set, it's a mind-set, without understanding what these terms mean in practice. Most things in life are done with a mind-set so be more precise. It's crucial that you know the meaning of why a young person becomes mentally imprisoned to the street. Because once you do know, you'll no longer view them as knife criminals. The only real crime they are committing as lost young children is survival. Most young children are just trying to survive a mind-set which they didn't create for themselves.

'Everybody from the Street aint Street.'

Me and another guy I grew up with delivered a workshop to some youths. I remember that I did my talk first and mentioned how I got shot at and stabbed and why those things happened. Then the guy I was with spoke after me. When I heard him speak he left me lost for words. He said something that blew me away. He started doing a talk similar to mine. Then he claimed he got shot in the hand and I looked at him thinking, *'No you didn't.'* This is the first I'm hearing of that one. Then I spoke to him afterwards and he said he got shot in his hand by one of my enemies. Years later we fell out and I asked the people who was with him on the day what happened. They told me he didn't get shot nowhere. They made a joke and told me he was running with them when the guys pulled out a gun. And out of fear he tripped over and fell on a stone, they said the stone must have shot him. I was in stiches at first but when you really peep game and think about it that's quite a sick minded thing to do. You mean to say you've lied so much about who you were on the street that you had to spice up your own story. Who would lie and say they got shot? I know who - someone who hasn't felt the pain of steel insert their body. And they need to feel like they've survived something street just to feel like they are qualified to talk on the street.

I can't talk for everyone but a lot of these guys going around doing youth talks weren't really on the streets. They played the game of the street and now there playing the game of the youth field. Acting like they were really out here on the streets but they wasn't, there experience is limited.

What is this issue some might say? I can't really explain it but it's like those people who make films and books about the streets when they didn't really feel the pain of being on the street. So once again, it's like they are profiting from our stories. Being on the streets means you can't go on the pavement when things got hot.

Last year I featured in a little short film called Armani's story it's on YouTube now. He told me he got stabbed and he was making a film and he wanted to make a difference. I said, *'bro that's a good look.'* He told me his story briefly and said he wanted me in this film. I liked the fact that he respected the book and that he wanted to introduce it into the film. But I was always sceptical about how the film was going to be presented, and if the film went in line with what I was teaching in my philosophy. Anyway, I told my mate who did the film, *'You got stabbed at 21 right?'* He said, *'Yes.'* So I said, *'Do you know that at 21 you're not even considered a youth?'* When we were getting stabbed at 14 and going jail at the same time, we were youth. And while my mates were coming out of jail at 15, 16 my bredrin who made the film about the streets got arrested for the first time at 15 for a fake looking gun. What I'm saying is if I was a yute man and you came to me with this story I would most likely get up and leave the workshop. In other words, you're not reaching me with that story. In fact the younger me would've thought you're taking the piss. You had a good life at home and you were out here at 15 trying to dumb yourself down to fit in? We might be from the same pool of mentality but to me that's the shallow end. As a youth I couldn't see myself sitting down and listening to anyone deliver a workshop about the streets. Unless that person can relate to what the deep ends is like without a life jacket. Someone who knows the pain of what it's like to have to learn how to swim or drown.

I'm not referring to my brother Armani when I say false prophets, but I think a lot of these guys jump into youth work out of fashion. They had love at home; they had less reason to become prisoners. They lived in safer areas. Even though we ourselves didn't need to be on the streets, a lot of us in the deep end had more reason than them. Most of these figure heads on the subject had next to no reason, like I said privileged prisoner to the streets. I'm still saying the streets are fake, but we were more street than them. And there acting like their some ex-street guys coming back in telling their stories as victims of knife crime or ex-gang members and all the rest of it. Some of these prophets are even lying about their experience on the street. But the people learning from them wouldn't know that.

So what I'm saying to the people is stop listening to everyone who goes around talking on the subject of the street. They get the platforms to preach about what we need to do to fix the streets. But they fall short in understanding the mind-set because they didn't do enough road life to tell you how to come off the road or what the roads are truly about. Their experience is limited. It's third hand information. What did they do? What was their part? And even the ones who were on the streets to the fullest. Some of them are so lost or programmed that they can't be honest enough to realise why they did the things they did when they was on the roads. So they sell their story as, *'I was a gang member. We did this, we did that.'* Or they play the victim card. You sell the story differently to what it is. You didn't keep it real. Now people believe that this is a gang or criminal issue because you failed to give an honest portrayal of the streets. That's my issue with it just tell the truth. False prophets love to keep the glory but hate to keep it real. Your lies create more confusion than solutions think about that

'It's not every youth worker who knows how to work with the youth.'

One thing I've learnt about youth work other than it's not a solution to youth violence, is that not everyone in youth work should be working with the youth.

I believe it was 2013 and I got invited to do a talk in a (Youth Offending Service) YOS in Hackney. I asked my main man the mental farmer if he wanted to roll with me. At the time I had just undergone some major surgery on my leg. I was still on medication and I had a leg brace covering my injured leg, and a pair of crutches also. I remember sitting in the room with a group of youths and their probation workers. Anyway the Mental Farmer was in the corner observing and I was getting ready to start my talk. Just like Coach Carter I believe in respecting each other and knowing boundaries. At first everyone was talking and I just sat down waiting for their workers to get involved and get some order in there but they were timid. They kept asking nicely, *'Erm... guys can you be quiet so our guest can speak please?'* I was thinking, *'How can an establishment working with the youth be too scared to tell the youth to be quiet?'* I wasn't impressed. The talking didn't stop completely but I knew it wasn't going to get any quieter. So I started to talk.

But while I was talking setting out the boundaries one guy in particular kept talking to his friend. I thought when are these workers going to address this but they went cold turkey on me. So I asked the young man to please be quiet. I told him, *'No hard feelings but if you don't want to be here you can always leave King.'* The yute looked at me laughing and carried on talking so I nicely asked him to leave. Then he felt embarrassed and he started acting up, running his mouth. Then I asked him, *'If it was me and you on the street corner do you think you could chat to me like this?'*

Obviously, that got his back up more and he stood up saying something rude. I grabbed my crutches and lifted myself to stand up and we were both in each other's faces grabbing each other. I kept saying, *'You better thank God were not on the street bro, thank him.'* Now I know youth workers would say that's not professional conduct. But I'm not a youth worker and I don't care about what they think is professional. There was a method to my madness, and they were too scared to control their client list.

Anyway after about a minute of me holding this young man, the workers finally got the courage to break it up. I sat back down to continue the session and the workers asked me to leave. They said they couldn't let me continue the session after that altercation. I couldn't stop laughing. I then asked, *'Are you lot serious? You mean to tell me you stood there all for a good minute and watched this escalate. You had no control over this young man and now you want me to leave? Are you for real cuz?'*

When they said they were serious I laughed even louder. I looked at the Mental Farmer and said,

'Lyn come we get out of here.'

Lyn just shook his head in disgust. As we reached the door I turned around and said, *'You guys don't deserve to work with these youths it's just a business to you lot.'*

Then the Mental Farmer said,

'Look!'

I turned around before I walked out, and all I could see was the youth shouting at their workers, *'What are you lot doing? Let him stay, let him stay.'*

When I turned around, who do you think was shouting the loudest for me to stay? You guessed it - the same boy. I was grabbing. I left that place feeling like Coach Carter for real, for real. I was still vex at the establishment but I was happy to see they got some sort of message from me that day, it wasn't all in vain. I learned a lot that day. One thing that stood out to me was how scared those youth offending workers were to intervene. I mean, how can you be a youth offending worker who's afraid to work with youth who offend? That's like being a police man and running away from crime. Lol - Mental!

Then there was another time I was walking past a youth club in Holly Street. One young king was being rude to the youth worker effing and blinding. As I was walking past the youth worker asked me to have a word. It's like he knew he couldn't manage the situation. Don't ask me how but me and my friend who were walking past ended up having to try and calm him down. I could see the young boy was hurting but that didn't excuse he's behaviour. I told him to have some respect for his olders. Then he started being rude to me. The young king was about 12. I took off my belt and was so close to just beating him. The boy was my son's age so I couldn't let him talk to me like that. Then I caught myself in the madness and put my belt away. I asked him who he's dad or mum was I told him when I find out he's finished. But he kept getting angry so I knew that the parents might not even be around.

Long story short, after about five minutes I grabbed the boy and hugged him, He kept screaming,

'He's gay get off.'

I laughed and said,

'I love you young King but I'm definitely not gay.'

Me and my friend kept telling him how much we cared about him and he couldn't digest it.

He kept saying,

'You're gay, you're gay.'

After a while we left him alone. All his friends were surprised how much we cared. I went home thinking - *when I find out who he's family are, he's finished. Because he's from my area he's parents could most likely be my people.* I did my research and found out he never had his parents. I was so glad I didn't put my hand or belt on him, because that would have been a major failure on my part. On the other hand, I was glad we told that boy how much we cared about him because he obviously never heard that before.

Then there was another incident of inadequate youth work. I was picking up my son from a summer activities thing from the same youth club in Holly Street. Two young guys were talking about stabbing each other. The youth workers didn't know what to do but they asked me to intervene and resolve the conflict. So I came in and dragged the two youth away from the crowd of youth outside, who were hyping them on. And I spoke to both of them with love and firmness, Coach Carter style. Anyway they came back out that centre and stood next to each other like kings. They didn't feed in to the prisoner's mind-set. I was so proud of them. As I was walking back to my car with my son in the crowd of youths I saw the same young king who thinks I'm gay. He came up to me very humble like and apologised. I spoke to him and explained to him why I got upset with him. And then the youth gave me a hug. All I could see was a younger version of me. A child who is behaving in anger but really just upset. I went home thinking the same thing I always do about the youth field. A lot of these youth workers don't know how to work with the youth. And to think I used to work in this field and they made me redundant. That's funny.

The worst scenario I found myself in happened when I agreed to deliver some boxing sessions to a youth club. A young lady I met along the journey through my first book asked me to come down and train some youth. I agreed and we started our sessions. The first week of any boxing session I do, I always set the rules and the boundaries. The rules are simple - no swearing in front of me; no rap if it's full of profanity; no lounging and no trousers swaging; I don't want to see no one's Calvin Klein's please and if you come twenty minutes late don't bother come in my session. Because it's me one trying to teach 20 people boxing that have never boxed before. For that to work we will need some sort of order with the young people. Other than that, if the young people listen and work hard then we can have a little fun too.

A few weeks into our session I found myself getting frustrated with the order of things. It's like every week was the same. I would come in and start the session positively. Then about twenty minutes into the group session the young ones would come in smelling of skunk. Now I'm not judging. I've been 15, 16, high on skunk in my GCSE's but this isn't the place for that. It shouldn't be me as the boxing coach that has to turn them away when they are late. My job is to teach boxing not manage who comes into the session high on skunk.

Anyway, after a few weeks I realised this was the only boxing session that was draining me. I came in late one Thursday and I ran in to continue the session. The music was playing some foul lyrics. About lick this and suck that and a couple B and N words. So I stopped coaching and asked a young king lounging in the session by the stereo to put it on a next track because there were young children there. So then the young king feels like I put him on the spot and looks me up and down then goes back to his phone. So I'm thinking - *Who's this little facety rarse looking up and down?* I felt violated but I held my temper as best as one could.

I walked up to the stereo turned it off and said,
'*What you saying young blood aint you got no manners?*'
Then he looked up at the youth worker and said,
'*Talk to your boy,*'

You see at that moment I had to do a lot of deep breathing because I'm not a youth worker I'm a boxing coach and nobody was intervening.

So I lost my cool but in a calm way I said, *'Your boy? I can't see no boys around here except for you.'*

Then I realised we wasn't alone talking, and I always forget young people like to act up harder when people are watching.

So the young king got up and said,

'Come we go outside then. Come then man will...'

When I saw he was talking all this knife talk I just wanted to fuck him up. A lot of people don't own when they're in the wrong. So I opened the door and happily walked outside. People might say well this guy is supposed to be a youth worker and author. Yes I am an author but I'm not a youth worker because my temperament and disrespect don't mix too well. I'm also raised in an era where if you disrespect your elders you get seen too. I think the youngers of today call it 'chat shit get banged'. Well, same difference. As I walked out of the gym with the boy I remembered it was just me and him alone without the audience watching. I thought let me give this guy a chance to explain his behaviour before I do something I'll later regret.

So I stopped and asked him, *'Yo, young blood, are you sure you want to do this? Cos, once we get outside that's it, you're not a yute anymore.'*

Naturally, he started running his gums again.

Apart of me wanted to school him, then a part of me wanted to do him over. I'm a human and I fight them prisoner to the street demons daily. That's another reason why I don't do youth work no more. My patience is gone. At this point the youth worker finally came over to intervene after watching the whole thing build up.

A part of me was relieved to see her I felt like she was going to handle the situation but she surprised me. She said, *'Everyone's looking guys; this isn't a good look for the gym.'*

As if to imply that she was more interested in losing her spot renting the room in a snazzy Gym, than she was about the conflict itself. I just gave her one look.

Then I looked at the young boy and said, *'Look, I'm going upstairs to finish my class bro; wait for me outside if you want. It's on you.'*

Then I went upstairs to finish what I came out my house to do.

As I started teaching two eleven year olds the basic stance, I looked in the mirror and saw the youth worker had brought the young man back in the session. I acted like I didn't see it but I was mad that she did that. The boy had a weapon and was possibly smoking skunk before my session. This same boy who's not even participating in my session, but she let him back in. What ever happened to good old safeguarding? Then I saw her walking up to me in the mirror. She said she needed to have a word. I said ok well I'm teaching a class so it's going to have to wait.

Then she was insisting that we talk now so I said, *'What are you saying, you want to have a word or you're telling me we have to?'*

She then said, *'Yeah. If we don't sort it out then...'*

I then interjected and said, *'Then what you want me to leave?'*

She responded, *'Well!'*

So out of principle, not stubbornness I decided to leave and never looked back. I was so vex I think I even slammed the door.

In my eyes this was just another prime example of poor youth working. The worst part is when we spoke after-wards. It took me a good week to calm down seriously. She called me and said she was disappointed in the way I left. She said I was wrong because the young people said I was rude to him about the music. I was so mad with her. It was like when you see two parents being played by their children. But I realised she doesn't even need an explana-tion. You see I remembered that this same lady told me the youth were throwing eggs and fireworks at her and the other workers weeks before. So I should really be mad with myself. If they can throw that stuff at her then they clearly don't respect her and if they don't respect her, the so called youth worker, then how the hell was they ever going to respect me?

All I know is most youth workers need to keep the numbers high when they are running a project. If not they won't get any funding to run further projects. Remember the youth field is built on numbers not challenging the mind-set. So I see why her priority was those children over me. She had to keep the loyalty to them because they don't respect her. So if she loses their trust the youth work goes bust. Other than all this youth work politics I think the lady who I fell out with is a lovely lady. I just don't think she is the best youth worker yet, but I have faith she will get it one day. I really do mean that, no sarcasm intended. You see, outside of all of our views and opinions, youth work is just youth work and people are still people. Moral of the story to be a good youth worker you cannot be scared to intervene, or challenge reckless behaviour.

One of the main frustrations outside of this false prophet mentality has to be the funding process. All these pots of money for this and for that but to get funding you have to sell yourself and your ideas to people on a panel. Or people in the system who know absolutely nothing about youth work calling the shots on what project is worthy. I've learned it's not about solutions in this field; it literally is about ticking boxes. There are a few organisations I know out there doing some good work in their respective fields. Sometimes I wish I was a secret millionaire. I would go around seeing who deserves funding to work with the youth. Then I'd dish out the funds appropriately. Unfortunately, false prophets are controlled by the establishments that don't seem to want to see the real change. But in order for people to get paid, they roll with it, instead of challenging the youth work establishment. *False prophets.*

CHAPTER 16

CRABS IN THE BUCKET MENTALITY - REVERSED

'Prisoner to the bucket'
mentality?'

Growing up, I learned and became familiar with being told that my circle of people had a *'crabs in the bucket mentality'*. I wouldn't argue it because it felt like there was some truth to it. What I didn't like about the statement was my intelligence being compared to a crab trapped in a bucket! I mean surely, if a group of humans were trapped in a 'crab mentality', we would have the sense to just get out of the bucket? No? I mean after all we are not crabs, we can communicate. Then it hit me that we are those crabs. We don't communicate with one another, so how do we begin to organise things to get out? The only way those crabs can come out collectively is if they can have meaningful communication. It's that simple.

If we make peace in the bucket between ourselves then we won't have to complain or worry about the police. If we make peace among ourselves the police won't have any reason or excuse to come and bother you and your children in the bucket. And if they continue with the harassment we can take affirmative action for justice. If we worked with each other rather than trying to pull each other down, we can build in the bucket, we can build in the community. We can actually have a community in the bucket. At the moment we don't have a community in the bucket because everyone is acting with an *everyman and every woman for themselves type* mentality. The community spirit is broken because everyone is looking out for number one - me. We want to get out and not look back to the others like we are better than those coming from the same place.

I stopped focusing on systematic injustices years ago. I haven't acted like they don't exist; I just refuse to fight those injustices. We all know that we can't fight the system. You might be able to affect change to a specific law or win an injustice act against yourself in the court of law. But you can't fight the system. It's sad that we live in a world where the system which one lives in isn't designed to empower the people. It's sad when parts of the system use their platforms to assassinate the character of a certain set of people. Yes it's sad but you can't change what is bigger than you. However you can create your own system within the system. Or create your own system within the bucket.

Last year I got invited by a brother named Howard to come and deliver a talk in Huddersfield. It was one of those events were everyone is talking in the same language about what they presume knife crime is. I had ten minutes to break down what prisoner to the street meant. As I was talking I saw a few police officers at the front of the crowd. They didn't seem impressed by my speech, some sat with their red faces and their arms crossed. When I noticed that I thought - *Why don't they like what I'm saying?'* I think it was the night before on social media I saw a child getting beaten up by the police. And so many have been killed by them and defended in the court of law. But every time I say policing isn't the solution police get upset. So I made it a thing to elaborate on why I said that. I closed off by saying, *'I don't hate the police I hate the way some police deal with my people. Especially young black children because they seem to be the most targeted.'* Then I went on to explain. *'I don't look to the police for solutions or help because they're job is to make arrest. Outside of my own beliefs, the only way police or the system can influence change is if they change themselves. A lot of people in power know what I'm talking about - corruption exists and institutionalised racism exists. If they change their hearts and start thinking like humans then they will learn how to truly care for other humans. That's the only way I see the system making a positive change.'*

After I said that I didn't really feel the need to say anything else. Whenever I talk to a room full of strangers who don't know my work, I struggle to see how I can reach them in that short-lived time. I walked out of the lecture hall while they was still clapping and went to the bathroom. When I got home later that night I heard one of the police officers had given me a standing ovation for the honest statement. Not only that I heard they had tears in their eyes a real emotion. When I heard that I was happy it gave me a small sense of hope that one day people in the system will realise it's not them against us. It's us against us. But in the meantime, while we wait for the world to have a heart, we the people have to create safe spaces for ourselves and our children in that bucket.

When it comes to solutions, we act like it is impossible to change things. They've given up hope - it's every crab for himself. But imagine if those crabs in the bucket stopped feeling defeated about being in the bucket and fought together to get out of it. Imagine they all use their crab claws, climb to the top and all manage to make the bucket tilt over. I know it sounds farfetched, but the reality is there is always a way. But, like I said, we've become those crabs. So instead of us figuring a way to get out of the bucket, we invest our time, feelings and consumed thoughts about who put us in the bucket. Or about who keeps throwing more injustices in the bucket and who created the bucket for us. At the same time of thinking like this we are still pulling each other back. What I'm saying is - the solution is internal.

Part of the solution is intervention. Once again I'm not talking about intervention from outside, an outside source that we're waiting for to put things right for us. I'm talking about us, the crabs in the bucket, putting things right for ourselves. Some of the older roadmen from the community need to help out and admit this mentality isn't working for us. In fact it's killing us. We all need to be honest about the fears we really face. We need to all be men and set positive examples. Otherwise we become part of the problem and not part of the solution. Their truth is so valuable that it may be older roadmen who can actually set these young boys free from the streets. If as older roadmen, as individuals, we don't choose to have a conscience and help out our young brothers. Then sadly we are making a decision to leave those crabs to figure it out on their own, instead of helping them to work together to tip the bucket over.

The primary part of the solution has to be to focus on the younger generations. Leave the older crabs to keep pulling each other back if after trying we can't get through. That might sound harsh but there's an old Caribbean saying -*Those who don't hear must feel.* We can't waste energy on trying to get people to change if they are stuck in their ways. There are so many other things we can do to help solve this, but I feel the objectives would be much better met if us crabs in the bucket lived in togetherness. That way we could build our own businesses and have our own schools and colleges teaching Black history, economics, culture, etc. That way maybe we wouldn't even have to be quick to leave the bucket, maybe we could build upon it instead?

Nothing isn't wrong with the bucket we can build a wall street in that bucket, but only if we can communicate effectively. This bucket is not a black one. This is the working class bucket. You can be white, Turkish, Somali, whatever. This bucket isn't a description for black people. All thought people have associated this bucket with our condition. It is actually a universal condition for people who have less than others.

Live by the gun die by the gun, is basically the same thing as live by the street die by the streets. What I'm saying is we know the streets come with a risk of death. If I was living the road life pass the age of 18 then I've made a conscious decision to live with whatever consequences come with that life. So if while I'm living that life I happen to get caught and go to prison then I can't complain, can I? If I am on the streets selling drugs for a way out of the bucket and another group of crabs set me up to get robbed, can I complain? Well we can complain but we would look crazy doing so. Because we chose the roads to get out of the bucket, so who are we complaining too?

When the riots of London kicked off in 2011, it was over the killing of a man who was unarmed. The murder of that man really hurt me and I didn't even know him. Not just because I knew the mother of his child and one of his children, but because the brother wasn't armed. In the mist of the madness I was ready to ride or die for the uncalled murder of another brother. My thoughts then and my thoughts now were, There's no justice, there's just this.

I stood in the middle of the road that day in Tottenham and witnessed what seemed strangely normal to me – chaos.

I saw people genuinely hurting for a friend or a family member who was killed unjustly and I was ready to defend them if they moved to the police. I turned my back and saw another group of people who were clearly confused about what the focus was and they began to see opportunity in breaking glass windows to steal items from people who didn't kill the brother. Though I understood it, my spirit didn't sit well with the looting. It only took focus away from the main focus. During the bottle throwing and the tear gas exchanges, I turned my back to see a journalist taking pictures. At this point I thought why is this non-crab photographer taking pictures when he doesn't care about anything but getting front page?

As I had that thought a couple of the other crabs decided to take his camera and rough him up a bit. Being the crab that I am I couldn't have that. I knew that would only mess up what the real fight was about. Instead that story would be the new focus. So I ran over and grabbed the camera and gave it back to the journalist. The other crabs looked confused at first then they realised what I was doing so they all let him go. I didn't have any qualms with them making the journalist leave because I knew he wasn't there for us crabs. At the same time I knew that camera wasn't ours to take. After realising all the crabs weren't on the same page for justice I decided to go home. I dropped off one of my friends at Wood Green station. Then I drove down the high road.

As I got to H & M store on the high road I saw a group of 30 plus crabs smashing up the shops. They were *bally'd* up with hoodies on running rampant with no direction, they were rebels without a cause. I was driving with my friend getting closer to the lost crabs when we saw them begin to turn their anger from the shops to the innocent drivers. Two cars in front of me these young crabs decided to start smashing car windows with bricks bringing the traffic to a halt. I had the opportunity to save myself the drama and turn right by the Boots pharmacy, but I couldn't do it. I couldn't act in fear. My friend saw the right turn also and by then the crabs were in the process of smashing up the car directly in front of me. My friend shouted to drive but like I said I couldn't act in fear. It wasn't out of ego, it was about justice, and it was about standing up for my beliefs. Although another crab was killed in our community I didn't think it was fair that these crabs were terrorising the innocent guys. I knew I didn't have the power to stop them from what they were doing. But I did decide that they weren't going to smash up my car without a war. I was ready to ride for what I believed in.

They came up to the car and surrounded us at fast pace. I wound down my car window as the boy with the massive rock was about to throw it at my car like when a footballer takes a throw on. And when he pulled that stone back over his head I leaned over my friend and shouted, *'Oi, I'm not your enemy don't make me your enemy!'*

I saw the twitch in his eye through the masked up face, he hesitated the throw on and went to throw it again. So I shouted it again, *'Oi! I'm not your enemy bruv, don't make one.'*

I don't know if it was the fear of me or the fear of righteousness bunnin his eardrums, but he decided to put the rock down. Then he told the rest of the crabs to back up, and they let me drive through without any violence. I would have been vex if we had to get it cracking because when you think about it we are all in the same bucket so we are not enemies.

A lot of other mad stuff happened around this time of the riots. A lot of what I saw during the riots and writing my first book gave me this crab in the bucket awakening, but it was this next incident that really cemented and changed my perspective on the word justice. I was in Tottenham marching with four other people to Broad Water Farm estate for a young man who was murdered by police. The reason there was only four of us is because police said we couldn't march and the people listened to the police. At that moment I realised these crabs aren't really activist they don't really understand what fighting for justice means. And I said to myself - never again. I will never march again. It reminded me of my past on the streets when I was riding front line for my friends but they never backed the beef. I even had two of my daughters march with me that day. When I got to Farm I decided to take my daughter's home as it was getting late. It didn't feel like a movement when I was there it felt like confusion among us crabs. I saw a rap video taking place under the garage and many old faces but it just didn't seem like we were there for the same thing. I was getting ready to go but I decided to go to the shop and all I heard was, 'Pap, pap, pap...'

I saw children running, I saw the blood, I heard the screaming, and I had to grab a girl frightened in search of her mother. I grabbed the young girl to console her from what she just witnessed. Then her mother came and I saw it was a friend of mine from school days. For some strange reason which I put down to past trauma when I see these things I'm not scared enough to run, I have the ability to think in the mist. During the post chaos I turned my head to hear a voice shout out, *'Good! He deserves it, he deserves it.'*

His ignorant statement broke my heart. It killed my hopes for waking up the fellow crabs to freedom.
'Why does the guy deserve to get shot like that? Why? Because of what, some street shit? But are we not out here trying to fight for justice of police killing one of our own? Are we not in front of children? What if one of your children got shot by a stray? What if those children become damaged for life because of what they witnessed? What are we saying here? It's ok for us to kill us but it's not ok for people outside the bucket to kill us.'

From that day I don't go marching or shouting no peace no justice because I realised were the peace and justice needs to start. And that's here at home.
I could use a lot of different examples to explain the point I'm trying to make but I won't, I'll use just one more. Just a few years ago the police killed another young brother from my bucket. When he got killed I was so pissed I can't tell you what I wanted to do. I saw the boy grow and even protected him a few times in passing. Plus I have a good relationship with his dad. I'm not one to cry easily but I was so angry at this one the tears just came flooding. I was angry that the officers sat on the back of a young man who had cuffs on his back. The procedure was fucked up and every time I played

the video back on my phone I saw another way it could have been handled without killing the young King. I was angry that the young king was still a prisoner to the street and nobody tried to rescue him. After his killing I heard the two estates ended up in war. How disgusting to beef at a time like this? No matter how much people may have disliked the young child, that is not the way. By doing that, you give the police more reason to justify killing us. You give them reason to talk about introducing guns in to our bucket. Is that what you crabs really want?

The message to my brothers here is simple live by the streets we die by the streets. You can't shout justice for the person killed if the person you are shouting justice for was on the road life when police killed them. Because anytime we break the law we give the police a reason to come in our bucket and dictate to how we live. By being on the roads we give them reason to search us, abuse us and at times even kill us. I'm not justifying it; I just understand the street life. If you live by the street code you can die by it too. The police still deserve to go to prison for it. But they probably won't. So my thing is instead of spending our lives fighting the people outside the bucket killing us, let's make peace and bring in values and opportunities so the bucket remains safe for all that sounds like justice to me.

CHAPTER 17

FEAR IS SILENT, BUT OH SO LOUD

*"Anger is a disguise for other
something else."*

*'What do you know about fear Trav? You're not scared of any-
thing.'*

Someone once asked me that question while assuming
they knew the answer.

I was 15 when I first heard someone say that to me. I
left them to believe that the statement was true. But as an
adult I'm wise enough to know that statement couldn't be
any further away from the truth. Growing up I learned two
fundamental things about life from a very young age. One

was - never let people see you cry and two was - it's not ok to show fear. Because showing fear wouldn't stop someone from troubling you. In fact it may motivate someone to trouble you some more. I learned this very early on in life, the concept was drilled in my head - *Hit him back Robin. Stand up for yourself.* Or something we all may have heard - *Go your bed, there's nothing to be scared of.* Most children I know weren't open about their fears so I guess our fears stayed silent.

When I look at the period of my life when I was a high risk prisoner to the streets, I can see why the perception of me being fearless existed. From 13-19 I was active in so much violence that one would think from the outside I didn't have any fear. My street story shows I would run and fight groups of enemies when they had knives. I told a man to do his thing when a gun was put to my head at 15 years old. I ran after the guys who were shooting at me after they stabbed me. And I held my own down in jail in Jamaica. I'm sure there's a bunch of other stuff which would give the perception that I had no fear. But sometimes actions speak louder than fear.

'What are you scared of? Better yet, what was you scared of as a child?'

A lot of people like to act like they were born road-men. Like there wasn't a process of life experiences that moulded them into the characters they later became. According to my mother, I was born into fear. I was born prematurely and as a result they're were complications that left my mum fighting for her life, but so was I. Apparently I was in the incubator for weeks upon end fighting for life and my mother was on another ward going through her fight to stay alive. A psychologist once told me that I must have experienced a lot of trauma while I was in the incubator away from my mother. At first I found it funny but she definitely wasn't joking. She said, *'Can you imagine how fearful you must have been in the incubator?'* I laughed and said, *'I can't remember.'* Then she said, *'Of course you don't, but that doesn't mean you wasn't traumatised by it. Can you imagine a baby crying out to their mother for comfort but nobody coming to pick that baby up? Can you imagine how scared that new born child would be? That child is already learning how to deal with his or her fears alone. Well that child was you.'*

I thought about what she said. Then it made me think about the time when my mother claimed she saw me sleeping in the cupboard out of fear. I don't have any recollection of sleeping in no cupboard but if my mum said it happened she isn't lying. She said I was about 4 years old when she found me sleeping in the cupboard. When I asked her why would I be scared? She said because the NF were banging down our door late at night and harassing us. As strange as it sounds I can't remember the banging on the door. But I do have a vague memory of seeing fire at the door and sensing my mother's panic. But whenever she talks about it for some reason something triggers off in me. The silent part of me which I believe chose as a child not to remember those bad days.

There are a thousand things I remember being scared of before the age of 6. Those things remind me of my childhood innocence before the prisoner. I remember being 6 and my brother started teasing me for being scared of a film that we'd both watched 4 times already. Up to this day I don't know why I was scared of a film I had seen four times before. I remember I used to even laugh at the film. But for some reason *Little Shop of Horrors* messed me up the fifth time I watched it. I think I digested the thought that the plant was eating people. It stuck in my psyche before bed and I would wake up thinking the plant ate me. I won't even mention how *Candy Man* frigged me over at 9 years old. If I'm honest I only watched that film Xmas Eve 2017. What's funny is I didn't even know why I was so scared. When I watched it as an adult I had to laugh because it wasn't even that deep. But I was only 9 to be fair.

Most PTTS I know will never be honest about being scared. They prefer to act up and front giving the impression they aren't scared of anything. Truth is everybody is or has experienced fear at some time. And the truth is its ok to be or feel scared at times, it's really ok. Fear is a part of what makes us human. It's what we do with our fear that can be the issue. Being scared doesn't make you a P word it makes you human. Fear is part of our survival mechanism. Look at Mike Tyson for example. One of the most feared ferocious boxing champions of his time. Believe it or not, in his early days he was scared to get in the ring and sometimes even cried before fights. He said himself he was scared every time he walked in the ring. But he managed to use that fear to motivate himself to be a beast in the ring. So it is not fear itself which is the problem it is what we do with our fear. It's been said, *'FEAR means False Evidence Appearing Real.'*

The fear factor became more silenced for me as I grew into a teen. And I believe that statement rings true with many other people who became PTTS. In fact I know people who it rings true for now. I know a lot of guys who was shit scared in primary school getting bullied. But by the time they hit secondary school that fear was silenced and their violence became loud. Some of the same killers that you think are fearless now were punching bags in school. But the fear of being constantly victimised made them change. I can relate to them in some cases. Although I was never the punching bag at school, at home my brother was the better fighter. Subconsciously I learnt that you have to be a mad man to get people to leave you alone. And that's what a lot of other people learnt who displayed extreme acts of violence. It's not always that bad man are bad man. Sometimes it's actually that the bad man's fearful. And when conflict arises that fearful inner child makes him act out violently as he always has done. And although the so called bad man is grown he doesn't know any other way of dealing with the fear of being a victim.

From my story you can tell that I was up for a good old fashion fair fight. Then when the guns and knives came into play it didn't feel natural. It's like everyone could be something they wasn't when the weapons became an option. So let's say a man who used to get beaten up in school decides he is a weapons man now. Then all of a sudden people respect him as a bad man. They fail to recognise that the individual is acting out his silent fears. Then the individual has to maintain that same level of badness because he becomes fearful and aware that he could get touched by weapons too. He now understands the saying - *duppy know who to frighten.* Some young men act violently with weapons because they are scared to do so without them - facts.

But like I said people only see the badman. I've seen films and heard stories from people I know who have killed out of fear. I've seen stories were a man might stand over the body and fire shots until his clip is empty. People will watch that and call it gangster. They wouldn't be wrong, the act is cold blooded. However, does this mean an element of fear wasn't inside them when they emptied the shots? The very fact somebody would empty a clip on their enemy shows me how silent their fear can be. I mean, imagine emptying your gun ammunition on somebody who isn't moving? In your loud actions, it's like you're saying - *I have to make sure my enemy dies. I hate them that much, but silently you don't want them to survive the shots and comeback to kill you.* Kill or be killed, right? Your subconscious knows that you have to make sure there aren't any comebacks. Doesn't that sound like silent fear to you?

A lot of people I know who have killed as children or young men tell me they still get flashbacks and nightmares. But nightmares are associated with fear, right? This is another form of post traumatic street syndrome. Some killers struggle with the memory or murder so much that they are now addicted to things like coke, crack and heroin. So we can't all be cold hearted fearless killers there has to be more to this.

Silent fear can come in many shapes and forms.

The media can really add to this silent fear in us. By sensationalising the issues it can create more fear. Moral panic is the feeling in my community right now and it has been so since the 90s. For example, the media dubbed a road in Hackney *Murder Mile*. I mean, really? Why give it a name like that? Even as an adult I still think of the area as *Murder Mile.* The impact of a name like that can stick in a community's psyche. Some people are fearful to live in London or anywhere else where there is violence and I don't blame them. All I'm saying is the power of moral panic and silent fear right now is at its strongest. The moral panic isn't only pushed by the media, sometimes it is our own people with platforms reinforcing the panic to create more fear and confusion.

I remember going on Facebook and watching a video that a man made with him interviewing one of the so-called groomers on our street. One of those older guys who lure kids in to *chasing dreams* for them. In watching the interview I found myself getting wound up by the presenter. It's like he was allowing the older to tell him how things go and he didn't put him in his place. He should have told the young man why he's a part of the problem for manipulating our young children to do things they don't fully understand. The interviewer should have smacked the man one when he said he doesn't care. Why? Well imagine a young child of I don't know, say 14 years old watching that interview, what is the young person really going to think? He's going to think the streets are more powerful than his dad or grand-dads opinion because when the interviewer was challenged he didn't put the man in his place. That message only transcends the silent fear to these young people that these older road men rule the world. We know that isn't true, but out of fear you didn't address him, and when people view it, it can promote that silent fear. All because we want to add to the conversation, instead of improve on the argument.

The late legendary boxing coach and manager Cus D'Amato once asked the question – *'What is the difference between a coward and a hero? There ain't no difference. They both feel exactly the same on the inside; they both fear dying and getting hurt. It's what the hero does that makes him a hero. And what the other doesn't do, makes him a coward!'*

Every time I think of heroes who stepped out on their fears, I think of the likes of Malcolm X, Marcus Garvey, Rosa Parks Harriet Tubman. I'm sure every one of these freedom fighters had some sort of silent fear within them. Scared they would get killed for being black or that they might be made a target for standing up for civil rights. But they didn't allow that fear to control them. They didn't allow the fear of death to stop them from being unapologetically them. For they knew some things weren't right in the world. They knew if they didn't stand up for what they believed in then they would still be sitting on the back of the bus scared. Their children would have to grow up in the same environment silently fearful. The same goes for many other places over the world. When the silent fear builds up its actions can result in a loud noise. It's not always as it seems. Sometimes fear is silent but so loud at the same time.

CHAPTER 18

NELSON MANDELA - FREEDOM FIGHTER OR A TERRORIST?

Freedom is a Must!

W ho is Nelson Mandela? To some he may have been considered a terrorist, but to others a freedom fighter. Nelson Mandela was born and raised in South Africa during a time were the government introduced the policy known as the Apartheid. The word *'Apartheid'* means legalised racial *'separateness.'* The history behind the Apartheid story starts off before the Apartheid itself in 1948. The origins of this story begin prior to this in mid-1600 when the Dutch invaded and settled in South Africa.

One hundred years after the Dutch settled the British invaded with the intentions of taking over the land because they heard the land was Rich in Diamonds. The British Empire was a large army who came with guns to take over, but they had to war with the Zulu Warrior tribe first.

Have you ever heard the saying -*'You can't bring a knife to a gun war?'* Well I don't think my fellow Zulu Warrior brothers cared too much about that saying there. When the British Empire came to kill them they literally ran towards the army who had guns shooting at them. Over 3000 Zulu warriors were killed as a result of this war. But in this first war the Zulu warriors came out on top. They managed to kill the entire army. This must have sent shockwaves back home to the British Empire. I mean who brings knives to a gun war and wins? Well after that the British Army re-upped and came back with more artillery and much more soldiers. And because of the man and gun-power they won the war. Years later the Europeans took over most of the land and its resources.

Over the years in between segregation issues took place. But it was in 1948 that the government of the land which was now owned by the settlers from the 1600's who decided they wanted to implement this Apartheid law. The government decided they were better than the black people of that land. They introduced this thing which was similar to the Jim Crow laws in America. Basically, the laws stated that certain areas were for whites only. They told the people of the land that they couldn't sit with them on the same train or bus. They couldn't send their children to the same school and they couldn't drink from the same water fountain. Like I said it was similar to Jim Crow laws. The only difference is the people were being segregated from their own land. Can you imagine being born black in Africa seeing signs stating - *No blacks white only?* The government also evicted some people of the land from their homes to build new houses for the rich, and make it white only areas.

Personally, I can't imagine being a black man in South Africa at this time. I honestly don't think I would have been able to be treated like a slave in my own country. There was too much oppression going on over there I would have had to ride out for that. And that's exactly what a lot of people did they stood up for their rights to freedom.

One person in particular that stood up against these separation laws was a young man by the name of Nelson Mandela. Initially Mr Mandela was a defence barrister in the courts of South Africa. Then he was approached by the ANC the African Nation of congress. An activist party that was willing to challenge the new Apartheid laws. At the time black people weren't allowed in certain areas if they were white. There were a few places that had an exception to this law. And if you had what they called a pass you could come in the area but if the police stopped you and you didn't have it, then boy you could be in a predicament. Nelson Mandela got triggered by the injustices of this law - a man he knew was beaten to death for not having a pass on him. This caused the ANC party to plan a peaceful protest to boycott the buses. Nelson saw this and was motivated by their action to argue this new law and joined up. The people of the land then went out and defied the new laws of the land and was prepared to go to prison for their beliefs and their freedom. The people defied the laws by running onto the trains and sitting down wherever they saw the *'No Blacks. European Only'* signs. Many of them were beaten and arrested for this so called act of defiance. Nelson himself was arrested.

Shortly after all that drama he had to go into hiding because the apartheid government saw him as a trouble maker who needed to be imprisoned. While on the run he married his wife Winnie Mandela. Then in 1960 there was a famous peaceful protest outside the police station in Sharpeville. The people of the land peacefully protested with their children singing songs of freedom. The people were protesting against laws requiring them to carry passes at all times. Then tensions rose high when the people of the land decided to burn their passes as a sign of rebellion. The police chief in command didn't like that and shortly after shots were fired. People were killed. They were slaughtered like a pack of lambs. Shot in their backs as they ran off, women and children included. Sixty nine people were shot dead for protesting for freedom and over 180 were seriously injured.

Up to this point the ANC was a non-violent group, but after that mass slaughter they said fuck it. They went into exile and fought fire with fire. *You can't bring knifes to a gun war, remember?* The ANC started bombing buildings they were putting in work. After that moment Nelson Mandela was branded a terrorist and one of the leaders of the movement. Then Mandela made contact with a foreign journalist to announce to the world that he wasn't a terrorist. He asked the government to resolve this in a peaceful manner. But Mandela refused to hand himself in to a government he didn't recognise. When he was asked by the journalist what he wanted from the government he stated, *'I want freedom. I want my children to walk free in their own land.'*

The fighting and oppression didn't stop there and shortly after the powers that be ran up on Nelson Mandela and his team and arrested them.

At court, the people of the land came out to support the man who was accused of terrorism and violent revolution. In response Mandela said, *'It should be the government in the docks not I. Not guilty.'* He then made a pre-sentence statement,

'I do not deny that I planned sabotage. I did not plan it, in the spirit of recklessness. Nor because I have any love for violence. The hard facts are that 50 years of non-violence have brought the African people nothing but more and more repressive legislation, and fewer and fewer rights. Africans want a just share in the whole of South Africa. We want equal political rights, one man one vote. I have dedicated myself to this struggle of the African people. I have fought against white domination. I have fought against black domination. I have cherished the idea of a free democratic society were all persons live together in harmony with equal opportunities. It is an idea which I hope to live for and achieve. But if needs be it is an idea for which I am prepared to die.'

After that passionate speech he came back in the court room to hear the verdict. Judge: *'I have reached my verdict.*

The defendants will rise... The accused are all found guilty of charged. The accused have made high moral claims for their actions. In essence they have fortieth martyrdom. At the hands of what they call their oppressors, but I will not give them that satisfaction. Let us show the world that we are a nation of laws. And were possible we temper justice with mercy. I have therefore decided not to impose the supreme penalty... The sentence in the case of all the accused will be life imprisonment.'

Would you believe the black people of the land were shouting chants of freedom while these men were being sentenced to life? Nelson was flown to Robben Island maximum security prison with the other so called terrorist to spend the rest of his days in a cage. While his wife Winnie and family were terrorised by the authorities on the outside. The inmates weren't treated like human beings they were considered wild animals. They were forced to do slave labour. Their mail was coming to them with important lines cut out the letters. At times the inmates were stripped searched and beaten in the rain naked. During the prison visits which was every six months Winnie Mandela had to talk to her husband through a glass window. Nelson Mandela wasn't able to see his children because they were too young to visit him. On the outside the oppression was still going on strong. People were still dying and Winnie Mandela was constantly being arrested leaving his children distraught. But Winnie continued to fight for her beliefs, even when imprisoned herself and tortured. She never let her spirit get broken for freedom was more important. On the long walk to freedom, Nelson's mother passed away and it was believed his son was killed in an accident. Everything was thrown at this man to break him, all because he was perceived as a terrorist.

The streets of South Africa had thousands of killings and the young people who rebelled were labelled terrorist also. Winnie Mandela became a fearless leader of the oppression and was also willing to die for her beliefs. After the riots and killings of 1976 the president chose to make a deal with Nelson Mandela. He said he is willing to grant Mandela his freedom if he would say he announces to the public that he rejects violence as a means to resolve political measures. Nelson Mandela's daughter spoke on behalf of him in public stating that he isn't a violent man. He stated that it was the president who needed to renounce violence and the apartheid as a means to make peace. He said his freedom and the peoples cannot be separated. Another meeting was set up with Nelson Mandela to make a deal with the minister of justice, and other powers that be. They wanted to offer Nelson and the ANC a share in power. All throughout his 27 years the killings of innocent South Africans continued. Winnie Mandela had to witness the war and oppression from the outside for 27 years. The day came in February 1990 when Mandela was freed from prison. The whole world was watching as he came out the car holding Winnie's hand taking their first steps to freedom.

At this point Mandela's release didn't cease the violence. The cheering didn't last too long. The relationship between Nelson and Winnie Mandela deteriorated because they were fighting by different means. Nelson wanted to fix the Apartheid by means of peace and negotiations, while Winnie was way past talks of negotiations. She had seen too much bloodshed of her own and the people of South Africa. She didn't want to wait another 27 years in hope of politics changing things. Not long after the couple's disagreement, Nelson Mandela announced his separation with his wife Winnie. She carried on fighting her way and he began fighting his way. The bloodshed however continued to plague the land and it was almost a civil war where blacks were killing blacks too. Then Nelson made his famous speech telling the people of the land they were wrong for using violence and that forgiveness was the only solution for peace. He said, *'We can't win a war but we can win an election.'* He encouraged them to vote not to fight. He later ran for presidency and became president of South Africa in 1994.

After hearing this story if you didn't know it already, would you say that Nelson Mandela was a terrorist or freedom fighter?

My next question to you is how would you perceive the Black Panthers? Would you view them as a terrorist group or a bunch of freedom fighters? Let's take a look at how they came into action. It began in Los Angeles in the late 1960's in a place called Oakland. This was during the civil rights era in America. I believe they were inspired by Malcolm X who said, *'We need to stop singing and start swinging.'* Huey Newton and Bobby Seale were the main founders of the Black Panther defence party. They decided they had enough of getting beaten up by police for being black and outspoken or in cases, for just being black. The movement was in its infant stages when a young black boy got run over in an accident. The accident was the third of the year. Which could have been prevented had it been that the system had listened to the complaints of the community.

The community was fed up of the *sufferation* on a whole. It was hard enough just being broke because of social exclusion. It decided to take a stand and march peacefully to get them to put up a stop light so another child wouldn't have to get run over at that specific crossing. They came marching with the pastor and their parents singing, *'We shall not, we shall not be moved.'* They were not only moved by the police, they were brutally beaten and locked up. After this Huey and Bobby decided the group needed to do more to defend themselves. They knew they were ignorant to the law. They realised they needed to educate themselves by exercising their constitutional rights to defend themselves against police brutality. They got fed up of praying and turning the other cheek. So they began educating themselves and got guns to defend the people. Their phrase was, *Power to the People, All people!* It wasn't about shooting cops it was about getting a man's attention. They wanted to show their community that they were protected. At this point the police were instructed to have an undercover watching them. They wanted to make sure the group didn't get too big. Personally, I don't know why they didn't just put up the traffic light that way they wouldn't have to send in an undercover police man.

The Black Panthers had good values. They educated the people, they fed the poor and they didn't let brothers hustle on the street corner. They weren't spreading any hate to any other race, and many people from different backgrounds supported the Panther's idea. At times they were policing the police with their guns. They defended a man who was being brutalised by the police and held their ground. This action made a statement to the people present. They gave the people hope of a safer community by not backing down. In 1967 the Black Panthers did some security support for the late Malcolm X's wife Miss Shabazz when she visited. After this the Black Panthers found out the other black group supporting them in guarding Malcolm X's widow, weren't prepared. They found out the group came with their guns unloaded. So Huey and the rest of the Panthers went and approached the Panthers in San Francisco and demanded them to change their name because they felt they made the real panthers look bad.

The group slowly got bigger and bigger spreading power to the people of all races. They recruited women who wanted to be a part of the change. All of this didn't stop the killing of innocent black people. Amongst six others in a matter of months another man was shot by police while he held his hands up in the air. Things got heated after this. More protest more attention. Then an undercover police officer infiltrated the crew trying to get them to break and turn on each other. The tactics to break the Black Panthers were increased once the Black Panthers famously marched into the state assembly but went in the wrong room to demand their constitutional rights and argue against the gun laws. For this Bobby Seale got sentenced for six months. The group managed to get worldwide attention for their actions but nothing was changed. In fact this is when everything started to change.

One of the Panthers was killed. They used one of the members called Judge as a way to break up the group. The undercover police officer forced him to do a robbery to defame the character of the Black Panthers, and set up its other members. But it backfired. Judge had outsmarted the police by robbing a blind man's shop. That way the shop keeper couldn't identify the accused. After this, obviously the police officer found Judge and gave him a good beating. At this point an FBI agent decided that the Panthers were becoming too much of a voice and a problem that needed to be eradicated. The Black Panther's offices were attacked. They were bombed, tear gassed, shot up and those alive got arrested and sent to jail. This didn't stop the panthers there were more riots more fighting more talks of freedom. *'We're non-violent with people who are non-violent with us. But we are not non-violent with anyone who is violent with us.'©* *Malcolm X*

Then Huey Newton got pulled over by the police in what they said was a routine check. Police asked him to get out of the car then they cuffed him. Then gunshots went off and the police as well as Huey newton got shot. The police gave Huey Newton a further beating while he was on the hospital bed bleeding. Then they sent him to prison as the co-founder Bobby Seale was being released. *'You can jail the revolutionary but you can't jail the revolution.'* - *Black Panthers.* Despite the crackdown on the Panthers, their power base in the black community continued to grow.

Then Martin Luther King the peaceful leader was shot dead. This sparked off more riots around the country. People were coming to terms with the fact that praying for freedom isn't helping. As a result of taking action inner conflict came into the Black Panther party. It appears one half wanted to use their brain and the other half wanted to use their guns and hearts. They ambushed the police with gunshots and ended up getting murdered upon arrest. After this so called act of defiance FBI agent Edgar Hoover decided that the community had to go. So it was arranged that heroin was flooded in to the ghetto community's to gain law and order. They knew the results of this would be fatal. The protest continued in the middle of all this drama. And the appealing of Huey Newton's court case was in procession. Then Bobby Seale was taken by police and they attempted to cause more division within the group by claiming Judge set up Bobby to get arrested.

You always get that one person in the community that can't see the bigger picture. You know, that one sell-out green-eyed thinker who would happily get rich at the cost of his people suffering. Well one guy from the community was given a warehouse of drugs by the police to begin flooding the black community. So the Black Panthers came out to stop it. When the police came to the scene one of the wounded Panthers sacrificed his life by burning down the warehouse with him in it. The police shot him dead in a shoot-out.

The drugs that were flooded into the ghetto were specifically meant for the ghettos but it fell into other parts of the country on their doorstep. The Panthers continued to provide breakfast, program sickle cell testing and even some schools for the community. Eventually the Panthers were washed out. Huey Newton was killed in a drug deal and Bobby Seale now teaches. It came out later that Hoover and the FBI used illegal tactics to destroy the Black Panthers. Several Panthers are still imprisoned on made up charges. This was the story would you describe these individuals as Terrorist or Freedom fighters?

How about Stanley Tookie Williams - the man who got sentenced to life on death row for killing four people. Was he a Freedom Fighter or Gang banging Terrorist?
Tookie Williams was the founder of the Crips. But how did he get to this place? A journalist who was interested in the topic wanted to find out what the origins of this Bloods and Crips thing was about. She wrote to Tookie a few times but didn't get a response. Then she went to a local youth club to ask someone who knew him to ask him to accept her letters. She must have caught Tookie Williams at a good time, as when she wrote he was in the process of making some changes. He was in a mode of redemption.

The writer came to talk to Tookie about a book she wanted to write herself on the subject of how both groups started. The letter was received and Tookie agreed to hear her out on a prison visit. Tookie didn't trust her on the first few visits. He believed she wanted to defame his character as a monster of the Crips and further stain him. She then gave him the ultimatum of having him trust her because she was going to write the book with or without his help. Eventually

Tookie made contact and said he would give her the story from the beginning. On the visit her first question was - *'Why did you start the Crips?'*

Tookie said he did it to defend himself and the neighbourhood from bullies and other gangs. *'So you started a criminal organisation to protect your neighbourhood from bullies?'* He explained that it wasn't a criminal organisation to begin with. He explained as a young child his mother moved him to Los Angeles from Louisiana in search for a better life. And when he arrived it was strife in violence and drugs. Then he got fed up of getting beaten up all the time. He decided he didn't want to be the victim or the victimised.

Sometime later he linked up with a guy called Raymond Washington and they decided to start defending each other and clean up the other gangs through physical combat. He admits it was really violent but they were building a reputation. And those who were scared of them joined up. He explains the police didn't care too much too make things better, they never intervened. A young Tookie Williams figured out he was on his own in this cold world. He didn't back down from anyone and chose to do the most savage thing on reaction. He tried to explain to the writer this was based on survival. But it seemed as though she couldn't accept that. She believed someone must have been able to guide and protect him through life. Tookie told her he had nobody he said his dad abandoned him so the streets became his family. And although those things were true Tookie still failed to take any responsibility for the wrong he had participated in. It seemed as though he put everything down to survival. During that visit they didn't see eye to eye so the writer left saying she doesn't need his story. After a while of reflecting Tookie wrote a piece of writing from his own perspective and sent it to the writer:

'I believed the people because they were afraid of me they would respect me. That was a mistake. Respect cannot be earned by using violence to scare people. Many Gang bangers are scared all the time, but they won't tell anyone, because they don't want their homeboys to think that they're not down. Gang bangers live by bad rules. Their rules make it be ok to be dishonest. Their rules make it ok to use violence against us. Their rules make it ok to put their own lives in danger. But you, you don't have to live by their rules. You can choose to live by new rules.'

Not long after the writer went to visit Tookie again and they made amends. Tookie then asked the journalist for her help. He said he wanted to write a children's book. After a meaningful conversation she decided to help him. The children's book journey begun and the journalist visited regularly to work. The journalist told Tookie on a visit that things were getting heated on the streets with the much younger Bloods and Crips. She asked him to reach out to them and he agreed. He knew it could get him into more trouble in the prison. As people might think, he was turning soft, but this didn't deter him. He said he saw it as his responsibility to do it.

'Twenty years ago I helped create a gang called the Crips. Today I'm speaking to you from death row. I never imagined

that the Crip gang would spread like hell throughout the nation, throughout the world. And I deeply regret the legacy that it left. Because it left a legacy of genocide, black on black genocide. And I apologise for my part in it. But I am deeply encouraged to see you here today. That lets me know, that I'm not alone in deeply regretting this legacy and seeing it for what it is. And no one can have a better influence on gang violence or gang culture than gang members themselves. And therefore best positioned to reverse its course of violence, we must do work. We must get out there, we must forge peace. We must stop exterminating one another. We must stop all of this madness, because at the end of the day we have only ourselves to blame. We must have a do or die attitude towards streets wars to rebuild our culture and to create a new lasting legacy a legacy of peace.'

The recorded video which was played at the youth club had a massive impact on the young Bloods and Crips in attendance. According to the journalist tensions were high gang signs were being thrown on both sides. Then peace signs started getting thrown too. The journalist was relieved to see that the recorded video had such an impact. Members in red and blue were embracing one another; some of them were even relatives. But they hadn't seen each other for years because they couldn't go to each other's neighbourhoods.

The journalist through all her efforts struggled to get a publisher for the book. The reasoning was nobody could see why they should give a platform to a man convicted of murdering four people. What qualified Tookie to be a voice to

people's young children? Until she said a quote that Tookie taught her, which means,
'They condemn what they do not understand.'

After that quote the publisher was interested. The book was eventually made and sent around the country. In child format the book was a preventative tool like a workshop to help change the mind-set. The book started to get recognition worldwide. They became such a success that Winnie Mandela even asked if she could visit Tookie. Who could imagine? On the visit Winnie Mandela praised Tookie for his words of peace and she encouraged him to stay strong and not to be afraid.

Shortly after Winnie Mandela's visit it so happened that Tookie Williams was nominated for the Noble Peace Prize. Obviously, this didn't go down too well with some other country leaders. The journalist was hounded after the Noble Peace Prize nomination. Tookie Williams was put in the news to have been accused of still dealing drugs and running the prison from solitary confinement. This was based on testimonies from other inmates. Tookie's death row appeal was denied he had six months to live before they executed him. Now if he wasn't a changed man when he received that news he could have *wilded* out in the prison but he didn't. Even when he was put back into general population with the other prisoners, instead of starting chaos he went to look for his enemy to call a truce. He managed to find his enemy in the prison yard and everyone thought it was going to be a violent showdown. But there was no violence. Tookie reached out to him in love. I think that proved to the people in prison at least what he now stood for, which was peace.

After all of Tookie's efforts the gang violence continued. Tookie continued to reach out to the youth for as long as he had life. Tookie Williams surprised the world when he won the Nobel Peace Prize. A small victory for a dying man, but a big legacy for what he would have wanted. After receiving the Peace Prize, Tookie Williams appealed the death sentence but it was denied. A few years later in 2005 he was executed by lethal injection.

So what are your thoughts? Was Nelson Mandela, the Black Panthers and Tookie Williams's terrorist? Each to their own but my opinion is that Nelson Mandela wasn't a terrorist he was a prisoner to the corrupt politics of South Africa. In other words as the streets would say he got drawn out. If I had to put myself in Mandela's shoes I would have probably done the same thing. Other than I wouldn't have made it to prison. I would have gone out guns blazing like Queen Latifah in the movie *Set It Off.* Not saying Mandela was wrong, I'm just saying I don't think as clearly as Mandela does when I feel oppressed. The people of South Africa was terrorised for a few hundred years and in return they rebelled. I don't believe anyone has a clear state of mind after being the victim of oppression for so long. And that brings me to another thought was Winnie Mandela a terrorist or a Freedom fighter? Like Nelson Mandela and the other ANC members my belief is - no she wasn't. If I put myself in Winnie's shoes only God knows how I would have reacted. They say hurting people hurt people. I say terrorised people terrorise people.

In the case of the Black Panther Party, how do you find those accused of terrorism, guilty, Or not guilty? Again for me I find the defendants not guilty. How can a group of people who have been victimised with police brutality and social depravation be labelled terrorist? Is it because they educated themselves about the law? Or is it because they educated the people on a whole? I see no crime in wanting to protect the people in your community when others in power fail to do so. I see no terrorism in getting guns to defend yourself against unreasonable individuals who have the right to shot you, and the protection of the law to defend them. No thoughts of terrorism come to mind when I hear of what the Black Panthers stood for. However the thoughts of terrorism do arise when I think about the illegal tactics used to destroy the Panthers. Just remember the world loves to label the black man as the big drug dealing criminal. In this story the terrorist was the one who flooded the communities with drugs. If that isn't terrorism then I don't know what is.

Last but certainly not least Tookie Williams. So was this man a terrorist or a gang banging criminal?

Some might feel this one is an easy one. He started the Crips as well as being convicted for four murders at a robbery. How can I possibly defend what this so called terrorist has done? First of all I don't condone any of the actions that this man has committed. Second of all I don't have any knowledge of any of the crimes he has committed, I only know what he's been a part of. He openly took responsibility for starting the Crips Gang. He himself stated that he regrets being part of such a self-destructive legacy. I can't say Tookie wasn't on the streets terrorising people because it sounded like he became a very violent individual. Notice I said he became violent, but this wasn't by choice. When he told his story he said as a child he was punched in the face when he first moved to LA, and constantly troubled by groups who already existed. He explained the environment was filled with drugs and violence was encouraged by some elders. Could this drugs and violence have anything to do with the batch that FBI agent Edgar Hoover left behind?

What I'm saying is before Tookie started terrorising people he was just an innocent child who moved to a new area which was foreign to him. An area plagued with drugs intentionally sent to destroy those within those communities. I didn't agree with Tookie when he said that he was to blame for all this gang violence that was going on in LA. Although I respected him for taking responsibility I strongly disagree he was to blame. Especially when I heard him say the Bloods fired the first shots which started the gang banging. I'm not saying that I blame the Bloods for shooting first either, although that behaviour can't be condoned. Between Tookie Williams himself and co-founder of the Crips Raymond Washington these guys were only 16 years old when they started the group. And I'm sure the bloods weren't much older.

I wouldn't say they were organised crime members; the gang wasn't built on criminal mind-sets. From my observa-

tion, it started from two young people who became prisoners to the streets but convinced themselves they wanted to
be gang bangers.

I won't say Tookie was or wasn't a terrorist. What I will
say is he started off as an innocent young man. Then he
became a prisoner to the streets, and then he acted in some
terrible ways to get his message across. He caused terror
to people in his community. As a result he was punished
for a crime which he denied committing. He left this world
with a different mind-set than the one he got lost in. He
chose to share this information with the world. My verdict
for this one really doesn't matter. Tookie Williams was
already serving time for a crime he said he didn't commit.
Instead of the governor making the decision to have him executed he could have been used to be a voice to help further
influence others in the community. The system could have
let him serve the rest of his days in prison but instead they
chose to make an example. They chose to carry out the
death sentence.

What does this teach people about the system that they live
in? It teaches them that mercy can't be shown. It teaches
them that we must act in revenge to achieve justice. It
teaches them that the system doesn't care about a man
changing - once a criminal always a criminal. It also teaches
them that the same system doesn't care for resolutions only
law and order. Sometimes I wonder if those same corrupt
people in power will be punished for the years of terrorism
they've caused worldwide. Brother Tookie, you were once a
high risk prisoner to the streets. You became so influential
in your last days that it rubbed off on people like me. The

word Redemption is tattooed on my neck. I cried real tears when I heard Arnold Schwarzenegger rejected your appeal to live. I know you never released yourself from the physical prison, you never regained physical freedom. However I want to thank you for digging deep within yourself to discover freedom in your mind while imprisoned on death row. That alone makes you a freedom fighter!

You might be thinking what this chapter title has got to do with Freedom from the streets. Well, it's simple this is what the confusion is. The other day I was on Facebook scrolling through as you do, and I came across a few RIP's. This month there have been a lot of killings and stabbings in my hometown of Hackney. This naturally evokes emotion and the people become expressive or reactive to how they feel on the subject. This specific day I saw a post stating,
All these young children doing the killings should be hung to death.
To which I felt I had to reply. Not to start a debate but rather to enlighten. I commented and told the sister that her post and comment was ignorant. I then elaborated and said,
'Sister while all this death in the community is tragic, we can't lose focus here why the death penalty? Have you ever been trapped in this mind-set as a child? It isn't about condemning our young ones for their evil acts. It's about enlightening them. We need to show them from scratch the mind-set they are trapped in. RIP young kings.'

The sister disagreed, she said, *'They need consequences and punishment.'* I agreed, but was it not that same government who took the power away from us to discipline our children? She then made reference to the riots of 2011 highlighting that the people were acting wild until the police intervened. Almost as if to say she'd forgotten that it was the same police who started the riots by not giving answers to the family of the man they killed. I then in so many words tried to explain to her that the same government that she feels should kill our children for their sins have already been killing our youth, but she didn't get my point. Instead she went on to tell me that I was too stuck on American slavery, at which point I stopped trying to explain myself and I just told her to go fuck herself. I know it wasn't called for but I came into this field of work to be a voice for the young people. I came here to stop us from being criminalised and hearing such ignorance being broadcasted on the media just wound me up. When I swore I should have known that would make it harder to get my point across, but fuck it.

After a few more exchanges she made the statement, *'I see you as a threat too. Just look at the way you conducted yourself on this thread because my views opposed yours. I'm convinced you'd have attacked me if we were face to face. You strike me as someone who has no control over his emotions. Look at the way you are no longer even using punctuations, you're mad huh?'*

The truth is she was right. Not about me being a threat but she was right I was mad, mad passionate. It was the overall statement. I wasn't angry that we opposed views. I was angry that she was talking from a place of opinion and spreading it like it was fact. It was this exact mind-set

of her post that I feel stops us from discovering or applying the solutions. She went on to say, *'Typical of someone of
your calibre to resort to insults when all fails. You are the type
to go and kill others I'm convinced, disrespectful, and very
likely ruthless. Hence your morals on this topic. You are the
one sending these young kids to do all types of foolery. You are
the 'older' who should be held accountable and punished also.
Look how you say it with such pride.'*

When I read what she wrote for some reason I wasn't even
vex by it, it was more of a revelation. I realised I was talking
to one of those people who my editor James used to speak
about. The type of people who have already made up their
mind based on their pre-conceived ideas about the streets.
The exchange of comments finally came to an end, with me
admitting I didn't need to swear but not taking back anything else I stated. I left the conversation thinking of that
same Tookie Williams quote -
'They condemn what they do not understand.'

She had the right to get on to me for the swearing but to say
I was responsible for the youths killing one another that
made me think about how others might view me. So I had to
ask the question - *Who was Robin Travis? Was he a part of the
problem or is he a part of the solution?* Am I part responsible for the way the streets of today are? It's not even a question I should ask myself. How could I even ask myself that
question after I wrote *Prisoner to the Street* and explained
in detail what a child does when he is lost? It's evident as
lost children we participated in the violence and the mind-
set but in no way do I feel responsible for anything. I didn't

make the best choices as a child, none of us did. And I may have done a few things in repping my ends that brought more attention to it negatively. But there is no way I can blame the children for the mess they live in as children. The mess was here way before they were. Whoever thinks the youth should get hanged for their misguided actions. Well what can I say? Maybe it's that same killing for control attitude you support that got us here in the first place. Maybe thinkers like you are the bigger part of the problem, what do you think?

Whenever I do a workshop I ask those involved whether they see themselves as *gang members or prisoners to the streets*. I ask this question before the workshop then again at the end. In the beginning when I ask the question most people say they are gang members. Then by the end of the workshop their eyes are open. Every single person says they were *prisoners to the streets*. So now I've explained my theory in detail I have to ask you the question one last time, '*Are we dealing with gang members or prisoners to the streets?*'

If your answer is prisoner to the streets then I'm glad. You finally get what I was doing here all these years. Now you can take the baton of freedom and finish off the race.

DESTINY - DESTINATION

'I can't change the direction of the wind, but I can adjust my sails to always reach my destination...'

Jimmy Dean

I made a promise to myself that I would leave the youth field and stop talking on the subject by the end of 2019. With the intention of training people who want to continue the workshops in my absence up to 2020. I have discussed this over the last few years with those close to me. A lot of people don't understand why I'm leaving this field. Some of my friends in the field think I'm quitting and some of them think I just need a break, but it's not that. My mind is made up - it is time to stop talking. My friend in the youth field asked me the other day, *'Trav why are you leaving the youth work conversation we need you at the table?' I replied, 'What table? I'm good - I've done all that I can do to contribute to this subject.'* He didn't want to hear that response. He got frustrated by that and said, *'But bro, there is so much more you can add to this.'* I didn't know how to explain to him in words why I was done. So I gave him a visual explanation instead.

'Bruv, try and imagine you're in a classroom setting. And the teacher has asked the class of students for an answer to the question. You fling up your hand first knowing that you have the answer to this question. You feel enthusiastic to begin with while you're waiting for your answer to be heard. Then the teacher points at another student and you have to wait. Which is Ok, she then points at another student behind you. Then another student and another, who wasn't even holding his hand up. By this stage you start to lose the enthusiasm to give your answer. Your arm starts aching in the shoulder area, so you start to lower your hand. The teacher turns and says, 'Is that everybody?' fully well knowing that your hand was up for a minute. You decide to sit up straight and give your answer. You shout out, 'Christopher Columbus didn't discover America he was a murderer who killed and took over the land!'

The teacher then laughs nervously because she realises you are not one of them children who believe everything they hear or learn at school. The teacher realises you are a person who does their own research outside of what they've been taught. And for being a freethinker with facts you are told to be quiet or leave. You argue with the teacher for a few seconds then you start thinking to yourself, what is the point? The teacher carries on teaching about how great Christopher Columbus was and you realise the establishment made its mind up. So you say fuck this shit and walk out of the classroom. You realise that the establishment is bigger than you are and they don't care for your truth which is the truth. You dismiss yourself from class and begin to home-school yourself.'

This is why I'm leaving the conversation for good. If I don't leave now eventually I will go mad. If I keep banging my head against a brick wall or earholes filled with ignorant wax, were will that get me? It doesn't mean that all the hard work goes to waste though. If people have read this book and believe this is the way forward and want to be a part of the solution, the workshops will be passed on and the work will be done in my absence. I don't believe my work was done in vain by any means. I finally feel like I've fulfilled the purpose I set out to achieve. One of them being that there is a difference between a gang member and a prisoner to the street. I'm over grateful for those people who have been touched by my work. Every single message I got kept me motivated to complete this book. There were many deaths and injuries around me at the time of writing this one. And I'm grateful to the most high for using such a flawed individual like me to deliver this message. Let's just hope the people can get to action it so they can get a real resolution and some freedom from these streets.

After thoughts

A few people have asked me if this will be my last book. If I'm honest, I feel like saying yes because this one just drained out my spirit. This year will be my last year writing on the street subject. I can't keep writing books on the street if I want to be free from the streets. And I don't want to fulfil a stereotype of only being a street author.

Personally, I think I can write on any subject. And if the time and opportunity presents itself, I will explore those avenues. I'm not afraid to step out of my comfort zone creatively, especially when it comes to writing so let's see what happens. You never know - I might write a horror film, a Sci-fi or a comedy script. Who knows? I might even write a romance novel and call it 50 Shades of Trav. Over the last few years I've been putting pen to paper to write a TV series with my co-writer Darwood Grace – (Preventing the Cure) the plan is to start filming this year. Whatever I do with this purpose filled gift, it will always have substance in it. I learnt that from watching films written by the Late Great - John Singleton. May he rest in power. I have ideas for days when it comes to writing but I don't have the days to fulfil all those ideas. And the author game isn't the most lucrative so whether I write again or not only time and motivation will tell. All I know is that I'm going to check out a therapist so I can get the rest of the freedom that I deserve - Freedom from the streets. Freedom is a must!

Bibliography

Long Walk to Freedom - Movie - (Justin Chadwick , 2013)

Redemption: The Stan Tookie Williams - Movie - (Sue Budgen et al, 2004)

Malcolm X - Movie - (Spike Lee,1992)

Black Phanter - Movie - (Ryan Coogler, 2018)